Books by
Pia Smith Orleane, Ph.D.
& Cullen Baird Smith

Pleiadian-Earth Energy Astrology–
Charting the Spirals of Consciousness

Wisdom From the Stars Series:
Book One – Conversations With Laarkmaa
Book Two – Remembering Who We Are
Book Three – Pleiadian Manual of Accelerated
Evolution & Ascension

Books by
Pia Orleane, Ph.D.

Sacred Retreat –
Using Natural Cycles to Recharge Your Life

PLEIADIAN MANUAL
FOR ACCELERATED
EVOLUTION & ASCENSION

LAARKMAA'S STEP-BY-STEP GUIDE

PIA SMITH ORLEANE, PH.D.
&
CULLEN BAIRD SMITH

Onewater Press
Santa Fe, NM

Pleiadian Manual For Accelerated Evolution & Ascension ~ Laarkmaa's Step-by-Step Guide

Pia Orleane, Ph.D. and Cullen Baird Smith

Copyright © 2020 by Pia Orleane, Ph.D. and Cullen Baird Smith
Published by:
Onewater Press
369 Montezuma Avenue
Suite 525
Santa Fe, NM 87501

Order books through booksellers, or through Onewater Press at
www. laarkmaa.com

Cover and book design by Chris Molé
Author photos by Judith Pavlik
Printed in the United States of America
Softcover ISBN: 978-0-9967835-9-0
eBook ISBN: 978-0-9967835-8-3
Library of Congress Control Number: 2020909801

DEDICATION

This book is dedicated to all of the Light Bearers who
have used their courage and perseverance in working
to evolve and create a better world!
Heightening our vibration has been essential
in the evolutionary process towards
Unity Consciousness.

CONTENTS

INTRODUCTION

This book is the third in the *Wisdom from the Stars* series, providing up-to-date information about our evolutionary path and the changes that are occurring on the planet at this time. We have presented the information in this book exactly as Laarkmaa gave it to us, with only a few grammatical changes. The information in each chapter builds upon the wisdom of the previous chapter. At the end of each chapter you will find a Questions and Answers section. The questions are from our International Live Call participants, with answers from Laarkmaa. We have included them here because they are relevant to the material presented, and they are timely. We trust this will open more doors and windows to the true reality, as Laarkmaa shares their Wisdom From the Stars.

This book has been specifically designed and written for those of you who have consistently worked to raise your vibrations through the conscious choices you have made. It is written for those of you who have mastered and mostly completed your psychological shadow work by attending consciously to your emotional lives and blocked memories from childhood traumas and parallel lives. For those of you who have regularly applied the guidance and wisdom of Laarkmaa, which they have lovingly communicated with humanity throughout the years, this book is for you. The principles included in this Manual will accelerate your progress toward achieving ascension, rather than repeating the old karmic loop of learning through the pattern of birth and death and rebirth, previously known to humankind. This text will help those of you who are ready to ascend to stimulate and enliven your path toward ultimate spiritual evolution at this precise time as humans on planet Earth. If you are reading this book, you are certainly ready to accept the responsibility of holding a tremendous amount of light, which will ultimately guide you on your glorious way. This Manual provides a jumpstart for those of you who are seriously ready to evolve and move forward in your ever-spiraling journey toward Cosmic understanding and enlightenment.

Congratulations on achieving this status and moving toward Cosmic Citizenship. We honor and respect you for working through your hearts so diligently in this process.

> With love and light,
> Pia and Cullen

PORTALS OF OPPORTUNITY:

PREFACE

We are Laarkmaa, a group of Pleiadians here to bring human evolution to the front of your consciousness. We are here because we love you and we wish to help you on your evolutionary journey. Therefore, we have created this *Pleiadian Manual for Accelerated Evolution & Ascension* for you. You are living in an amazing time that is bringing opportunities never before experienced by humanity. This is the time that all of you have been waiting for. You have been living under the shadows of human history, clinging to the same old, tired beliefs about reality and what is possible. This Manual will guide you to a deeper understanding of what actually is possible and how to attain it. In this Manual, we will share a broader perspective of concepts that you have thus far grasped at a mental level but have been unable to realize in your everyday life. This moment brings you a potent opportunity to change everything that has held you back from who you really are. With our guidance, you will find yourselves stepping into the possibility of discovering and being able to look closely at what has prevented your remembering the truth of your divinity and remembering the power that you possess. Remembering your ability will magically make changes in your lives and in the lives of others. This Now moment holds all of these possibilities.

You have already begun to experience planetary alignments and cosmic energies that bring into the forefront of your awareness certain forces that considerably alter your human experience. We are speaking of the Schumann Resonance, the Solar Minimum, and Cosmic Rays. The Schumann Resonance is the resonant frequency of Earth's magnetic field. Resonance occurs when energy can be stored and transferred easily, which is how Earth's energy supports your presence on the planet. For millennia and generations of humans in the past, Earth has vibrated fairly consistently at a rate of 7.83, which has supported the human physical body and all life on Earth. However, in very recent years, the Earth has experienced sudden and frequent spikes in vibration, causing the scale at which you measure these energies to register much, much higher than what you perceive as a normal Resonance. These spikes affect human heart rate and blood pressure and can cause such symptoms as dizziness, nausea, and extreme fatigue. Your bodies are having difficulty matching the new frequencies. What you will discover in our Manual is the blueprint for change as you transform from the dense carbon-based physicality that you have always believed to be your essential selves into the higher frequency liquid crystalline waveforms that you truly are. You are waveforms, not static, unchanging particles. The heightened Schumann Resonance supports that change.

These cosmic forces are opportunities for moving into actually being different, thinking differently, responding to life in a different way, and creating a new reality. The opportunities that are here through the above-described influences also bring forth conflict to be resolved in a more harmonious way. As you face and learn to harmonize these conflicts, you will begin to understand the concept that conflict does not even have to exist; you will automatically find yourselves moving more into alignment with the understanding and implementation of possibilities for unity, as each of you brings your gifts and talents into the Now moment. You will attain a more comprehensive understanding of duality and move towards a deeper unity.

As you move into higher vibratory forms, you will need a deeper understanding of Universal Laws. Our Manual for Accelerated Evolution will expand upon existing concepts of unity, objectivity, and judgment. We will guide you through ways to step beyond patterns and beliefs that have kept you stuck. We will discuss the power of your thoughts, your liquid crystalline body, how to truly heal yourselves, and the real definition of love. We will discuss the changing structure of your reality and explain the concept of Liquid Time, that is, a perception that time does not have a perceived past or a perceived future, but instead, you are in an eternal Now moment, and that Now moment stretches into the next Now moment according to what you think, feel, and believe. We will address the question, "Where is your consciousness?" Our Manual will prepare you for a different world, describing the process of ascension and the Rainbow body[1] you can attain, helping you to prepare to be the New Human on a new Earth.

If you have not already begun to experience feeling a different sense of your "self" and your reality, you will feel it as the changes we discuss intensify. You are human; there is no way you can avoid the necessary adjustments to changing circumstances in your evolutionary process. Now, this will require some work on your part, but we know that everyone drawn to this book has already been working for a long time both individually and collectively for personal evolution and for changes in the world. So, it will not surprise you that as the changes accelerate and intensify, your own work to evolve accelerates and intensifies as well.

We would like to begin by discussing portals with you. Portals may manifest as energetic openings in a myriad of ways. You may sense their presence energetically, or they may appear physically as waves in a mirage-like fashion as gateways that invite you into other dimensional experiences. You may experience portals opening in specific places around the planet (or even in your very own home) as you do your personal work. Remember that everything is energy, and as you work to open yourselves, you will find that portals shift, appear, and open. They will open, offering opportunities to all who wish to change with the evolving Earth. They will automatically raise the vibration of anyone entering into them, working with you as you raise your own vibration by measuring your lives through *energy* rather than *time*. This is important because *time* as you perceive it is an illusion. Remember, time only exists on planet Earth in the third dimension. The reason we focus on Liquid Time is to help you understand that time is not static measurable minutes on the clock that tick by linearly, one by one. Time is a flow of energy that proceeds according to your thoughts. We cannot say anything more important than to emphasize that you must monitor *each* thought you think to raise your vibration to meet the incoming energies for your own evolution.

This Now moment brings grand opportunities for doing just that, grand opportunities in which you have enlightened moments of being able to see that your old thought patterns no longer apply. You will begin to understand that you don't have to worry, that you don't have to hold on to belief systems that no longer fit the true reality. You don't have to believe that old patterns of experiences will be repeated and that you are powerless to change them. You will have the opportunity to discover and act upon the knowledge that you create your reality by what you think, and in monitoring your thoughts and choosing them carefully, you can then begin to actually create a better reality than the one in which you have been suffering for so long. As you change your thinking and your beliefs, you will begin to expand your consciousness so that you will be able to have a greater connection between yourselves and Source as co-creators and re-awaken to your own power and divinity.

You are about to experience changes for the entire planet, for not only is Earth changing, but humanity is changing too. You will find that individually, people are becoming more harmonious by nature as they open to possibilities and begin to interact differently with each other. As more light pours into the planet and people work with higher vibrations, these portals of energy will open all over the Earth to help you raise your awareness. You can match your own energy to the portals that are appearing by requesting that you have access to a portal of higher energy. Then go into a deeply quiet state and experience what is possible. Just as time does not really exist, space also does not exist. Everything exists simultaneously and in unity, which is another way of saying that you are a conscious being living in a multidimensional and conscious experience. Multidimensionality means that you step beyond what you think is over here or over there. Other dimensions exist side-by-side with the one that you perceive now. As you change your thought patterns and open your hearts to more possibilities, you will begin to experience a more multidimensional way of being in the world. You are not moving in a linear progression from the third dimension to the fifth, although many, many channels are quite fond of saying "fifth dimension" as a marker or an all-encompassing term for the next level of vibratory awareness. We disagree with that terminology because we know that there are differing levels of multidimensional awareness available all the time having to do with opening to the understanding that space and time do not exist in the true reality. Dimensionality is moving between experiences in a liquid, flowing way with the trust that you have the power to make an effective difference by the choices you make, the thoughts you think, your beliefs, and the love you hold within your hearts.

We will speak about what humanity is becoming, what we

call the Authentic Human that will be the New Human and how you may begin to perceive yourselves differently. Throughout the book, we will use Cullen's term, which we very much like, your "Future Selves". As a species, you have always seen yourselves through your physical eyes or through concepts only fixed in your mind as mental pictures. But in ancient days, as measured by your linear perception of time, you also incorporated the spiritual aspects of yourselves. That has been lost for various reasons. You have come to see yourselves as static beings who are in the physical realm only, perceiving only through the five physical senses. You organize your lives according to your physical experiences or what you believe to be real. The energies that are now present are opening you to remember that you are larger than this, not just the mental concept of understanding that you are a spiritual being in a physical body, but an actual experience of being in a larger state than you experience yourselves at present. You are, as we have often said, waveforms. You are energy in motion. In other words, nothing about you is the same in any given moment, for you are continually changing. Yet the rate of change according to your perception is so slow that you do not perceive it at all. In the energies of Now, things are speeding up to such a degree that you will have to actually begin to understand that you yourselves are constantly moving, constantly in change, constantly in a flux of moving out of who you were and becoming who you are in the next moment.

Your ability to remember that you were in waveform before you became so attached to your physical bodies will help expand your remembering and knowing who you are and what you are capable of. It will solidify your awareness of where your consciousness lives. For those of you who agree to release your collective and individual perceptions of who you think you are, this will enhance your ability to do what you now consider to be magical things. When you perceive yourselves as you were before you so attached to the physical form, you will remember such things as communicating telepathically. You do that somewhat now but on a limited basis. You may know when a friend is going to call, or you may complete someone else's sentence because you have joined the water[2] of their thoughts and understand what they are about to say. That is a limited use of your ability for telepathic wisdom. When you open up your First Sense[3], or your intuition, more fully because you recognize the waveform that you are and begin to act from that understanding, you will be able to send telepathic messages anywhere at any time to anyone. Others who open up will be able to receive those messages. That means that the need for speech will be much less important. The need for communication will be much more streamlined and flowing. You will be able to say "I need" telepathically, and if you are in a positive vibration, the Universe will provide whatever you need because that telepathic need reaches out to everyone across the planet, as well as beyond the planet. Your needs can be met because you are communicating them more clearly without the internal conflict of your belief systems and your limiting thoughts based upon your earlier experience about what you can or cannot have. Your telepathic communication will open up new worlds for you. Once you begin to understand how to express to the Universe what you need, adding your own creative energy, you will be able to manifest more readily as well. Your lives may become more like what you view on the television show "Star Trek" of having replicators that you can ask for a specific breakfast and instantly it manifests in front of you without the preparation. This is the import of knowing how you can communicate telepathically.

You have believed that manifestation comes only from positive intentions and positive thoughts, and indeed, that is a great part of how you manifest. And yet, you are so conflicted in your thoughts as a species at present that often you cannot consistently hold the positive intentions and ideas that you wish to manifest. Instead you move into an emotional state and re-enter old patterns of reaction and old behaviors rather than continuing to constantly hold the trust that you can have whatever you want and need at any time. Always remember that when you manifest and when you communicate, you must consider in your heart the principle of *In Lak'ech*, a Mayan phrase that means, "I am another yourself." Our Chapter on Unity will enforce principles on how to regularly incorporate that consideration. The principle of *In Lak'ech* links you to everything and everyone on the planet and beyond. It helps you to remember that you are connected, and it is through that sense of connection that you must always honor the highest good for all. As you raise your vibrations and begin to remember to include that all of your requests have to match the highest good for all, you become more synchronized and joined with harmony. Therefore, it is easier for the Universe to provide collectively what you need upon this planet. Our Manual will help you understand the higher reality so that you can begin to participate with the Universe in this profoundly wonderful way!

In the accelerating energies that support your evolution into the New Humans, you will learn to step away from separation and fear if you choose to do so. But it is your choice. If you remain afraid of what is happening with Earth changes, or the weather, or war, or in your family dynamics, or in your job, or your finances, if you retain patterns of thought that say, "I am afraid of these things because this has been my experience," then you cannot consistently be in the higher vibration. So, you do have a very big choice to make in each Now moment—a choice to abandon who you thought you were or believed yourself to be and how you believed the world to be. You have a choice to instead adopt a viewpoint that says, "What I believed to be real is an illusion, and I trust that I am larger than what I see, for I am a fluid waveform that is connected to everything." Operating from higher vibrations with this awareness of your connection to everything allows you to make choices for the highest good for all. You will do it with such a feeling of joy that it cannot help but manifest. This will be a major change for humanity.

We are telling you that you have the opportunity Now to move beyond everything that you have believed to be real, and we are providing steps to achieve this! You have the opportunity to let go of everything that has caused suffering and separation on this planet. As we mentioned earlier, the Earth and humans once understood the nature of change—that change is in every present moment, and that you are flowing waves of energy. When the realization of your waveform sinks in, the possibility to create a new peaceful kingdom arises. You can collectively manifest a reality where you do not struggle in opposition to each other, Nature, or the Earth, but thrive in the harmony and grace of interwoven waves of love and joy! You will have the ability to connect with the concept of *In Lak'ech* and align that concept with every animal, every plant, every person on the planet, and then extend it beyond the planet into all those other beings that you know exist but may or may not have met quite yet. You have the opportunity Now to begin the pathway to co-creating a peaceable kingdom with each other and with Source. You have been given an opportunity to understand that your life is an energetic experience and that every experience you have alters your energy. It is to your best advantage to focus upon the higher vibrational aspects and respond to everything that comes to you with love and compassion.

We trust that you can raise your vibration and do the work required to release the shadows we spoke of earlier and step into alignment with who you really are, stepping out of third-dimensional reality and stepping into multidimensional reality as waveforms of energy, light, and love. We profoundly wish you a wonderful journey of heightened awareness and possibilities stepping into, experiencing, and loving all, from this moment on. As you apply our Manual for Accelerated Evolution, you may, if you choose, enter a magnificent portal on all levels to finally bring about the momentous positive changes you have been envisioning and have been waiting on for so long.

One thing that is important for you to know is that we have never been interested only in one-way dialogues. We have always been interested in two-way conversations because while you learn from our perspective, we also learn how to better support and help you by listening to your perspective. We see this as our job—one that we love—to be connected and listening to what is important to you. Therefore, we include Questions and Answers from our previous Live Calls[4] as an important part of this book. We trust sharing in this way will even further enhance your understanding and evolution.

We love you. Good Always.

~ Laarkmaa

STEP ONE:

UNITY CONSCIOUSNESS

You have been hearing a lot of words from light circles around the world; all the different avenues for bringing forth evolutionary wisdom are using key terms like Unity Consciousness, Anchoring the Light, Light Worker, and Light Mover—all manner of terms that speak of higher vibratory resonance. We would like to bring those key terms into your everyday vocabulary in a way that makes them real to you and not just as mental concepts. We are going to start with the idea of *Unity Consciousness*. First of all, as we have said before, nothing is ever going to be the same again. Some of you may grieve that you cannot get your favorite this or your favorite that to which you are accustomed, or that things are changing so much that you do not feel comfortable without your familiar settings. But whatever discomforts you are experiencing now will be offset in a very large way by the things that are coming to bring you harmony, peace, joy, uplifted spirits, and more love. So don't be too annoyed or too frustrated when things to which you are accustomed fall away or are no longer available, or when things change suddenly, or the formats of your technology or third-dimensional structures shift just a bit. It will happen. Just take a breath—breathe in; breathe out—then ask how this can be better, and then look for how to participate in or with whatever is there. For a very long time now, your world has been built upon ideas of separation, competition, judgment, and blame. And yet, those of you who are working with the light know that there is a higher reality. There is such a thing as Unity Consciousness. When we have spoken to you about the principle of *In Lak'ech* (I am another yourself), you have understood this to mean that every single one of you is connected. If you love yourself, you love everyone else; if you judge someone else, you are judging yourself; if you blame someone else, you are blaming yourself. Whatever you do to yourself, you are doing to everyone else. And whatever everyone else is doing is impacting you. This becomes a little bit "touchy" when you start to look at the unconscious behavior of many people all around you. But whenever you witness that, simply shrug and say, " I will give them compassion, for I have experienced exactly what they are experiencing in a different situation—a lack of understanding, a lack of awareness of the highest good for all. " Instead of being frustrated, extend your compassion, for you have all suffered.

We want to give you a particular principle to work with to help you move away from the separation that has been such a part of your reality in the third dimension. That is to examine everything in terms of *we* instead of in terms of *I*. In the western world, there has been a strong push over the last hundred years or so to individualize and stand up for who you are, to speak up for yourself, to put forth your own point of view, and to speak your own truth. These are the ways in which you have been trained; in fact, psychological training in books and universities for therapists instruct therapists to teach you to say, "I *feel*" as a preface to any problematic conversation to prevent your saying things that blame one another. We are telling you that you need to take it one step further. Rather than simply saying, "I think or I feel" to make sure that you are being heard, try fully listening to what someone else is sharing also. Listening is far more important than speaking, for if you do not truly listen from your heart, you cannot know how to respond when you speak. Ask yourself, "How often do I think in terms of I?" The modern cultures of society are very narcissistic. You are trained to be narcissistic because you do live within a narcissistic culture. And in order to break that pattern, you need to make a very strong conscientious choice to begin to speak in terms of *we*. If you are talking about a problem, you can say, "We can address that in this way," or "We can pay attention to that", instead of "I'm going to do this" or "You should do that." When you talk about yourself and your life, start to notice how much you incorporate everything into terms of your own personal self: *"I'm* going to do this", or *"I'm* going to talk about this now because it is important that *you* hear *me."* Instead of saying, *"I'd* like to speak about something that we can all benefit from," say *"We* need to speak about this." In other words, bit by bit, begin to curb the way you think and change the way you speak to *we, we, we.* You are connected. You are in the light together.

All of you who are reading this are working with the light, and the more you band together with the sense of *"we*-ness" in unity and the oneness of what you are, the stronger the light becomes. And the stronger the light becomes, the more you can use it with precision and a laser-like focus, sending it into any area that is troubled, to any person or place that needs healing, and to anything that needs the attention of the light to bring it out of darkness. What we are saying is for your own personal good, for the highest good of all beings on the planet, and for the highest good of the planet itself. The more you focus on *we,* the more you automatically are incorporating light into your cellular structure. You move away from individuation and separation cell-by-cell, changing the individual organism into a unified blend of connectivity, in which all cells are connected and each one affects the total impact of how the organism functions. That organism can be a person, a family, a business, a corporation, a spiritual group, or a political group; the organism can be anything. But you need to understand the liquidity of cellular structure, how all cells flow into and impact one another, and how when you fill them with light and are aware of the connection and how everything is impacted through this connection, you strengthen your light, and you become a stronger organism as a whole. Focusing upon unity is going to help you to *be* the light, rather than simply "anchoring" the light. That is not our terminology, but we have certainly heard it a great deal recently. We would say *bringing in the light* and *shining your own light.* You know, we changed the term Light Worker to Light Mover many years ago when we told you that your job is to *move* the light, not to *work* with it. And then we changed the terminology again from Light Mover to Light Bearer. The terminology was changed to help you recognize that you are a light being and begin to think and act like one. You bear light. And everywhere you go, every thought you think, either reflects shadows that you have not yet cleared, which cloud your perceptions through continued fear and separation, or the light that you are, which reflects clarity. As you focus more and more upon *being* the light, *being* the love, and sending that light and love out with every thought, with every breath, with every choice, your light becomes brighter and brighter. The fire within you is more directly connected to Source and to the Light Bearer who is standing next to you or across the planet working with you to shine light into dark places.

We want you to focus upon being the light that you are. We have spoken with you before about individual projects where you should focus attention such as clearing out your shadows or doing some work in the third-dimensional realm; we have suggested that you look at what is going on there and focus upon what you need to do to awaken others and make them aware so that conscious actions can be taken. This is best done through demonstrating by example. We have also told you that now it is time to simply focus upon sending the light into any situation. We give you guidance and suggestions according to the errors that humanity is making or what humanity needs in order to evolve. We know that all of you, with your open hearts, your willingness to serve, and your desire to reach your highest versions of yourselves, are willing to listen to our suggestions and incorporate them along with your own choices and your own intuition that guides you.

When we tell you to think in terms of *we* instead of in terms of *I,* know that we are already doing that and setting an example for you. Ever since we first began speaking to you through Cullen and Pia, we have always said, "We are one of six and six of one."[1] By this, we have been instilling the idea within you for a long time that each of you is an individual spark of great importance, and yet all of you together create a flame, a band of light that cannot be denied or ignored. Together you can be a bright flame that influences everything on the planet. Be willing to stop thinking in terms of *I* the way your culture has trained you and begin to think and speak in terms of *we.* Don't say *you* or *I,* but say *we* at every given opportunity. If you are speaking in terms of *we,* it certainly is impacting everyone in a more obvious way than the subtle ways you impact each other through your current self-reference, for every thought you have and every thought you voice sends out an energy. You might as well begin to think in terms of, "We think this, and we would like to see that, and we would like to focus on this" because you are already impacting everything and everyone with every thought, with every word, and with every choice you make. When you begin to think and act through the concept of *In Lak'ech,* you will automatically move closer to Unity Consciousness, understanding that what is done to one is done to all.

We trust that we are giving you a different vantage point on Unity Consciousness and Oneness. From our perspective, Unity Consciousness and Oneness have previously been understood by humanity as a joining of hands together and doing something for a like cause, in which you decide to focus on something together, and each one of you brings your part into the whole. Now we are saying, still join hands, still join spirits, but look to each other and understand instantly that the *we* that is doing something is the totality of all the *I's* that you have seen before. You are each other. You are we. We are you. And the more you focus upon this perception of Unity, the more you begin to see yourselves as changeable energy that can transform itself into any shape or form, rather than static, unchanging physical forms. Energy can direct itself to anywhere that it is needed with its own intelligence. So therefore, begin to think and speak in terms of "We are energy. We are light. We are love." And in that *we*, incorporate all of humanity who is listening, all of humanity that is willing to step into that place of unity, abandoning ideas of separation, pain, judgment, and competition.

Competition and judgment have done nothing but cause more separation and more fear upon the planet, and it is time to put that aside. Many of you are putting a lot, if not all, of your energy into bringing this Unity Consciousness together in a form so that you can live together, eat together, work together, have projects together and not have to worry about paying individual bills, who got a job or who didn't, who won or who lost a competition or a game, or who is better than someone else, all those judgments that have kept you separate before. The new communities that you are almost ready to build (as you are now working out the last struggles and last kinks of old paradigm competition) are built upon concepts of *we*. They are built upon concepts of energy and the understanding that everything is energy, and as energy, with conscious intention, you have the ability to bring forth light in every single moment. From our perspective, what you are doing as Light Bearers is much grander and reaches out much farther than simply "anchoring light" into the planet. You are not simply passively accepting the light that you know is there, receiving it into yourself, and then anchoring it into the planet. No. You are doing more than anchoring light. You are *bearing* light yourselves because you *are* light. You are joining together so that your light becomes stronger, brighter, and more effective. Simply joining together in unity can heal everything that needs healing. Light is love, and love in its unconditional form is light. This is the true understanding of Unity Consciousness. We gave you the Mayan Calendar and the Pleiadian-Earth Energy Calendar to help you begin to live your lives through the understanding of energy rather than using time to guide your lives. Each Universal energy and each Earth energy present circumstances for you to explore and expand your consciousness.

Pleiadians and other light beings have watched your species for a very, very long time. We have seen those of you who are reading this now begin to choose things from a higher vibrational perspective, making higher choices on a more regular basis. We want you to know that as long as this experiment on Earth has been ongoing, humanity as a species has been evaluated to see how you are progressing. We have explained to you about the Choice Point[2] that was reached some time ago. The evaluation is now over for us, but you may certainly continue to evaluate *yourselves* as you continue to grow and evolve. You are no longer being evaluated as a species. Those of you who have chosen to ascend with the Earth have made your choice and are moving through the ascension process. Others may be slowly awakening, but while they are being watched with love and guidance, they are not on the same ascension path as you are. We want to give you an understanding about energetic places where you can evaluate yourselves. You are able to sense the need for evaluation and correction within yourselves whenever you feel yourselves a little off center, that is, emotionally unbalanced or mentally stuck.

A particular energetic point has been the evaluation point

for humanity ever since the Pleiadians were helping the Mayan people over 5,000 years ago. That point holds the energies of 3 *Loving* as shown on the *Pleiadian-Earth Energy Calendar*. Three is the Universal energy of creativity, providing you ample room to create something new every moment. When the Universal energy of 3 is present during the same moment as the Earth energy *Loving*, which is the energy that most contains Venus's guidance of how to blend duality into unity through justice and love, a portal of opportunity is present for you to make leaps in your evolutionary process. The energies of *3 Loving* provide an excellent place to evaluate yourselves and make self-corrections, asking,

> "How am I doing?
> Am I on track with my evolution?
> Do I understand reality from a broader perspective?
> Have I achieved a state of balance and unconditional love for all life?
> Do I make all my choices for the highest good of all?"

3 Loving has been an important evaluation point for humanity for thousands and thousands of years, but you were unaware that you were even being evaluated. Now you know. And now it is time for you to use that energy as the divine sparks of light that you are to begin to evaluate yourselves and take charge of your own process of understanding and evolution.

This Manual for Accelerated Evolution provides the basic principles you need for your evolution and for ascension into Rainbow body form. We have already discussed your consciousness and unity. We have talked about love, and we will discuss it more later in this book. We will also speak about family. Most of what we have to tell you has to do with letting go of old viewpoints and beliefs from the old paradigm while you are changing into a new paradigm with new ways of thinking and relating. There are a few key energies we wish to discuss now in more detail. The words describing these energies are *flow, flexibility, freedom, and abundance,* and they are infinitely connected. There is no way that you can separate the meaning one of these words from another. We would like for you to practice being flexible rather than clinging to old ideas of right versus wrong or clinging to old ways of doing things simply because they are familiar and comfortable, or you have always done things in a certain way. Inflexibility has plagued humanity for thousands of years. You call it "tradition." As you are now evolving more quickly and increasing your vibration, you must become more flexible, as you will melt into what we call Liquid Time[3]. Time as you have known it is melting away; you cannot use it in the way you used to. Increasingly you are experiencing that there is not enough time to do what you have been able to do previously. This is occurring because you are learning to be rather than to *do*, which means you don't have to fit so many things into your daily lives. You are beginning to actually experience time as flow of energy, moving away from the structures of time. Liquid Time is the dissolution of all the structures of past and future, keeping you in the present moment. Liquid Time is deeply connected to the energy of flow, allowing you to move in flow from one synergistic experience into another. Liquid Time is energy; it is about being in the medium of flow with water, air, consciousness, and vibration. Whatever medium you want to choose, being in flow means that you are very much aware of what is going on around you in the present moment, and you are also very much in contact with what is called for in the current energy for the highest good of all. Being in flow allows you to ask, "What is being asked of me in this Now moment that will carry me fluidly into the next Now moment?" That is being in the Liquid Time experience with flexibility and flow, a new concept, yes?!

As you step into being more flexible, you may notice that plans do not work as smoothly as they have before. You may begin to do something you planned, and the Universe presents you with an alternative. The plan fails, but success arrives when you listen to the energies that are present and see what the moment asks of you. For example, if you plan to have lunch with a friend and your friend cancels at the last minute, you have a choice to be disappointed or to accept the change, asking what else does this moment want of me? Perhaps the space opened up to meet someone else who needed your council and light. Or perhaps you were protected from being exposed to a toxic situation of some kind. These are just a few examples of possibilities. When you approach everything in Liquid Time, you are experiencing life with an attitude of gratitude and acceptance. This attitude opens you to all good things flowing toward you because you are in alignment with the highest good of all.

The ability to flow with whatever is, to be present, to do whatever is necessary with gratitude that you are flexible and can flow into a different pattern brings a gift. This way of living with a grateful heart and acceptance of *what is* provides the doorway to ultimate freedom. When you are flexible and in flow, you become free. You are no longer confined by limits of time. You are no longer confined by belief systems or expectations or even hopes. Instead, losing all expectations, you live in grateful acceptance of whatever is before you. It is best for you to look at all experiences objectively, being grateful for them even if they may be challenging or uncomfortable at the time. Whatever comes to you, be grateful for the experience and ask, "How can I use this experience for the highest good of all?" That is learning how to understand and appreciate true freedom. When you have true freedom, you will find you no longer have that feeling of lack. You will lose the fear of not having enough: of not having enough time, enough money, enough love, enough food. The fear of losing whatever you have thought would not be enough will be gone. Once you are living as we are suggesting, with flexibility, flow, and a grateful heart, you will find yourselves experiencing more freedom. The wonderful thing about being completely free is that complete freedom leads you to complete abundance.

Abundance is not simply about money. Abundance is about having enough of everything you need and enough of everything that makes you smile and feel happy and joyful. Having complete abundance fills your heart so full that you want to share everything you have with everyone else in the world. This is true abundance. But you cannot achieve true abundance without being truly grateful, truly free, truly flexible, living in true flow, and honoring the principle of *In Lak'ech*. These principles are part of the abundance that you seek. Now your monetary systems are upside down. You may have noticed that there is a lot of control of your monetary systems at present. (There always has been, but it is more obvious now that you are more awake.) We have been telling you for at least a decade that this monetary control was going to increase and that your financial structures would fall. But many of you are also noticing *that it doesn't matter!* Suddenly you don't care; you are simply not worried about having enough money or paying your rent. All of a sudden you are beginning to experience a deeper level of trust that was not possible when you were living in constant fear. You have a sense of freedom and understanding that everything will be okay. You may not know how it is going to unfold, but you sense and trust that you will be fine. You are doing your part by being grateful, flexible, and continually asking for guidance on how to make higher vibrational choices for the good of all. You begin to understand how to live within Liquid Time, moving synchronistically from this Now moment into the next Now moment. As if by magic, you know what needs to be done and everything is taken care of. When you are living like this, you will find both more freedom and more abundance in your lives.

We want you to stop and think about freedom. Although you have been told that you live in free societies, how many of you feel truly free? How many feel the freedom to do exactly what you want in any given moment? We think not too many of you have that freedom—a few, but certainly not many of you. That is because you have obligations that keep you from being free. They may be chosen obligations, but they are still obligations. You have not learned to manage your lives in unity, in Liquid Time, in a state of gratitude, flowing with *what is* for the highest good in every single moment in every energy. Because of the old, habitual ways of thinking and living, you still feel like you are imprisoned here on Earth. You are imprisoned by time; there is not enough of it to do what you want to do. You are imprisoned by monetary systems that keep you in jobs you don't like to pay for things that you don't actually need, or sometimes, even want. Families that you feel obligated to by birth, not by choice, imprison you. (We will talk about that in more depth later.) You are imprisoned by choices you have made that are no longer appropriate for your life. You do not understand that you have the freedom to choose something else, something truly better. Freedom, flexibility, and flow are three key principles to help you move into a state of gratitude and abundance. Abundance comes from freedom, and freedom comes from abundance; they are interlocked, intertwined. You cannot have one without having the other. Freedom comes from flexibility and flow. Most people think that if they had enough money, they would be free to do whatever they want. But it doesn't work like that. Abundance is not simply having enough money. Abundance is recognizing that you are free by living from your heart in the present moment, aligned with the new paradigm and the ascension process. The freedom that you are obtaining moment-by-moment as you make higher and higher choices provides the thrill of feeling a sense of higher vibrational living. As you feel light pouring in, changing you at a cellular level, you are becoming more free. And yes, we will speak about the challenges you feel during these changes: the confusion, physical symptoms, and forgetting. Think how free you will feel when you have forgotten everything that imprisoned you through your sense of obligation, as you learn to make appropriate choices moment-by-moment in a spirit of unity, and as you remember who you are as divine sparks of light who are free to make choices related to the highest good of all. It is important for you to understand that these suggestions in no way dismiss the importance of keeping your word to others. If you promise to show up, you should show up. But as you begin to live in the way we are suggesting, you will learn how to make promises from your heart, using your intuition about the right timing, rather than making empty promises from your mind, promises that fall apart and then leave you feeling guilty. True freedom and flexibility require consideration of everyone else, for you are all linked in unity. When you make your choice in the spirit of *In Lak'ech*, you are making a choice that affects everyone else. As they do the same, making choices for the highest good of all, they, in turn, are bringing you a higher vibrational energy. This is your light working together for freedom for all. This is your achievement; it is what you are here to accomplish right now.

There has been so much confusion and fear heightened recently by your governments, your media, and your medical authorities (who do not understand the possibilities of true healing). All of them are telling you to do as they say, or the "boogey man" (the latest illness or threat) is going to get you. We think that when you are living as we suggest and taking responsibility to discern and stand up for the truth, you will not be impacted as greatly by these real or imagined threats. When you are not afraid, you have your own shields of light protecting you. Refusing to be fearful and simultaneously taking responsibility to act appropriately in the third dimension supports your continued safety. You are being responsible when you do not react with fear, but instead respond objectively to what is present. When you respond to outer circumstances objectively, being flexible and changing as the situation changes even if you must change your plans, you earn more freedom. You recognize that you are moving in flow with Liquid Time, with the power of light that you are, giving you the freedom to become who you truly are, your Future Self. That is how you will attain true abundance, including abundance of good health.

Always, always remember to be grateful. Cultivate feelings of gratitude. Instead of being disappointed when you cannot find what you think you want, be grateful for what else you find, or what shows up instead. Cultivate gratitude for everything that happens to you and recognize that as you are flexible with outer third-dimensional situations, you are protected because of the light that you carry that refuses to acknowledge fear. When you are objective in your third-dimensional reality, and you respond appropriately to whatever the moment brings; you flow through all challenges in a state of grace. We bring higher vibrational energy of trust, especially during these times of intense change, to help you step into truly remembering who you are and trusting the evolutionary process you are currently experiencing. Remember, remember, remember who you are, divine sparks of light, grateful sparks of light, flexible sparks of light, fluid sparks of light flowing through Liquid Time, reaching and obtaining abundance and freedom moment-by-moment.

QUESTIONS & ANSWERS
STEP 1

Thank You, Laarkmaa. I like that you are always listening in the ethers out there. So, thank you.

You are welcome. We remind you that we have never been interested only in one-way conversation. We have always been interested in two-way conversations because while you learn as we share our perspective, we also learn how to better support and help you by listening to your perspective.

Was our experience with the Coronavirus a new step for humanity to come back to ourselves on an inner basis, for inner growth and inner light?

You are living on a planet of duality. Those who chose to remain on the wheel of karma and responded with fear did not see what you have just described as an opportunity. To them it was seen as a threat. Because you have a dualistic experience at this time, as you begin to separate your path of choice from the path of the collective, those who are working with the higher vibration and who maintain a higher perspective can recognize that the virus was a doorway of opportunity. This was an opportunity to step outside of your fear and to learn to be objective rather than fearful. Those of you who maintained this higher perspective responded objectively to what was happening rather than reacting in fear. It was an opportunity for you to learn how to keep out of harm's way by simply refusing to be harmed! And by being objective, you were also able to discern the true cause of the symptoms, most of which were not virus related. Yes, indeed, the presence of the virus could be seen as a higher vibrational opportunity for those who are looking at it from this perspective.

In such situations, we do not recommend that you simply

say, "I can't be harmed; it is never going to touch me," and then walk into the middle of an infected area or a crowd that could be contaminated. That would be equivalent to saying a prayer over a spoonful of sugar believing that then it won't hurt you. Both of these examples are ideas held in the mind, but they are mind ideas only, and they are not remotely connected to the truth or reality. A simple affirmation is never enough. You do live in the third dimension and must pay attention to real third-dimensional challenges by taking positive action as well as using positive thoughts. Use your objective discernment and decide where it is appropriate for you to be and what you need to do in changing circumstances. Keep fear out of your discernment. Instead, trust that you will be okay, and then make wise, objective choices. You will be okay if you are combining trust with your objective choices. You will be okay if you do not focus on fear, but instead use your energy to prepare yourself for whatever is happening. As most of you reading this have already made your choice to ascend with the Earth, it is always a good idea to choose the higher perspective of whatever experience you are having. To descend into the lower perspective takes you back into the energies of the Collective, which do not belong to higher vibrational states. There is no reason for you to enter into that doorway of fear and reaction ever again.

Thank you for your suggestions and your guidance to help us make wise choices. You have spoken before about the coming control of the monetary system, and I have been reading for years that the monetary system was going to crash. It has been mentioned that the Coronavirus would cause the freezing of our bank accounts. Is it appropriate to change paper money for gold money in this time of transition, or is there something else we might do to get through such a challenging period, or should we just let money go?

The Coronavirus was not merely a simple biological virus

that evolved. It was intentionally instituted with the increased presence of 5G to control you more than ever. The idea of controlling your money is only one of two ultimate systems of control; the other one is more forceful, requiring you to have vaccinations, restricting your travel if you refuse, and possibly even restricting your ability to leave your own homes. All of these outer restrictions are aimed at controlling you and your freedom. Freezing your monetary accounts may well be a last attempt to control you if they cannot create enough fear to control you otherwise. It is a possibility. But the value of your money is already failing, as we told you it would. When sources mention freezing your bank accounts, there is an implication that there is not enough legitimate backup for the paper money that is printed (in any country). In such cases, governments are admitting that money has no value. Freezing bank accounts allows them to take whatever money is there for themselves. Ten years ago, five years ago, two years ago, we would have (and actually have) recommended that you have precious metals for currency. At this point, with the ultimate control they are seeking, it is likely that personal gold and silver would be seized as "property of the state." It may be a temporary tool for bartering for food, but once it is known that you have such precious metals, attention would be drawn to you, and it would likely be seized by those who wish to control you.

Our suggestion for the transition is to objectively use all forms of currency available in the moment, knowing and understanding, that at any given instant the rules can change. If something isn't working to the satisfaction of those seeking control at any given moment, they will try something else to control you. Your ultimate abundance will come from joining together and saying to one another, "What is mine is yours." When you do that, whatever they seize from you will not matter, because together you will find a way to manifest what you need. Your ultimate abundance will come through the spirit of *In Lak'ech* and the ability to be flexible and fluid around whatever is happening. Have enough on hand of all your essentials, knowing that everything can change in a moment.

Hello, Laarkmaa, thank you so much for your powerful Live Calls during this amazing time to be alive on this planet. Also, thank you so much for your message to humanity and other messages on YouTube.

You are very welcome, Dear One.

Someone asked me how I drive my motorcycle on the freeway, which is a dangerous place with a lot of traffic and inconsiderate people. I don't have any problem at all driving on the freeway because of my general inclination toward unity, beginning with consideration and compassion on the road. It has turned into just a general flow, where nobody impedes on me because it is part of the unity I experience. I believe that is why I don't experience traffic the way everyone else does.

That is exactly accurate, and what a beautiful example! If only we could help more people to understand that when they actually change their consciousness to incorporate everything around them as part of themselves, they will stop having obstacles and challenges, because everything will flow. It is a beautiful concept you have mastered and expressed perfectly. When you worry about something that you think is going to be a problem, when you perceive something that is happening as a problem, you are creating more of the problem by judging what is happening through the lens of separation. When you acknowledge what is there with compassion as part of you, you change the energy. In this way, solutions to problems are discovered much more quickly, or problems even cease to exist at all. Many people spend most of their time worrying about something that never happens or judging what is happening without realizing it is part of them. If there is traffic, and you are on the road, you have contributed to the traffic. If you see it flowing, you are contributing to the solution to the problem, and it ceases to exist as a problem for you, because you have enlarged your vision. We encourage you to focus on what you need to accomplish rather than worrying about potential problems so that you do not drain your energy worrying about the negative "what ifs" that simply build boxes around your experience and keep you trapped. When you understand that you are all the same and that everything is energy, you begin to understand that you can flow as you need to, and the energy changes to allow that to happen. Thank you for your very, very wonderful example.

Can you give us a physical example of how we can move from separation into unity?

Yes. During these changes deep breathing is important, especially because you are moving. You are moving from a system of duality closer to a system based on unity, and you must rely upon your breath to remind you how to unify opposites. Breathe in and breathe out, and pay attention; think of your inbreath and your outbreath as one unified breath. Half of it is in and half of it is out, but it is one breath. Slowing your breathing down, slowing your movements down, watching what your body is doing to de-stress, and relaxing in the moment is very helpful and will help you understand exactly what to do and when as you are moving toward unity.

STEP TWO:

OBJECTIVITY, JUDGMENT, & EXPERIENCE

Our Manual for Accelerated Evolution will now take you further into understanding what needs to occur as you evolve, beginning with a deeper understanding of duality and unity. We last spoke about the concept of unity; now we will discuss the concept of duality and your dualistic experience from our perspective. Duality, as we have always said, was never meant to be about the polar opposites in which you continually find yourselves engaged such as right versus wrong, us versus them, and all of those other seemingly polar opposites were never intended to be part of your experience in duality. Rather, duality has always been meant to give you a larger perspective. Nevertheless, you now find yourselves in a world that is continually focusing upon dualistic opposite extremes, and your attention is focused on the conflict between the dualistic perspectives. Everywhere you look, everything you hear has a different perspective, often with an underlying argument or assumption behind it, either subtle or spoken, that implies, "I am right, and you are wrong." That is not the way to evolve, when you consider that you are all connected. You are all one. The way to evolve is to begin to listen and consider what you hear (or see) that is resonant with your own energy and what is non-resonant. Then from a point of discernment and objectivity, you can join the varying perspectives together into a more unified and holistic form of thought about whatever the issue may be, rather than contributing to the continued separation of ideas that is so prevalent on Earth. Meld the differences together to achieve a better and more balanced whole.

Objectivity

Our theme in this chapter is objectivity. For you to evolve more quickly, you must learn to be objective. You are living in a period where the energies encourage bringing up whatever shadows need to be cleared so that you can objectively see and participate within a larger reality. Whatever shadows of misconception or misbelief that reside within you or within the world must be cleared through a conscious desire to do so. When the need for clearing old patterns surfaces, you will most likely experience a sense of "pulling" on your emotions. You may find yourself overreacting to people or situations. You may find yourself feeling unhappy, angry, frustrated, or deeply sad without really knowing why you feel that way. You may find that you simply want to leave the planet and don't want to be here anymore. That should be considered as a temporary feeling state only, not a reality, for you are here because you are on the verge of accomplishing what you came to Earth to do. But it is quite natural for those of you who are working with the light, on occasion, to feel that it is just simply too hard. The way to work through these feelings so that you can evolve more quickly is to obtain objectivity within yourself. The Trauma Clearings[1] that we offer are helping people across the world bring up things from this current life and parallel lives and dimensions that are now entering into their everyday consciousness and either causing them to struggle or keeping them blocked from what they need to see. We offer the Trauma Clearings as one avenue to boost you over the hurdle to become who you truly are.

Our Trauma Clearings offer objectivity, which some can

achieve through their own personal work if they choose; however, most of you will achieve more success with our assistance and a broader perspective. With objectivity, you can lessen your reaction to whatever is causing the problem. That does not mean to put your head in the sand and not look at the problem. Nor does it mean to ignore your shadows. What it means is that objectivity allows you to see everything from multiple perspectives without emotional reactions that cause pain, suffering, and separation. Right now, as shadows come up to be cleared for humanity, most people do not even want to look at or examine the pain because it simply hurts too much. Or they are tired of reviewing their shadows over and over again. And yet, this is the most crucial time for shadow clearing, trauma clearing, or working through blockages so that you can finally and fully be the light that you are.

We have noticed in working with you that many of your traumas stem from your families of origin. In working to clear trauma from your systems, it is important that you understand our perspective of family. We see each person's family as a personal training ground, and we will discuss this in more depth in a later chapter.

We are here to help you transform from the divine spark of light that you are into a blazing flame of light that can change the world! That is our purpose: to help you evolve and find your power so that you can achieve your mission, your purpose, what you came to this planet to do. We have always told you that your sole (soul) purpose, the primary thing you are here to do, is simply to *be love.*

By that we mean live each and every moment in the presence of love. And when you accept that as your purpose, and you live your life moment by moment from that place of being love, you will automatically shine light everywhere you go! And what is your work to do right now with this purpose of being love? Your work is to shine light and receive light. It is not just "anchoring" the light, as we have already mentioned. It is not just passively letting the light come in. This is a much more engaged process than that and a much more accelerated expression of light. It requires you to be diligent in your task every single minute of the day. This is the process of being the light and allowing yourself to move from spark to flame so that light shines out from you to wherever it needs to go, even without your conscious direction. And your reception of the light is simultaneously and equally important, that is to receive light from Source, from the Universe, from those of us who are shining light around you, and from the other Light Bearers who are connected in this web of light that is helping the planet. You are here to help the light come in, to accept it, and to reflect it back. As you are nourished by the light, you nourish others. We trust that is clear for you in the way that we state it, and we know that the instruction manual for how to do this is already written in each of your hearts. You simply have to access it, remember it, and then do it!

Judgment

If you find yourself unable to be objective, one of two things is usually happening. We are going to focus on both of those things now, so that you can more easily achieve your soul (sole) purpose at this important time of evolution for humanity and the ascension of the planet. The first issue that prevents objectivity is something that we have discussed many, many times before[2] but not a topic that we have discussed in this particular framework: *judgment*. Often you do not even realize that you are judging someone or something. You are very accustomed to the polarity and the misuse of duality that categorizes everything in terms of "right or wrong" or "me or you" or "us or them." That overlay of judgment from the collective, of which you are quite unaware, will often cause a reaction to someone or something before you even think about it. Thoughts or feelings of, "I don't like this; this makes me angry or unhappy" are not discernments; they come from an emotional place, which classifies those thoughts or feelings as a judgment. We are asking you to increase your attention around judgment. Pay more attention to the ways that you judge. That frown you may give when someone else makes a suggestion; that turning away from someone in your family or at work who says, "Let's do it this way," when you had something else in mind. All of those things are tiny versions of judgment.

We are asking you to slow down and find these patterns within yourself so that you can change them. Evolution is speeding up, and the way to accelerate your own evolution, as strange as it may sound, is to slow down. You need to slow down your reactive response while you are intensifying and raising your vibratory response. Your vibrations go up as you do this work, and your reaction time goes down; your reactions slow considerably. By lowering your reactions and raising your vibrational response, you enter a state of *non-judgment*. Responding is always more gentle than reacting. Cullen reminds us that, "You cannot be in a state of compassion if you are in a state of reaction. Conversely, you cannot be in a state of reaction if you are in a state of compassion."

Non-judgment promotes unity, which we spoke about in the previous chapter. Unity promotes your evolution, and to achieve non-judgment and unity, you must become objective. It is keenly important that you look at your reactions and determine how you can be more objective; ask yourself where you are being judgmental. It is not just about judging other people. It is also about judging ideas that come to you from outside yourself. And it is about judging things that come from within yourself too, from those parts of yourself that are still fractured and are seeking your attention for clearing and healing from family training and traumas in this or parallel lives. Unhealed, those experiences have louder and louder voices, and until they are healed, when you hear those voices (or thoughts or feelings within you) you may become judgmental, asking yourself, "What is wrong with me?" instead of simply acknowledging, "Here is a piece of myself that I have ignored, or a piece that needs to be loved, or a piece that is presenting shadows for me to clear." All of those kinds of thoughts or feelings can constitute judgment. We are asking you to pay more attention to what you feel, and following that, to pay attention to what you are *thinking* about what you feel. Change your thoughts; change your judgments into discernments; change your feeling state by changing your thoughts and your judgments. This is a key point within objectivity.

Experience

The second point within the topic of objectivity also comes from the misperceptions of duality. Here in duality you have a keen attachment to pleasure over pain, a keen attachment to right over wrong, and a keen attachment to good over bad (as you perceive these things). To be objective you must detach from what you "know" in your mind is right, wrong, good, bad, us, them, all those separators that have been a part of the collective overlay of thought. They do imprint themselves upon your consciousness because the world is infused with this kind of thinking. Your job is to change the collective way of thinking by changing how *you* think and respond to life.

We will start this portion of our conversation on objectivity by speaking about experience. To be objective, you must learn that every experience has a purpose. Every single experience you have has a purpose of fulfilling something you have set in motion by a previous choice or is an experience your High Self is bringing to you to show you where your work needs to be focused. You also have experiences that are projected onto you because of the collective. You are part of the collective: you are connected to everyone, and the collective unconscious imprints its thoughts, judgments, and ideas of polarized separation upon you. It is your job to raise your vibration and light, so that you do not react from such an imprint of collective thoughts that are heavier, denser, and sometimes darker than your own vibration or thought field. To do this you must take your most uncomfortable experiences and stop judging them. Stop wishing them to be other than what they are. Do nothing except objectively look at your experiences and tell yourself that they are just that—experiences. Then ask yourself what you can learn from the experience, what benefit can be found from the experience, or what is the experience asking of you? Sometimes what is found is a new way of seeing things. Sometimes what is found is compassion for others. Sometimes what is found is a renewed conviction that you will persevere because you are here simply to *be love.*

In giving each experience the freedom to move, the freedom to speak to you, the freedom to change, the experience has space to begin to change from something you do not want into something that is more palatable to you, something that is more in alignment with who you truly are and your real vibration. You have the power to do this the moment you stop judging the experience and accept it as just an experience—nothing more. However, if you spend your time thinking such thoughts as, "This hurts and I don't like it" or "I don't want to do this because it is painful" or "I don't want to be here like this," if you spend time focusing those feelings into thoughts that express negative outcomes, you are contributing to the dualistic split that causes humanity so much pain, rather than contributing to the unity that we are all seeking and that can bring you peace and joy. Instead contribute to the objectivity that will help you to transcend these experiences so that you can receive their benefit and then quickly move on to what comes next. As we have already said, objectivity is our key second point in your Manual for Accelerated Evolution. You are working toward unity, and to obtain that, you must master objectivity. Now that does not mean not to use your heart. It does not mean to distance yourself in such a way that you do not interact with others; nor should you distance yourself so that you do not wholly give yourself to listening to what is occurring around you and what is being asked of you in every situation. Objectivity is intended merely to remove the emotional component. You have been told for a long time that emotions,[3] which we distinguish from the higher vibrational feelings of love, joy, trust and compassion, are your signposts for how you are out of balance. Well, emotions are appearing all over the place right now as the energies are intensifying to be cleared and cleansed for further progress. Therefore, it is most important that you pay attention to your emotions, but distance yourself from them objectively so that you can really look at and really objectively study what the emotion is telling you. Explore why you are feeling this way from an objective point of view rather than through blame or judgment. Ask what is the essential pattern that is arising for you, and examine your thinking about that pattern. What your emotion is asking of you is to break the *thought* cycle in which you are engaged. Those thoughts that you have stored in your mind from all of your previous experiences that have been categorized as good or bad, me or you, all of those dualistic splits are coming to the surface now for you to be able to see that they are simply *different*. You can then discern if they are in resonance with you or are not in resonance with you. You are moving toward an enlightened field of being and an enlightened sense of who you are as you move from divine spark to divine flame. Therefore, you become more liquid yourself, more mobile, more flexible. This is the liquid crystalline body to which we have referred in the past[4] and which we will address again later in the book. To do this, you have to master objectivity. You have to learn to be objective and still use your whole heart. Use your heart to listen. Use your heart to make decisions. Use your heart to move forward but remain objective every time an emotion arises. Every time you get emotional about an experience, every time you have a feeling that reflects a judgment, remember that emotions are there to help you evolve by changing your thoughts. They are merely (and very importantly) signposts to point the way and to help you achieve the next level of vibration. We have always told you that emotions are signposts for change. But now, the necessity and intense desire and intense need for change are showing up in emotional signposts all over the planet. We are asking you, the Light Bearers, to intensify your focus and ask, "How can I be objective? How can I see what my emotions are pointing to and pay more attention to what I am thinking so that I can break old patterns that are looping in my mind, old patterns that I return to over and over again when things are not what I perceive to be comfortable or good?"

These are uncomfortable times, Dear Ones. You must go through this discomfort to evolve and fully embrace your true selves. It is necessary, and the more uncomfortable you are, the more work you have to do. That does not mean that those who are being called to do more work are of a lower vibration; it means that you are being asked to do more because you are more. Each of you reaches a place of being more light as you do this work. Remember, the dark does not want the light to win this battle of circumstances on your planet. Therefore, when the dark sees one of you moving from divine spark to divine flame, the dark is drawn to your light and then gives you more challenges to try to stop your evolution. Your job is not to simply throw up your hands and run the other way saying, "This is too hard," for this gives the dark more negative energy and allows it to feed upon your distress. Your job is to say, "Yes, I see that you are throwing something at me; I see that you are challenging me; I see what you are trying to do, and guess what? I'm going

29

to send light back to you. I'm going to focus upon the good in every situation. I am light and love, and therefore, the way I am going to respond to this challenge that you have put in front of me (whatever it may be) is to send light into it." Shine light into yourself, into every aspect of who you are, every problem that presents itself, every illness, every depression, everything that comes, shine light into it. Objectively realize that some of these challenging experiences are coming from the dark, which in its own ignorance and forgetful separation, is trying to prevent your growth because you are making such progress in your evolution. Other challenges you experience arise from parallel lives because they wish to be cleansed, cleared, and reintegrated into the fullness of who you are. When you evolve, you change everything. The dark is afraid of that, for it has forgotten that it is also part of the unified field of light. Under the veil of illusion and separation, the dark believes itself to be separate, but we can see and share the larger picture that even the dark serves the light, because through light and love everything is connected, even the dark.

We trust you will spend time with the perspective we have shared here. Feel into your heart and find the pathway that is the best for you to obtain objectivity moment-by-moment as you are sending out love and sending out light.

QUESTIONS & ANSWERS
STEP 2

You have talked about the negativity we experience either from parallel lives or that others project on us; would it be easier to not try to analyze where it is coming from, but to simply be love in that moment? I find if I try to just be calm and as loving as I can be in every situation, it takes the blame out of the situation, and I'm able to concentrate on what I should do. Is that a suitable approach to negativity?

Absolutely. It is absolutely the best approach for discerning what is happening. When you try to analyze it, you get stuck in the mind, and the mental sphere is too imprinted by the collective and your own previous similar experiences. All of those old patterns are coming through in a stronger way. Take yourself out of the mental loop by simply saying to yourself, "It doesn't matter where it is coming from or what it is, all that matters is that I return to my heart, that I am love, and that I send out light in this moment." That is all that matters. Begin in that moment by sending light to yourself, so that you are not unbalanced by what is occurring. Then send light from your heart outwards. That is an excellent way to proceed.

Should we send light into particular areas where we perceive difficulties?

We would prefer that rather than picking one particular problematic area that you send out light everywhere. And let the light contagiously connect with other light. Each time one of you sends out light, know that someone on the other side of the planet is also sending out light, and those loving energies join together to create even more light. Places that seem particularly dark receive the light because you are continually sending light all across the planet. When you do it this way, there is less of a separation between "problem" areas and "okay" areas, or between "bad" and "good." You are changing that sense of separation between areas by helping to create one world of harmony and peace as you send light *everywhere*. You can do this individually and collectively. Through the power of your intention, the power of your thoughts, and the power within your hearts, you send light. And because light is energy, in its intelligence, it knows exactly where it needs to go.

A lot of chaos is coming up in the world, things that upset us. I understand that I'm a part of the creation of all these things. Am I somehow creating it because the world mirrors what we are thinking and doing? If so, how can I change that?

By acknowledging what you see objectively and moving away from the emotional space and then bringing your vibration up through kindness, compassion, grace, love, ease, and flow, thinking thoughts in alignment with those energies and sending them into any situation that may appear to be troublesome. Do not feel responsible that you have caused all of this individually. No one person is individually responsible for the global distress you are seeing. It is a collective problem. Be objective about what you are observing, and then consciously choose to align your thoughts positively. Acknowledge what you see, what you hear, what you know to be real from the third-dimensional perspective, then invite in the multidimensional perspective by raising the vibration around the situation through thinking higher vibrational thoughts. You can always choose to send love into any situation. If you or someone else is upset, the best thing to do is to back away, become objective, and then send compassion.

Thank you very much, Laarkmaa. It makes the heart feel good, all the things you are telling us. We appreciate that very much. What challenges or potentials lie in the upcoming Collective Shadow Cycles we will experience?

The upcoming Shadow Cycles[5] will be a collection of all Shadow Cycles previously experienced. You will experience the accumulation of humanity's deepest fears rising to the surface. There are likely to be cataclysms and changes where everything falls apart. You will also likely experience expansions and openings, heart awareness, and opportunities for growth. You have already experienced such a Collective Shadow during the period when the world was moving toward a global lockdown. Such periods will continue until you learn to work together, take back your power, and make different choices for the highest good of all. These are likely to continue to be unsettling times because humanity has not responded to the opportunity of Shadow Cycles in the past. And now as the planetary influences are affecting Earth so much more than they have before, you are likely to experience a greater intensity of a push towards evolutionary change. Therefore, you must be ready for anything. You must be ready to feel, see, and know that darkness is surfacing, and use all of your light and all of your love to address whatever issues are put in front of you. In other words, instead of saying, "I didn't want this, I didn't ask for this" say, "This has been put in front of me, so I will send it love and light, whatever the circumstance may be." Instead of grieving or becoming angry or upset every time you find some sort of darkness coming to the surface say, "Here is a place that needs love and light". If it is something that you can address in the physical third dimension such as fighting against 5G, vaccinations, glyphosate, or the geochemical engineering of your weather or saving your food sources—all of these things—if it's something that you can do in the third-dimensional realm, by all means do it. Don't wait until the next Collective Shadow Cycle arrives and then try to act. Do it now; do it today.

Send light and love into your body and mind and then into the world first thing when you awaken in the morning. Then look around you and ask, "What do I need to do to protest what is happening on my planet?" And then after you figure out what third-dimensional action to take, invoke your multidimensional awareness and your higher consciousness and ask, "Please guide me, show me what choices to make, show me how to make a difference, show me how to be the light that I am." You will be bringing in the higher consciousness of multidimensional awareness to address whatever is in front of you. It is a challenging time. It is also a time of opportunity for growth. It will probably be experienced more strongly than what you feel right now. As you feel the waves, remind yourselves, "This is our opportunity. Change is coming. We've been asking for change, so we must live through the chaos while the change arrives, and we must do our part to orchestrate and navigate how we will participate with this change, how we will use our energy and our light to make a difference."

Most of us have seen situations where someone says, "Well, the Universe will provide everything," and then things fall apart. What is the difference between allowing and creating, or do they work together?

That is a beautiful question. The Universe provides 50% of what occurs, and humanity creates 50% of what happens. To fully participate within your 50% of creation, you must give 100% of your attention, attitude, and higher vibrational choices. So, if someone does not participate in using her or his 50% power to manifest, merely saying, "I will just trust the Universe, and the Universe will bring me what I need," that human is not doing his or her 50% to co-create and manifest for the highest good of all. That type of choice can be aligned with choices made by those who put their total faith in the church or government, rather than taking their own responsibility. Sometimes people think, "The church or the government will take care of me; I don't need to do anything but be good." Well, who is defining what is good?

Who is making the rules? They do not realize that part of being "good" is being responsible to make choices for the highest good of all, not choices that are dictated by a particular government or religion. And what freedom of choice are they giving up by turning all their faith over to a structure of organized religion or to a government, expecting it to take care of them? Many humans find it too easy to give up their power, and they refuse their own responsibility of choice, simply abdicating to what they consider to be a "higher power." But you are divine too. You are intended to be co-creators who have been given the gift of choice. Giving up that power and refusing responsibility through "faith" is not the same as doing your best while simultaneously trusting that the Universe is also working for the highest good of all.

Nobody in a human experience is asked to do everything on their own, nor is anyone in a human experience asked to completely surrender in pure trust without continuing to do their part. You are divine sparks of light. You are trying to become more conscious. This is what we are hoping to do: awaken you into activating your power so that you can work with the Universe to make things flow in a more harmonious way. There is so much chaos on the planet right now that there is very little harmony. People are still separated, still fearful, still competitive, and still acting from greed. These choices of attitude and behavior stem from judgment and fear, where people have no trust and are not working in cooperation. You need to learn to release what you think is right and say, "This is just my perspective, but I am open to other perspectives." Most of you reading this book know this, which is what prompted the question.

In order to function more fully in universal cosmic citizenship, you have to do 100% of your 50%. That means that there is not a moment that goes by that you don't trust that the Universe is providing exactly what you need, and simultaneously there is not a moment that goes by that you don't also do your part—choosing positive, non-judgmental thoughts and positive intentions and actions with trust, love, joy, and compassion. The moment you let in worry, fear, doubt, or judgment, you are no longer doing your 100% of your 50% to co-create a better world. You will be cosmic citizens when you have incorporated the true meaning of the highest good for all and continually participate in what manifests through the combined energies of trust and positive intention. Everything that you think and everything that you do will not only be for your own satisfaction or your own soul's purpose, but it will be for the highest good of all because you will finally realize that each individual is a spark of divine light joined together with a common purpose: to be love and to shine light everywhere. Light is needed. So, when you see those who just surrender completely, abdicating their own responsibility by saying (or thinking), "I am turning it over to the Universe," and then you watch as things fall apart for them, you need to remember that they are starting with a very good idea, for they are working on their trust. They are working on trusting that they can be safe or working on trusting that the Universe is a good and safe place, but they have forgotten that they must also use their own empowerment and their own responsibility. Without that participation, things will always fall apart for them to rediscover that they need to find their own power and use the gift of human choice. Thank you for such a good question.

I've experienced that very often things will totally fall apart in surrendering to the Universe, even though I'm doing my 100% of my 50%. Things might still fall apart. I've come to understand that when this happens, I'm making room for a higher frequency of energy, and what was in my life before wasn't the right resonance. I just want to share that if someone's life is falling apart and he or she feels like they are doing everything right, it might still be ok. You might be doing all of the right things, and it still might fall apart.

That is absolutely true and a very good perspective. Thank you for sharing that. Yes, of course, things can completely fall apart to let in a new frequency. That's what's happening in the changing structure of reality right now. We do not encourage anyone to turn it over completely in surrender, trusting that the Universe will do everything and that you don't have any responsibility to make any choices. You still have the opportunity and the power to choose your attitude and to understand and grow more deeply. Your 50% participation is still important. So, the true way to participate is to say to yourself, "I have a responsibility every single moment to take each challenge and turn it into an opportunity." With that way of thinking and intending, whether things fall apart or whether they don't, the Universe is right there with you providing the next higher level of vibratory experience. Thank you for sharing that perspective.

Laarkmaa, Pia, and Cullen, thank you very, very much. I've been working with a psychologist for a number of years and, of course, that involves processing past trauma. Are your treatments, Laarkmaa, a more targeted way or a different way to process trauma? Or can I use your treatments together with my psychology treatments?

You may combine anything in your own individual circumstance that helps you achieve clearing of trauma. What we do in our treatment is to empower you by working with you to simultaneously either remember the source of the trauma or imagine the source of the trauma, and then change the outcome. You cannot change what actually caused the trauma obviously, but with our help, you can change the energy of its impact on you. We use certain tapping programs so that you tap on certain portions of your body giving positive energetic messages that go through your body at the rate of your heartbeat. We guide you to where to tap, and we help you understand what you must know or may have forgotten as you safely look at the trauma with us.

We see where it comes from, ask what is necessary for you to change and feel better. When we approach it in that manner, you become empowered to change the outcome. You no longer have to carry around the heaviness of the trauma. Instead it becomes simply an experience, and you become free to move on to living a life in a different way. That's our process. We do it in several sessions, rather than making you go through it for years, as many psychologists do. You have your first level in one session, thirty minutes long, and then we give you homework to do. After you have completed your homework, we give you another thirty-minute session, and again we give you homework to do. When that homework is complete, we give you the third session. Through the three levels we are generally able to access all the traumatic places that are causing difficulties within the patterning of your life. Whether it is childhood trauma, trauma as a grown-up, trauma from another dimension or a parallel life—it doesn't matter where it has come from—you gain the power to see into it from a different perspective; you gain a different outcome energetically to help you be free from the impact of the trauma.

Is hypnosis an appropriate way to work on one's shadows from your perspective?

We feel hypnosis may bring things to the surface before you are ready to have them revealed. Things will reveal themselves on their own when you are ready to incorporate them if you do not force it; pieces of memories or emotional triggers will come to the surface, causing you discomfort. Hypnosis *can* take you to a parallel life, but it may be unsettling for you if you are not ready to deal with that aspect of yourself yet. Therefore, we do not recommend hypnosis *per se*. We acknowledge that it is helpful for some, but it pushes many people beyond where their soul is ready to work.

What can you tell us about facing our fear of judgment, fear of death, and so many other fears?

Many of the fears that you are facing now are connected to other emotions as well—anger, frustration, grief. All of your emotions are rising to the surface now for healing. If you are feeling afraid, you don't know why, and you have examined old childhood fears and patterns, then the fears you are experiencing could be arising from a parallel life. The purpose of our Trauma Clearing sessions is to clear the experiences that created the fear and caused these blockages, both in this life and in all parallel lives, so that you can integrate all aspects of yourself. Facing one's fears requires the courage to face all different aspects of yourself in multiple dimensions and multiple parallel lives, and through looking at them, realize that they are not as scary or big as you had imagined. Putting all of these things together is not necessarily easy, but it is a necessary part of integrating all that you are. You must not allow yourself to be gripped by fear at the emotional level, even though you know at a mental level that there is nothing to fear. You must use your feelings and your emotions together to move beyond the problem. Crying and asking why you are suffering will not help you move beyond your suffering. When you are having an unpleasant or a painful experience, you are being offered the greatest opportunity for shining light into a dark situation and changing it by using light and love instead of allowing the fear to define the situation. You must objectify by moving the emotion out of the way—the sadness, the questioning, the disappointment—and change your thinking. Do not attach to labeling your experience as bad or good. This is the power you have within you that we are trying to help each of you to discover and integrate into who you are. Here on Earth you will have things occur that are painful, but the more you focus on the pain, the more you close windows and doors that allow you to change the pain into something else, simply another experience.

Laarkmaa, what language would you use to describe or define, if possible, the fear that comes up in the human condition? I sometimes lose some of what I have, and I think I experience a fear of leaving the human container, the attachment to the container. Can you can give us a definition of what are the most basic fears that we experience?

There are two basic fears that humans experience. Many, as you just described, have a fear of losing the human container because that is what is familiar to you and what you remember. The other fear is the fear of not being loved or not being good enough to be loved. These are the two basic fears that humans experience. But you asked about the language of these fears. We would describe both of those fears with one word: separation. Both of these fears, and actually any other fear that you can name, come from the origin of separation because you fear that you are separate from everyone and everything in the Universe and from Source and all that is. You are not separate. That is part of the illusion. That is the part of clinging to and wanting to be in a physical container because you think that the physical container defines you and proves that you exist. As you raise your conscious vibration and become more and more aware, you begin to see that your consciousness is much more than the physical container. Yes, the body is conscious, but your consciousness goes beyond even that, for you are part of the stars as well as part of the Earth. As for the fear of not being loved, that also comes from the fear of separation. When you feel that you are separate, you think that no one can love you or that you cannot find someone to love you. This misconception comes from feeling that you are separate or cut off from Source, the ultimate connection to love. So, when you're trying to work on your own fears, we suggest that each of you ask yourself, "From what am I feeling separate?" Then remind yourselves that it is just an illusion because there is no real separation. Separation is just a game you all chose to play to demonstrate your different perspectives and to be able to share those perspectives together when you reconnect to the whole. Separation is an illusion. And it is completely irrational to be afraid of something that does not exist. You should work with that idea a little bit and see how you feel. Then as you breathe in say, "I am connected." Breathe out, and say, "I am no longer separate." Breathe in and say, "I am connected." Breathe out saying, "I am no longer separate." You are consciously breathing out the illusion of separation, and you are consciously breathing in the concept of connection, which is the truth. The concept of separation is the illusion. Breathe the correct concept into your body, telling your mind that it is the truth. You will know it is true because your heart confirms the truth for you, giving you a feeling of peace.

Laarkmaa, your Trauma Clearing sessions were more powerful and more helpful than years of psychological therapy for me. Why pay a psychologist for years when we have you to help us move beyond our trauma and our pain?!

Thank you. We appreciate that!

What does true love, or the largest version of love look like?

The larger version of love is being able to accept people just as they are. You don't have to agree with them, but you must accept them and their path. True love begins with compassion, so you must start with compassion first before you can experience the wonder and the bliss of true love. You have moments of this when you "fall in love," so to speak. You fall into a place where nothing else matters but your connection with the other person and each choice you make considers the highest good for the other person as well as for yourself. This is an example of unconditional love. But you "fall out" of love very quickly because of your human behaviors and patterned beliefs about what should be and what you should not be, what you need and what you do not need. All of those things become mingled, and you begin to question if it is really love or even if it is the right person. If you are sending your love and your light to the other person, you are expressing love. If you feel resonance from the other person, and you feel a smile in your heart from the other person, you are receiving love. Use that as your basis of understanding; we will speak more about this later.

STEP THREE:

HEALING

It is our wish to give you as much information as possible to add to what you know in your hearts (or may be just discovering) and to put it into practical terms so that you may begin a faster evolutionary process. We are presenting topics that build upon one another and join together to make a whole picture of what is necessary for an accelerated rate of evolution. This Step is about *healing*.

You have been living under the spell of duality for so long that one of the things that influences and impacts your thinking about healing is the idea that there is a difference between physical (or material) healing and spiritual healing. We wish to merge those boundaries, blurring some of the sharp edges you use to define one or the other. The possibility of understanding and achieving true healing is more possible now. Two of the ultimate goals of healing are to understand exactly what it is and how you can attain it.

The first point to understand is that you must redefine your interpretation of healing. Many consider healing to be curing. But curing is to make a situation go away. Sometimes an imbalanced or dis-eased situation is there for a specific reason and benefit. It is to your benefit to be able to view each circumstance objectively simply as an experience, as we have explained previously. Do not label your experiences as good or bad. Moving beyond defining your experiences as either good or bad helps you to stop categorizing yourselves as sick or well. Stopping this pattern of dualistic compartmentalizing teaches you to look at what you need to *be*, rather than what you need to *do*, which is the first step to healing.

The physical is a manifestation of thought energy—not only yours, but that of the entire collective. Each thought, second by second, contributes to either the continued negative density on the planet, which in itself needs to be healed, or contributes to a lighter, higher vibration, which is healing. That is why it is so vitally important that you monitor every thought, not only for yourselves and your own wellbeing, but also to do the job you came here to do: to bring light to eradicate all the old patterns of density, pain, suffering, and separation, which brings ultimate healing.

That's right. Your job is not only a physical one. We have told you many times that the idea that you are here to be a teacher, healer, or leader is over. That idea no longer fits your job description. You are here for one purpose only: to be the light, to be the love that brings and sustains healing to all. In doing this, you bring that light into the collective of the planet to make positive changes.

It's easy to keep your thoughts positive and your vibration up when things are going your way. But to do so when you are experiencing illness, emotional distress, or any kind of separating energy, is not as easy. It's far easier to fall back into old patterns of thinking, "This is too hard", or "I don't want to be here like this anymore." Listen to yourselves! Of course, you don't want it to be like that! That's why you are here. You are here to change the experience by bringing in the light through being light yourself.

You don't have to be well or happy to do your job. In fact, your work is more valuable and cuts through the negativity and density more when you are able to be light, keep your vibration up, and create positive thoughts *in spite* of being miserable.

Remember what we said about experience? *Even* when you are having a very miserable experience, or are very, very ill, your job is to ask, "How can I bring light into this experience?" "How can I be positive in spite of the pain?" "How am I to remember that I am light and shine my light into this experience?" Those are the questions you should continue to ask. There is so much more freedom, connection, and *joy* if you transcend these old patterns and replace them with a set of *real* positive energies that are attached to you. You achieve these positive energies not only when you can feel that you are making a difference, but also when nothing *seems* to make a difference. *You* make the difference. *You* are the light. *You* change the experience. This is your job, and it is an absolutely essential part of the ascension process, for we are helping you to remember who you are—you are light.

Those who cling to old thoughts like, "I can't do this," will just take the thought patterns from which they are creating their reality with them as they transition, and it will take them longer to reach the vibratory place we are now helping you to understand. You all take your thought patterns with you, whether you ascend with the body into Rainbow body form, or whether you die. And you will find that when you make the change in vibration *here* in your current physical forms, it is actually easier to ascend with your body because you are *seeing* yourselves as light.

Many of you may be experiencing acute symptoms that arrive suddenly and without warning. Perhaps you may have heart pains that make you feel like this could be your last day on Earth. Or maybe you have ringing in your ears and vertigo that affects your whole system, although you do not understand why you are having this experience. Some of you are experiencing intense muscle cramping or feelings that your muscles simply don't want to work normally. While going through these changes, sometimes the human body needs more magnesium, and an absorbable magnesium cream is the quickest way to get it into the body. Some of you are experiencing intense eye symptoms, which can range from floaters moving across your eyes, blurred vision, or even to stabbing pains. Your sense of smell may be heightened, leaving you finding many things offensive to you that once were perceived as neutral or pleasant. Even your sense of taste may be somewhat different. All of these things are being altered because you are being altered. Does this mean that you are sick? No. It means that you are healing from a misconception about who you are and how you manifest your own energy. Having chosen the accelerated path forward, you need to disengage and become objective about what it means to have a physical body and how to best care for that physical body. Nothing you have experienced in the past will ever be the same again; you *are* changing!

There is actually no difference between the spiritual and the material. Everything is spiritual, and everything, being energy, is connected. The material world that you see, evaluate, and participate in here in the third dimension is built by your thoughts, the energy your spirit puts out in thought form. Your thought forms, individually and collectively, manifest the reality you are experiencing in your material world. You raise your vibration through the thoughts you think, the choices you make in diet, entertainment, communication, and all other manner of things, with each choice offering opportunities to increase the energy field around you as well as within you, which mirrors the reality that you are manifesting. It is time that you move away from the dualistic perspective that divides the material from the spiritual. Certainly you can have positive intentions and visualize higher possibilities. Certainly it is a good idea to send love and light to all those who may be suffering, regardless of the symptoms they are experiencing. All of these things are of a spiritual nature. And it is a good thing to have a proper diet and not misuse your eyes, your ears, your stomach, your sleep patterns, and anything you perceive as part of the physical world. But that material body is also a spiritual body, and the more you begin to see the two as united, the more you will grasp the true concepts of healing and move beyond the ideas of needing to cure something or merely make the symptoms go away. One thing that has a direct bearing on your healing abilities is your objective thinking about any experience. You need to be reminded over and over again that what you think creates a field of energy in you and around you, and you need to remember that there is no separation. What you think goes out to affect everyone else; what others think comes in to affect you. When you feel something arrive that does not belong to you, such as a dark energy, your job is simply to send light into that energy, knowing that everything is connected and that you are doing your part to bring the darkness back into the light.

To heal completely includes healing all old concepts, all old judgments, and all old beliefs that no longer serve you as you are stepping into the new reality. You are evolving to become more than who you believed yourselves to be. This is a great time to slow down, reintegrate, and use your heart-guided thoughts to imagine the kind of world you wish to create. The old has to die before you can heal into the new. Remember that you are divine sparks of light, which gives you the power to heal yourself and extend the light that you are so that others can see how to heal themselves too. Your sole (soul) purpose at this time is to simply be light, be love, and shine light into the darkness. We remind you that it is very easy to be light and to be love when you feel good and things are going well in your world: you feel good; your relationships are harmonious; you have no money problems; everything seems to be in flow. In *these* circumstances it is quite easy to simply pick a time and decide to send light out into the world because you feel so grateful for all the things that are working in your life. But it is much more difficult to focus upon your job, your task of sending light, when you feel ill, when you feel miserable, when you have just had an emotional exchange with someone, when you are upset with yourself, or you just don't feel like you can go on. When you are experiencing any of those things you forget that your job is to simply be love and send light. Even though it may be more difficult when you are suffering, it is more appropriate and possibly even more powerful to raise your vibration at such a time and send light into the world no matter *what* your personal experience may be. This is claiming your responsibility and remembering your purpose, telling yourself, "That's my job, I will commit to it, and I will finish my job as long as I am here on the planet because that is what I am here to do!" Once you begin to engage in being and sending light as a regular practice—no matter what your outer circumstances, whether you deem them to be uncomfortable, miserable, or joyful and full of bliss—once you engage in this practice regardless of what you feel on the inside or what is happening on the outside, you are engaging in a process of healing. As you send light into the world, simultaneously your own light begins to build within yourself, and that in and of itself, raises your vibration. As you raise your vibration, healing can occur, and usually does at some level. It may not look the way you want it to look immediately, but you will be able to notice the difference by the thoughts you are thinking and by your desire to send out light regardless of what is happening within you. That is an indication that healing is already occurring, for you are accepting your responsibility and you feel glad that you have the opportunity to accomplish what you came here to do. These things are important for you to remember. You are light. You are love. You are here to send light into the world, and in doing so, raise your own vibration at increasing levels until you are able to send light *just* by being who you are. You as the Light Bearers of the planet have more potential for effecting personal and universal change than the entire collective put together because it is the Light Bearers who are learning how to work with the light and who are able to manifest a better outcome through being aware of and managing your thoughts, being light, and sending light.

Part of the reason for this Manual for Accelerated Evolution is to assist you in your ascension process. Now we will look more closely at healing as part of the ascension process. We have spoken to you for a long time about the importance of making proper choices for the highest good for all and raising your vibratory levels. Doing those things presents you with the opportunity to ascend with the physical body. Now that may seem almost impossible when you are experiencing extreme physical symptoms, but we tell you that the dichotomy between the two is based upon what you *perceive* as real. If you are placing more focus upon what is experienced as real in the physical world and not as much focus on what you know exists in the etheric, then you are seeing a division that does not necessarily exist. Your etheric body, or what some call the Light body is the blueprint for your physical form. If you are sending light and raising the vibration of the etheric, it therefore impacts the physical, bouncing back the vibrations that are required for healing the physical form. This healing may not look how you expect it to look, or it may be exactly what you envision. It depends on what is needed for the highest good of your own total personal healing. But the point is not to segregate it into thoughts such as, "I'm suffering, so I must not be healing," or "My body looks like it is not doing well, so therefore I cannot ascend."

If you judge how your body is doing and believe that you cannot ascend with your body because of its struggles, then you are closing a door to possibilities of what the blueprint of your etheric body is attempting to do through merging with your physical form. That merging between etheric and physical bodies can happen gradually, or it can happen all at once. You may realize it in an instant, or you may begin to realize it in a series of little moments. But the first step, the first clue, of the etheric merging with the physical occurs when you realize that you are having thoughts of an uplifting nature. So, continually question, asking:

"How can this experience serve me better (no matter what the experience)? "

and

"How can I be a better participant in sending light, even though I am having an uncomfortable experience?"

and

"What needs to happen or what do I need to know that I cannot see?"

When you begin to automatically ask those questions, you will notice that your entire vibration seems lighter. You will notice that you accept more easily that whatever is happening to you physically is only a *part* of who you are. Therefore, the movement from your focus and concentration upon the physical into the understanding that you are so much more than *just* the physical is accompanied by an accelerated process of evolution. We would like to see you accelerate your own healing by working with your light body and your thoughts, as well as with your physical body. We want you to understand that asking questions about how your experiences serve your evolution and discovering that you can continue to send light even when something unpleasant may be happening in your own reality is beneficial.

Change your viewpoint so that you do not see yourself as ill and possibly dying, but instead view yourself as simply changing. Recognize that in the old paradigm, what you see and experience may have led to death, but in the new paradigm, you are not attached to that end point. You can begin to see that your body is making some changes; simply accept those changes as your body's response to previous choices you have made. As you become more and more responsible in your choices, your body will decide to go with you when you ascend. Once you have established good communication to understand what your body needs and how to supply it (through light, through thoughts, through connection with the etheric blueprint, and through physical choices that impact the body), your body will change to ascend with you. Every conscious choice you make brings you closer to aligning your etheric and your physical bodies to create your Rainbow body form.

The acute physical and mental issues are happening to bring you back into a harmonious, balanced state and to take you away from the distractions of the world so that you can do your work. If you suddenly find you are having visual problems or cannot see, we suggest that you are being guided to stop doing so much outward looking. Close your eyes and look deeply into your heart or go deeply into a meditative state to see what is there waiting for you. If you are having trouble hearing, then it is time to stop listening to the outside world and begin to listen to the inner voice; listen to the messages that are coming from your heart, telling you what needs to happen next. If you are having trouble with your digestion, it is time for you to acknowledge that something is changing and that your dietary needs are altering. Explore what your body wants or needs.

There are many forms of ascension. Death is but one form of ascension. You eliminate karma from your path by making higher and higher vibratory choices. When no further karma is being created, you eliminate the need for ascension by death. As you eat only foods that nourish you without taking the life of an animal, you are, again, raising your vibration and eliminating karma. You understand that there is no need to eat animals to nourish yourselves. Killing them just causes more suffering on the planet. You simply cannot nourish yourself with fear or death energy as a food source. All of your choices link together to form the path of your ascension. Also listen to your heart. Most of you are not ready to be Breatharian yet, but dietary choices are a part of going through this process. You are making this transition by choosing lighter and lighter foods until eventually you will be able to live on love, light, and water, as we have reminded you for many years.

There are many things we can say about healing. But the most important thing we can share with you is that you heal most easily when you have joy in your hearts. When you find something that makes you feel joyful, something that makes you smile, something that makes you feel happy in every cell of your body, all cells of both your etheric and your physical body immediately attune to a higher vibratory range. In the higher vibratory range, the perceived illness cannot exist so easily. In the past, some may have referred to this as prayer healing, or spiritual healing, or trust healing, allowing someone or something outside of themselves to heal them. We remind you that you are the healers yourselves. The trust comes in knowing that you are powerful and knowing what is possible. The healing comes in focusing your attention on the light that you are and *consciously raising your vibration at a cellular level* by invigorating yourself with joy. It is such an amazing thing to feel joy! Most of you experience it infrequently these days, though not as much as you did when the world was less chaotic and the oppression of the masses was not so dense. Nevertheless, as you begin to focus on light and send love more and more and more, that sense of peace and sense of joy return to you because they are your natural birthright. As you spend more time in that place of joy, you are—more and more—raising each cell of your body to a higher vibratory level, a level at which illness cannot exist, even though you may perceive it existing through your third-dimensional experience of physical symptoms. Remember, perception is a very key event in noticing what is happening and how things are changing.

You are able to do this—each of you. However, you need practice because you have become concerned about your bodies, as the collective has been taught that you will live, get old, and die. All of these belief systems are embedded into you, as you have watched grandparents die, parents die, friends die, or animal friends die; you have engrained into your consciousness that this is the way of life. This *mis*-understanding has been engrained into humanity's consciousness for most of humanity's existence. But it does not need to be that way now. What you need is to have an objective perception of what is happening at any given moment, and from that objectivity accept each experience from a place of peace, rather than from judgment or alignment with outdated beliefs. Ask yourselves repeatedly what you need to learn from your experiences, and continually invite the vibration of joy into you.

There is one more thing you need to know about healing. We have told you for a number of years that during the times of Solar Minimum, you would feel more and more radiation coming in. Those who continue to fly often and regularly, wishing to hold on to the old paradigm for travel and not paying attention to the increased danger of Cosmic Ray radiation at altitude, will be more highly exposed to increased radiation. Even at sea level humanity is being impacted by increased radiation from incoming Cosmic Rays. You must be conscious of what this radiation does to your physical and mental forms. Regardless of the choice you make (low altitude or high altitude exposure), those who are afraid of the radiation and hold on to beliefs about the dangers of irradiation will actually feel themselves burning. Those who are not afraid of the irradiation and are making choices to adapt to the new environment (one choice being to fly less or not at all), may also feel a sense of burning, but you will experience it as a purification fire, burning out things that are out of balance within you and that no longer serve your form. Those internal fires that you experience as intense heat are burning you into a different level of existence. This is a level that will not sustain viral activity, negative bacteria, or fungus that has long been part of imbal-anced human systems. All of these things can be irradiated at the higher vibratory rates, whether that vibration is achieved from your own work with light or whether it is from the light that is coming in as Cosmic Rays and Solar Rays during this Solar Minimum. Your bodies are being given more radiation so that they can evolve and mutate into a higher vibratory form. Take care of your precious bodies, minds, and spirits, especially when you see that the Cosmic Ray index (Kp Index)[1] is indicating change. You may find during these times that you cannot think nor function as well as usual. Do not let it alarm you. Use it as a time for integrating light in a different way and sending out light differently. Use it with the wisdom that it is transforming you, changing you. This is important—you are moving through your choices from carbon-based human forms to liquid crystal-line human forms. We have told you for years that your natural form is not carbon based. Carbon-based forms are the result of the density you have acquired through the fog of negativity that surrounds your planet from thinking dense thoughts, and acting through competition, greed, selfishness, separation, darkness, and all of those dense energies that have filled the collective of humanity for years.

Your true form is reflective of light, and to reflect the light that you are requires the liquid crystalline content of your form. Your forms are changing. This means you are going to become a little more liquid, a little more flexible, and a little "lighter" in your physical presence. So, do not be concerned if you feel the density of the physical form to which you are accustomed is moving away or when you feel that your physical form is not as grounded as it used to be. *It is not meant to be.* This is your progression toward a form with more fluidity. This is a space for healing, where you can move easily between dimensions and where you can move back and forth in a Rainbow body from your etheric to your *new* physical body as you feel is appropriate. This is the way it is intended to be. We wish to help you achieve this in our Accelerated Evolutionary Program. We supply the new perspective through cosmic wisdom, and you supply the required release of old belief systems to make room for this new perspective. When you begin to live as if this is the truth, then you will be able to achieve what we are sharing with you. When you increasingly experience spontaneous moments of joy, you are freeing yourself from old paradigm fears and beliefs, raising your vibration, and moving toward your new form! In a liquid crystalline body, as we describe it, *liquid* means flexible, fluid, and wavelike; *crystalline* means transparently clear. One can see clear through you because as you become more transparent, you no longer need to hide from who you are or protect yourselves from pain. You are in a form that is meant to share from the heart, with trust, courage, compassion, and unconditional love, which radiates joy all around you. Crystalline forms are reflective so that you shine out who you are. The liquid crystalline aspect of higher vibratory forms is not something you usually see walking among humans on your planet in everyday life. Not yet. But it is something you can envision and something that you are moving toward yourselves, through your choices, and you will meet yourselves in this form if you go into deeper meditative states and visualize, asking, "How do I look?" "How do I appear?" "What do I need to associate with or connect with to accept myself in this new form that I am creating?" And the more important question to ask, of course, is, "How do I feel?" You will discover that your appearance of light and transparency is a result of your *feelings* of compassion, trust, unconditional love, and joy. What you *feel* is reflected in the form you manifest. It is true now, and it becomes even more true as you discard your old fears and beliefs and accept the wisdom of the perspective we are sharing. The liquid crystalline body is indeed your natural physical form, the form that allows your movement in Rainbow body so you can easily travel back and forth through dimensions. This is true shapeshifting!

You are changing. You have great opportunities. And the choices that you make moment-by-moment are enabling you to accelerate with these changes, giving you opportunities to heal beyond what you have believed is possible. Healing will become simply a forgetting of what illness even was. You will not remember because it will no longer exist within you or around you. You are not there yet, but you will be, and that is something to look forward to. Let go of those old beliefs. Open your heart to a larger wisdom and way of being. Release all the old emotions of fear, grief, anger, frustration, greed, or jealousy to make room for your natural feeling state of joy. Take in and consider all that we have said, and practice it every day.

We have spoken with you about the changing structures of your human form and how those changes are necessary for healing and for becoming who you truly are. Next, we are going to speak with you about the changing structures of your reality—the changing outer world that you perceive and how those changing structures support the evolution of the New Human.

QUESTIONS & ANSWERS
STEP 3

Thank you so much for the lovely and clarifying messages. So much appreciated. Occasionally when I feel pain or illness, or I'm in a circumstance where I am upset, I immediately try to send love and light. I know that I need to have a positive feeling when I send love and light, but quite often it's difficult to have a positive feeling when I am in pain or upset. Perhaps you can give us some help in how to bring positive feelings in these circumstances as part of the sending love and light. Thank You.

Yes, we are happy to address that. When you are suffering, and you are not feeling very well, it is more challenging to send love and light, as we have said. But it takes both positive thoughts and positive feelings to make change happen. We suggest that you simply begin to breathe in and out, telling yourself that whatever you are feeling is just an experience and that it will change. You can breathe in love, breathe out trust, breathe in joy, breathe out compassion. You may say to yourself, "I am breathing out this pain or emotional distress. I am breathing out this unhappiness. I am breathing in peace; I'm breathing in acceptance." Give attention to yourself first. And then when you become calm, you are in a better place to search for something to be grateful for. From a feeling of gratitude, you can more easily and more effectively send love and light into the world, or into whatever situation has caused you distress (including to your body that is experiencing pain.) That's a difficult thing to do when you are hurting and focused upon the pain. Change your focus, step by step, until you can find the feeling of gratitude for something. If you force yourself to try to send love and light when it is beyond your ability at the moment, you will simply feel unsuccessful, questioning why it did not work. Instead do the breathing, accept the situation objectively, until you feel calm, peace, and gratitude in your heart. The moment your feelings are more positive, and it may not be in that instant, you can successfully send love and light to change whatever is out of balance. Do not expect it to happen instantly; it may not happen until minutes or even several hours later. Those positive feelings may arrive when you see a butterfly, or when someone smiles at you; you suddenly remember how it feels to be grateful and at peace. In that moment, take in the gratitude, take in the joy, and send out love and light, because in that moment you're in a positive feeling space. We love you and appreciate all of you who have the courage to find new ways to approach challenges. We understand it is hard to step away from old patterns of focusing on your pain and suffering and turn your focus into the acceptance that is required to move forward. We understand that. We also know that you can accomplish much when you change your feeling state.

I've noticed that when I clear the way for higher vibratory living through healing old wounds or ways I have lived in separation, I have a positive impact on other people. Can you comment on that, and can you tell us how to work on our wellness and health in our changing environment?

We are giving you an instruction manual for how to move forward in your changing environment. This manual is meant to guide you through hands-on experience, rather than simply providing mental concepts that you understand or like. As you practice higher vibratory living, you can actuate the changes that are necessary. All things that need healing can be healed by light. This manual provides hands-on instructions of what to do and how to do it. The most important thing you can do right now is to monitor your thoughts; always strive for positive thoughts. Do not deny that a problem exists. Recognize the problem, acknowledge it, and find the solution. Instead of worrying or talking about the problem, look for and find or create a solution. The instruction manual provides practical guidance on how to move into oneness and unity and how to speak differently in terms of "we." When you change the way you speak, you will change the way you think. When you change the way you think, you will institute choices that are for the highest good for all in your thoughts and your behaviors. In living this way, you automatically invoke the light. When you invoke the light, you remember that you *are* the light. When you remember that you are light and that you are joined to all other light, the light can heal anything and everything. Your health and your environment change for the better.

Thanks for your great teachings. I have a question about healing and crop circles. I have read that some people are able to heal themselves using crop circle images. Do you have any comment about it: how to use crop circles?

First you have to distinguish how the crop circle has been manifested. Is it man-made because someone wants to draw attention to it, or is it something that has been given to Earth by other cosmic citizens to help enlighten humans? You must visit the crop circle to feel whether humans generated it or whether it has been created by beings with higher cosmic awareness. In genuine crop circles, where the energy is there to give cosmic messages, designs, intentions, and symbols to help awaken humanity's consciousness, healing can, indeed, occur. However, the healing that occurs will depend upon the individual's level of need, level of development, and level of attunement. Healing may occur as a clearing out of something painful–something that does not belong– or healing can occur as a restful energy that uplifts you, taking you into a higher vibratory state. Each crop circle is different; each brings a different energy. Some are meant to be seen from a distance as symbols so that you interpret the symbols and raise your awareness from seeing them. Others are meant to be experienced by sitting on the ground in the energy to feel the message at a physical level or at a vibrational level. It's a very individual thing. And we notice as the lay lines are shifting and some of the politics of the planet are shifting, some of the crop circles are appearing in places that they have not been before. So, we suspect that no matter where you live, you will have opportunities at some point to experience a crop circle's energy. You must be in the country in Nature to find them, not in a city.

It's a joy to meet with you in a frequency of love. Since I have accepted fully the idea of ascending with this physical body, accepting the higher reality that exists all around me, I have a lot of symptoms with my body. What I have come to realize is that everything that happens with my body is an ascension symptom. And that makes it so much easier to go with the flow.

Yes, and thank you for reinforcing what we have been saying. Your bodies are simply changing. Understanding at this level allows healing to occur, as the dense carbon-based bodies shift into the liquid crystalline forms that you need for your evolution. It is good not to be attached to what was and to look forward to what will be. You are doing a very good job of transitioning and transforming yourselves.

How do I know if healing is complete?

Healing is complete when you no longer hold negative or painful thoughts about a person or a situation. You simply see it as an experience, and you are able to be grateful for what the experience taught you. When you can do that, there is nothing to heal. The physical manifestation of health will follow your thoughts.

STEP FOUR:

THE CHANGING STRUCTURES OF REALITY

We continue with our Manual to help you move through these challenging times that have so many opportunities in a new, different, and enlightened way! Previously we have told you about healing and how part of healing is the ability to join the vision of your material world with the spiritual world. We move now into the topic of changing the structures of reality, for your reality is, indeed, changing. As we have often said, you are moving from your third-dimensional perspectives of what is real into a more open awareness of and alignment with multidimensional reality. We continue to tell you (differently from other sources) that you are *not* moving from third dimension to fifth dimension, for we do not limit you to a hierarchal position of climbing from one level of awareness to the next. That is very third-dimensional thinking! Instead, we remind you that as reality shifts and changes, you lose all perspective of hierarchy; everything and everyone becomes more equal and unified when you lift the veil of illusion that overlays the third dimension. You begin to think, see, feel, and know from multidimensional perspectives. When this happens, you can be in the third dimension when necessary; you can also move to the ninth, the sixth, the twelfth, or the fifth dimension—to whichever one you are aligned with at any particular moment. As you consciously raise your vibration, aligning your energetics with the energetics of another dimension, you match your frequency with the frequency of where you wish to be. That is one of the goals of multidimensionality. It allows you to move between dimensions at will, as guided by your heart, and as called by love to be in a certain place at a certain moment, because that dimension requires your presence. You are aiming for this now. Ultimately, you will regain your ability to be in multiple places at once, as we are, if you so choose. If you can imagine being in other dimensions, and some of you are already either imagining or experiencing dimensional travel, practice will accelerate your ability to achieve this multidimensional awareness. In the third dimension everything is defined for you: "this is solid; this is liquid; this is gas;" or "this is hot; this is cold; this is night; this is day". Specific definitions for embodiment already are already defined for you. The most confining definition in your third-dimensional reality is *time*, followed secondarily by *space*. In true multidimensional *reality*, neither time nor space exists. If you wish to be across the Universe, you just intend yourself to be there, and there you are! There is no space to traverse, no light years to travel, no time to pass, nor aging while traveling from one place to another. Traveling is simply achieved through your conscious intention. The most limiting structure in your third-dimensional perspective—time—is managed by raising your awareness of energy. Third-dimensional limitations of time hamper your understanding of a larger reality, keeping you stuck through cultural use of the Gregorian calendar and clocks. Those false measurements are based upon twelve hours in a day and twelve hours in a night. Your calendars and clocks are readjusted periodically to line up with the artificial third-dimensional perception of time; they are not attuned with universal movements of energy. Therefore, they are not accurate.

In trying to step outside of third-dimensional reality and understand how your structures of reality are indeed changing, you must let go of your concepts and beliefs about scheduling your lives down to the minute by time. Instead, you must begin to plan your lives according to the energies that are present. Allow intentions to rise from your hearts to your minds, and coordinate your intentions with the energies that are present. Learn to harmonize your intentions with those of others for the highest good of all. This requires what we spoke about in the first chapter—beginning to think in terms of "we" instead of "I" and acting from a place of unity rather than from your individual desires. Currently there is some confusion and chaos because the varying levels of human choice are activated either by selfish, individual needs or expanded, unity-based needs. Some of you are very much attached to the third-dimensional structure of time and space. Others are moving out of those perceptions so quickly, that it is challenging to balance moving between realities of the varying dimensions you visit. In the third dimension, you still must agree on the "timing " of specific meetings or actions. But you can do that by choosing the most appropriate energy for each meeting or project. The *Pleiadian-Earth Energy Calendar*[1] we have provided for you helps you begin this process of changing your focus on time to a focus on energy. You can mutually agree upon the proper *energy* for each meeting or action, using this calendrical system.

As you are already experiencing some of the chaos of this evolutionary change, we ask you to navigate it by always allowing multiple perspectives to contribute to your decisions, especially when working together in a group. Let the energies guide you. For example, rather than becoming frustrated or angry because someone is late, try to find another perspective and flow around the delay that has occurred. If you are the one who is late, find a way to be in harmony with the needs of others. Learn to flow with the energies that are present, and allow them to guide you towards what needs to occur. Make your decisions from a place of harmony, unity, and peace. This is an important evolutionary step for participating in changing your reality to a more multi-dimensional structure that supports you as the New Humans.

While time and space form the basis of all other misunderstandings in this dimension, there are other things in your third-dimensional structure that are changing. You see Earth's foundation to be based upon the elements: earth, water, fire, and air. These elements are manifestations of the third dimension only. They are manifestations of energy, but energy can manifest into any shape or form in multidimensional awareness. Therefore, we would like you to understand the different foundation of the larger universal reality and begin to make strong, reliable structures around yourselves. The universal structure of which we speak consists of love, trust, compassion, and joy.

Building a new reality requires changing some of your beliefs, your thoughts, and your ideas. It certainly requires that you release your attachment to beliefs that *this is the way things are* simply because it is the way you have always experienced it. Change your thinking from, "This is how things should be" to "This is how I perceive things in this moment", or "This is how things used to be, but I am open to different perspectives." The truest foundation for the New Humans in multidimensional life is love, joy, trust, and compassion. We explained this foundation to you in our earlier book *Remembering Who We Are*[2] to prepare you for what is coming. We are telling you about it again now because it is already in progress, and you need to understand how to participate in creating a universal and more harmonious foundation on Earth for your evolving selves. When *Remembering Who We Are* was first written, you were able to comprehend it at a mental level. Now in the changing energies, you can understand it as you experience it at a multidimensional level. As things happen in your lives, you will have a choice of reacting in old ways and clinging to old beliefs about what is real, or responding with curiosity, asking, "What is this? How do I meet this energy? Where is my trust? How can I be compassionate with someone who is not meeting my expectations? Where is my joy in the moment of exploration? Am I being the love that I am?"

Begin to see how the ground beneath you is no longer simply Earth; your true ground of being is *compassion* for others and for all life. Think of the water that flows on your planet, in your blood, or in your emotions as the foundational element of love, the universal foundation for life in the cosmos. See the air that supports your breathing as the foundational element of *trust*. The element of *joy* replaces fire in the new foundation, for it is joy that feeds your highest vibrations and sparks your evolutionary growth! Responses of this nature shift your view of reality and help support what is being created. For those of you who are deeply committed to changing the structures of your reality, these questions will become the norm. They represent the inner changes you are making while outer changes are simultaneously occurring.

You are undergoing outer changes here on Earth in changing atmosphere, changing weather patterns, changing magnetosphere, Earth's changing positions, changing energetic ley lines, changing political structures, and changing financial structures. Your financial structures do not offer balanced exchange since they are based on greed and competition. All of these structures that are clearly not working will fall apart. Some already are. Your job is to remain free of fear, open to trust, and curious about what is forming and what is coming next. Participate with the changes by speaking out for what your hearts want in unity. Discern what is true and what is not, and expose lies to take back your own power. Things on your planet are accelerating, which is why we created this Manual—to give you a jump-start, to help you make the leap, to help you detach from those things that no longer serve you, to desist from saying (or thinking), "It always worked like this before, so why is it not working now?" Instead, say to yourselves, "It used to be like that, but I can see it is going to be working differently now; I need to become aligned with this energy. I need to discover what it feels like, looks like, sounds like, smells like, and tastes like. I need to be in alignment with what this energy is in order to function with it." As you do this, you attune yourselves vibrationally with each new energy that comes in to support you on your evolutionary path. The more you choose to respond to the new energies in this way, the more you will fall away from old reactive patterns based on fear, judgment, and separation. You will stop experiencing emotional reactions that make you so uncomfortable. You will stop clinging to belief systems that have been built by your education, your training, your religion, or your experience. You will release habitual thoughts that automatically occur simply because you are accustomed to allowing your thoughts to flow only in certain directions when stimulated by outer circumstances. We want to focus now upon what you can do to adjust, adapt, and thrive as your environment and current reality change, and the structures you believed to be real begin to shift under your very feet.

You may find the boundaries of countries beginning to change, and your attachment to being proud citizens of one country may suddenly change to be a proud citizen of the world as you become more aware that you are global, or even universal citizens! Circumstances will require you to change your thinking from "My country is the best" to "My country has something to offer, and yours has something else to offer. How can we blend these gifts together to offer them to the world?" Questions will likely begin to arise, such as, "What is my role as a cosmic citizen? How can I recognize and appreciate the variety of ways of doing things in the world, while simultaneously sharing my own views in ways that cause no conflict?" You will learn these ways to work with the changing structures of reality.

In duality, you always have two choices. When you move out of dualistic thinking, you have a multitude of choices, so we are helping you to move beyond your accustomed two choices into the multitude of choices actually available to you. Instead of having only "right or wrong" or "your way or my way", as we discussed at the beginning of this manual when we suggested that you begin to think in terms of "we," you will also have the choice to move away from the dualistic opposites of love and fear, which in duality have been the underlying guiding forces in all your choices. You may wish to be loving, want to give from your heart, and want to receive love; you may wish for all of your choices to come from a place of love. Yet you find yourselves reacting to unexpected change from a place of fear, worry, or concern about what the changes will look like or mean to you. You may question how you are going to survive. Being worried about surviving comes straight from the paradigm of fear, and that is how those who have controlled humanity for so long continue to control humanity. This is the way that you are manipulated—by stirring up your fear, and then telling you that someone will save you or protect you if you take this action or pass that law. You can be assured that whatever you are promised by governmental or religious agencies, your highest wellbeing is not their concern. Instead they intend to better control all the masses through belief systems based on fear and misinformation. Therefore, they paint the best pictures they can to stir you into a state of fear, and then they say, "Have faith in us; we will fix it for you; we will keep you safe." We tell you this is poor advice, and you should not follow it. Do not in your naivety have faith that someone else will fix your problems, even if someone else has caused those problems. Learn to see the truth through objective discernment. Have trust in yourselves and in each other. Awaken the divine power that lives within you, that divine spark of light that is connected to Source, that is connected to one another, and that receives all of its wisdom from your intuitive heart. This is what you must learn to trust. This is what you must learn to rely upon to resolve your challenges, for reality as you have perceived it is crumbling and falling at your feet right now. You will more and more need to shift your perspective beyond the third dimension to see the larger reality that is emerging. As you change your perspective, you will see windows and doors flying open, revealing possibilities you have yet to even dream of in multidimensionality.

Now is the time to move beyond all those questions such as, "Where should I invest my money?" What do I do to keep my money, my home, my family safe?" "What do I need to do to be sure I have a place to live?" "What do I need to do to make enough money to pay my bills?" Of course, those are realistic third-dimensional questions, and you must take responsibility for all of your choices. However, you are shifting out of the limits of the third dimension into limitless multidimensionality, where you can access whatever you need in an instant and then apply it to your third-dimensional situation. This shift requires changing the structures of your thoughts. It requires changing your belief systems, and it requires trusting in the power of possibilities. You must simply keep yourself at the higher vibrational levels of thinking, feeling, and openness. Rather than saying (or even thinking), "Well, I tried that, and it didn't work" say, "I see that in this moment I am limited by some third-dimensional structures or beliefs that are preventing me from achieving my goal." See the limitations of the belief systems that are surrounding your intentions. See the limitations of the feelings that you have that move you back into powerless states of worry, fear, or judgment. See all the things that are happening all around you, and immediately turn the channel from one that reacts in fear to the channel that responds with compassion, love, and trust. Act from that place, making empowered choices. Choose to align yourself with the new energies and structures that are arriving with confidence, curiosity, and trust, instead of spiraling down into old reactive patterns. Remind yourself that you are one of those who is here to greet and create the larger universal foundation of love, joy, trust, and compassion. Breathe out every difficulty that comes to you, and breathe in the trust that you have the power, with your human sisters and brothers and your interstellar friends, to help resolve whatever the difficulty may be. Trust, as you breathe out the next challenge or difficulty, that you will find solutions. Answers will come from the compassion you share with others; compassion will lead to connectivity, which will lead to sharing in unity. Sharing in unity will lead to abundance—not limited financial abundance, but true abundance where you have everything you need or want, without monetary restrictions. The old paradigm of monetary structures that have controlled you for so long is dying away.

As the structure of your reality shifts and changes, know that you also will be experiencing internal as well as external changes. They are mirrors of one another. When something outside of you begins to crumble and fall, you will feel something inside of you crumbling too. Rather than moving into old reactive patterns of worry or fear, remind yourself that it is simply time for that cycle to end, and open your heart to embrace and breathe in the new and better cycle that is arriving. This is the way to evolve, by creating the new structures of reality as you gain more understanding. Simultaneously, whenever you catch yourself feeling reactive, with old thoughts, emotions, or behaviors interfering with your love-based perspective, know that what you are thinking and feeling will be reflected in the outer world, and will cause the outer world to manifest exactly what you are experiencing in the inner world, causing a continual loop of the old paradigms. Your job is to continually release the old reactive patterns of thoughts, feelings, and behaviors and turn the channel to your higher vibration with a response of compassion and trust. It is going to take practice to get into the flow of automatically doing this with trust and compassion and love, until you step into those blissful moments of joy where you exclaim, "Look! It is working!" And you will have to practice doing this over and over until you find your structure is firm and solid, not solid in a third-dimensional way, but solid in a multidimensional way, where it is fluid but very strong. You know, water is fluid but very, very strong. You are fluid; you are water beings. You are also beings of light in waveform. Use that strength and fluidity to practice what we are sharing with you so that you can succeed in changing the structure of reality, both on the inner planes and in the outer world. You are in the process now of something big happening. We suggest that you go into it looking at what is not working and discard it immediately with understanding that the old way is no longer valid. Then immediately open your heart to the questions of "What can work better now?" and "How can I achieve multidimensional success?" Each of you is here to be love and shine light. That is your job. That is your purpose. Now approach that job by working with the finer details we have outlined for you in this chapter and use those suggestions to further understand the part of your job description that allows you to participate in changing the very structure of reality.

QUESTIONS & ANSWERS
STEP 4

How will life on Earth look when the institutions break apart?

Ah, that's the great question, and you have already seen some of this as circumstances around you have been changing. However, to answer more directly, it will look like whatever you co-create together. If you focus on higher vibrational thoughts, feelings, words, and actions, your Earth will begin to manifest a more peaceful and harmonious environment. If you focus on being afraid of the unknown, then you will manifest exactly what you are afraid of. Your thoughts have power. We have told you this many, many times. The future cannot be predicted because each choice you make as you are going through this process determines the outcome. You cannot define it in advance; you intend what you wish, but you cannot predict the outcome because the outcome is determined by individual and collective responses made either from fear or from trust. You must join together in unity to find out how much power you have to co-create different structures and a different reality. We have no other answer for your question. You, actually hold the answers to that question.

You have spoken about the foundations of the new energy, describing the four anchor points: love, trust, joy and compassion. When I first read those words in "Remembering Who We Are", I understood the foundation of the old, higher dimensional world, where water equals the foundation of love , air equals our trust for one another and the Universe, fire or the Sun equals joy as light arrives, and the earth element equals the compassion that actually helps us to evolve towards unity. Your description is a brilliant way to remember what is needed from each of us to truly integrate higher and more inclusive versions of ourselves into the Earth that we all share together as we ascend together. We are exercising our 50% of co-creation as an awakened humanity.

Thank you, Dear One, for sharing that, and we do appreciate your reminder of the foundation that we have suggested for humanity. It does bear remembering this because you are now able to embody it and to raise your vibration to incorporate it. It is a good thing to be able to review that perspective and focus on understanding it within your own hearts.

I'm feeling very heart-centered today, with a wonderful feeling of just sending love everywhere. But I'm suffering physically from a very unbalanced energy as I walk. The light-headedness I am experiencing is really challenging me.

We understand, and you are not the only one who is experiencing the light-headedness. It is happening to many people at this time. The more you are awakening into a sense of joy, a sense of purpose, feeling a sense of lightness, the more it will be a little challenging physically for a while, although not indefinitely. The dizziness and lightness you are feeling is actually movement away from third-dimensional form and reality as you begin to function multidimensionally. Do what you can to stabilize yourself, while simultaneously accepting that you are not going to be in the third dimension in the same way any longer because you have chosen to evolve at a higher vibratory rate. Having made that choice, you are opening to more joy in your heart and releasing things that have kept you bound for years in the old-style patterns of existence. We know it sounds a bit challenging to tell you to be grateful, but please remember that this is an expansion of opportunities for gratitude to grow and achieve new ways of being. Your third-dimensional physical forms are undergoing many, many challenges and difficulties because they do not know how to adapt to the new energy coming into Earth. Your job is to focus on the expansion of your consciousness. It is from enlightened vibrations and higher consciousness that your physical forms will learn to adapt and change. Walk with your hand on the wall to keep yourself steady in balance. Close your eyes and tune in to the multidimensional reality for a moment, and then open them again to participate in the third dimension to do what you need to do. Begin to practice moving back and forth between realities. You are moving in and out of a dream-like state, yet it is much more real than you imagine, for the very real experience causing you the perceived difficulty is more real than your illusionary experience of what you have lived so far in your lives.

As we are going through these adjustments, is it generally good for most of us to take Epsom salt baths or is swimming in the ocean beneficial?

It is good for most of you to take sea salt baths. Epsom salts have different minerals in them, beside just the sea salt. Some individuals need Epsom salts for the additional magnesium, but sea salt is good for everyone. To return to your blood's natural balance, sea salt is the most optimal for bathing. If you need other minerals because of your individual condition, magnesium or Epsom salts may be a good choice for one person, but not for everyone. Swimming in the ocean is the most excellent way to align yourself with the waters of this planet and the waters of your own blood. That is a first-choice option. Yet, sometimes being in a warm salt bath when you feel achy, tired, when your body is out of balance, or when you are emotionally upset, will help to rebalance you.

How can I be of service in the best way now?

The best service you can be at this time is to complete your individual mission of exploring the highest version of the energy you brought to the planet (Universal energy) and the energy you came here to explore (Earth energy), as outlined in our

Pleiadian-Earth Energy Book and Calendar.[3] As you continually raise your own vibration, your light reaches others. As your vibration and frequency become higher, you also intuitively know how best to be of service in any given moment. There is not one specific third-dimensional task to undertake at this time. The task is to master yourself, learning what you came here to master. Explore the energies, and pay attention to how you begin to identify the lower and higher vibrations of every choice, every thought, and every action.

Looking at my own shadow as I was walking, I attempted to lighten my shadow by consciously pulling the cells of my body apart so that more light could flow through. It occurred to me that if I am actually becoming a crystalline-based being, I will be shining the light out, reflecting and refracting it. There will no longer be a shadow, but a "light shadow." Is this close to where we are going?

You are creating more space within your cells and recognizing the light that you are. For a long time, we have been telling humanity that you are liquid, crystalline light. We do not mean that you are comprised of liquid quartz crystals. We mean that you are crystals of light that reflect and refract exactly as you are describing. When you are light, your crystalline essence allows light in and shines light out, and that is what you are. We say liquid crystalline light because you are becoming more and more fluid energetically and less and less stuck in a static physical form that is defined by third-dimensional observations and concepts. You are moving into forms in which you are defined by higher vibrational terms, such as unity, liquidity, crystalline essence, and light, light, light. You are now beginning to understand these ideas at a physiological level, rather than just as a mental concept, and as you do that, you become more light and less shadow. You are integrating them into your physical form and into your daily experience. As you do this, you will have physiological symptoms or signs of evolution. You may find yourself disoriented or feeling a little bit "lighter" (pardon the pun! hee-hee-hee)! As you do your personal work to clear out your emotional shadows or any trauma that may have kept you locked into old patterns of behavior or thought, you become lighter and lighter on all levels, freeing you to do the work you are here to do. Your creative idea to intentionally send light into your shadow as you see it when you are walking, is excellent for increasing your conscious connection to what you understand mentally and what you are experiencing physiologically. This is a great exercise!

So, one of the things I should do is to work with my shadows?

Yes, working with your shadows (both your physical shadow and your emotional shadows) is essential for your growth. You must work with your shadows and not be afraid of them. Because the shadows have been so dense and so challenging in these times, we have instituted our Trauma Clearing Program to support people in clearing their shadows more functionally and more quickly. You certainly may work to clear shadows on your own; however, at this time of intense energies, it is sometimes helpful to have an outside perspective to support you and help show you where you are blocked.

What is Reincarnation? Is that just a concept? What is the difference between Reincarnation and a parallel life?

The difference is perspective; parallel lives exist simultaneously in different dimensions. Reincarnation is a concept of looking at lives from the vantage point of linear lifetimes, one after another, stacked one upon the other. The concept of Reincarnation views every other lifetime as past, each built upon or created by the karma in that system. We see karma as an effect that unfolds moment-by-moment through the choices you make.

We do not see things in terms of past or future, because everything happens simultaneously. This concept is a bit difficult for most humans to accept because it seems chaotic to think of everything happening at once. Your species is focused upon linearity and the arrow of time. You believe that everything moves from past to present to future. That way of thinking has led to the idea of reincarnation. Many people wish to clear their karma from past lives to make this one better. That is equivalent to our helping you to clear trauma from a perceived parallel life so that you stop suffering in this one. The trauma is impacting you now because it is happening simultaneously in another dimension, but you are fragmented from that aspect of yourself. When you clear trauma from a parallel life, you can then integrate that aspect of yourself into a more fully functioning "Now" you. There are many, many parallels. For example, imagine you are standing inside a circle; now imagine twelve doors around you. Open any one of those doors, and you can step into a parallel life. The landscape may be different; the characters may be different; you may find yourself different—changing genders, changing physical appearance—and yet the experiences on the emotional and mental levels are real and very similar. If you go to another door, you find the same thing—different circumstances and different appearances with similar emotional and mental impact. Each time you open one of these doors, you open memories and opportunities to clear mistakes or misunderstandings that you experienced in another circumstance. As you clear those traumas and bring back a fuller sense of who you are, you no longer segregate that part of yourself as a "past" life because each of those selves is understood to be part of the current self and is dissolved or integrated into who you are now. You end this karmic pattern when you choose thoughts and actions from the highest vibration in every moment. Those positive thoughts ripple across all of your parallel lives, making each one better.

If you choose thoughts and actions of a lower vibration (such as worry, blame, or fear) you are impacting not only the lifetime of which you are conscious (your current third-dimensional life) but also every other life you are living in a parallel dimension. Each one is connected, and each one suffers.

Is it possible for different aspects of ourselves in parallel lives to affect us in a positive way in this reality and, if so, how does that work?

Absolutely. Many of you have abilities or gifts that you feel are quite natural to you. You have a gift of this or an easy ability to do that. These are things that you may have developed in a parallel existence and are implementing now, though you may perceive them as just natural gifts. It also could be something that you trained yourself to do and in which you now excel, so that's a possibility too. But if your talent comes to you quite naturally and you don't remember any training, you just have always been able to do it with ease and flow, then most likely you are integrating positive attributes from your parallel lives. As you clear up the traumas that exist in this and in parallel lives, more positive aspects come in to support you now because you are not spending as much energy trying to heal wounds from existing traumas. When you don't know where a trauma comes from or you are operating under a trauma in your currently perceived experience from a parallel life, you don't realize how much energy you unconsciously give, trying to stay "safe" from something that feels out of balance. Once you clear the traumas and you begin to understand more clearly where they came from and how to remove them, then you will gain more clarity, which allows you to more easily receive other gifts and accomplishments from your parallel selves.

Can you say something about organ transplants?

Yes. It's an interesting concept that has an impact on the individual person receiving the organ, her or his individual life path, and the evolutionary path of the person who is donating the organ. It's not something that we would classify as good or bad, for we do not judge these things. But we do say that it's not always a good idea to have an organ transplant simply because you are clinging to life; it may be time for you to move out of this particular body and on to your next assignment. So, we suggest that you not cling to this life out of fear. Choosing to have an organ transplant because you are fulfilling something required while you are here on this mission is a different choice, but no organ transplant decision should be made out of fear of death or a clinging to life. You must understand that you never lose who you are. If you have an organ transplant from another human being, however, you will incorporate something of who they are into who you are, so you are going to go through a change either way. You go through a change by implementing and integrating new parts of the organs that come from another person. You also go through a change by moving into a different form if you die. Either way, if you are considering an organ transplant, you are stepping into a position that it is time for a very big change for you. And again, we say the choice should be made individually. Each individual must look at her or his life, examine his or her feelings, fear level, and level of intention. All of these factors must be considered, as well as how it will feel to care for and integrate part of another into yourself. Ultimately, each of you is connected to starlight anyway. You are one species, but there will be individual differences that will be noticed through organ transplant. So, the question for each person facing such a situation is this, "Is this transition intended to integrate another energy into my form here on Earth now, or is this transition intended for me to move into another form because I'm ready for a new assignment?" That's the way we recommend you look at this.

Have these sorts of changes happened on other planets in the Universe or are they unique to Earth?

Yes, such magnificent change has happened on other planets and, yet, your changes are unique here on this planet. Each planet that goes through a transformation has its own set of parameters, its own set of transformative procedures, its own set of understandings, learnings, wisdom, growing, failures, and level of participation. Each one has a different way of proceeding through the process of evolution. This planet has something pretty unusual—that is, you have been given the power of choice that determines 50% of what happens. Most of you don't know this; you don't recognize it, and you don't utilize your power of choice for the most part. You allow others to control you, thinking you have no power. Part of the transition is your awakening to recognize the power that you do hold in every choice you make. Every thought you think has power. You hold the power of choice in every reaction, every emotion, every feeling state, every sharing—each one of those is a potent and powerful energy that ripples out across the planet, paving the way for the changes that will come next and next and next. One of the reasons we've been working with you all for these many, many years is to help you awaken, to remember who you are as powerful divine sparks of light so that you can properly use your power of choice for the evolution of humanity. This species is floundering. Humanity has the potential of dying out altogether, if inspired and great choices are not acted upon. Many choice points have already been reached, and you are now living through the choices you have made as a collective, which for the most part, have been made out of ignorance, separation, and fear. But the evolution continues regardless, as Earth moves through the process of ascension. Whatever you are doing now to raise the vibratory energy of the collective will still help those who are not ready to make the evolutionary leap. Your higher energy will accompany and help prepare them for the next opportunity at the next place they find themselves in their own evolutionary journey. So, your work here is still not done even if the choice point for each human has already been made. Does that help you to understand?

Yes, you've always said in the past that the only real power we have is the power of choice and your answer reinforces exactly what you have been telling us.

You also have something else that other planets have not had. You've seen many science fiction movies that comment about other species, other interdimensional beings, showing that interstellar beings are not, perhaps, as emotional as humans are. Humans are very, very emotional. We interstellar beings certainly have feeling states, some of us more than others, depending upon where we are from and our approach to this process of evolution. However, you have the benefit of being able to *use* your emotions as signposts. Emotions are clear and direct signals to show you when you yourself are out of balance and need to change. Emotions on your planet are an evolutionary gift that most of you have failed to use properly. That's something else that is different and unique about your evolutionary process here on planet Earth.

I've heard much talk about the increased involvement of star beings or interstellar beings around this planet over the years. I'm just wondering, what makes it different now?

Well, there are two reasons for this. First of all, have you noticed how much more interest is present at this time? There are more ships in the sky as more Earth changes occur and as more people become interested in interstellar presence. Have you noticed how many more people are paying attention to the concept that they may not be alone in the Universe and that maybe there is another intelligent species out there somewhere? That is half of the answer. The other half of the answer is that many people have managed to raise their consciousness—not everyone, obviously, but enough of you—to open into portals of multidimensionality. We have been here all along while you are going through this process, but you can see us more easily as you open more to multidimensionality. As you take off your glasses of familiarity, and you begin to talk about ship clouds, movement, unusual things in the sky, as you open to more multidimensional perspectives, then you're more able to perceive what is already there. Your eyes, your ears, and your hearts are opening to that type of interest because you are opening to multidimensionality yourselves. That means you have a choice. Although some people are frightened by seeing things that are unusual or different from the familiar third-dimensional paradigm, those who have chosen to read this book do not have a fear response at all; you have a more excited response like, "Oh boy, this is what we've been waiting for!" If you are moving in this direction, we encourage you to keep doing what you are doing. Keep doing everything to move towards unity with an open heart; that will open your mind. Let your heart lead your thoughts. Thoughts from the mind keep you in the third-dimensional perspective. If you let your heart lead you, you open to multidimensional perspectives.

You have mentioned portals opening in specific places around the planet, and that these specific places will shift in order to offer opportunities to all who wish to change with the evolving Earth. You said these portals will automatically raise the vibration of people entering them, as we raise our vibration by measuring our lives through energy rather than time. Will you please say more about these portals of opportunity?

Yes. They are not located in third-dimensional spacetime as you perceive it, but they will *appear* in your third-dimensional spacetime as waves of other dimensional experience. The way to approach these portals is to engage your intuition. The more you engage your intuition and allow it to guide you, the more you will be able to step away from Earth's spacetime orientation and experience other dimensional moments where the portals appear synchronistically. Humanity used to view stone circles in England and other places as portals. Today that is old paradigm thinking. Portals certainly did exist in certain places, such as stone circles for a long, long time on this planet, but the lay lines of the Earth are changing. Additionally, the energy of the Earth is changing through the arrival of Cosmic Rays, changes in the Schumann Resonance, and unfortunately, through purposeful geochemical engineering by humans. So therefore, the portals are also shifting and changing. The more you can open your consciousness to communicate with other realms, specifically, the Devic Kingdom, the realm of the trees, the plants, the Earth Herself, and the stars and the bodies of planets that you see in the sky, the more you open to portals that you can step through to other worlds. Opening your awareness to aspects of the Earth and the sky can open your awareness of a bridge that provides the answer to the question, "Where do I need to be in this moment?" Then you can find yourself at these portals in the moment that you need to be there. As we said, they will be shifting across the planet because the planet itself is shifting. The Cosmic Rays are impacting you with radiation, and the Earth's core is moving. In other words, you have both inside and outside forces culminating on the magnetosphere of your planet. You will do well to ask the question, "How do we find and navigate our way with these changing dynamics?"

Therefore, we cannot identify a specific third-dimensional location and say, "Here is a place to look for a portal." The best way to find a portal is to open your intuitive heart, allow it to lead you, and spend more time in Nature. It is in Nature that you will often find portals. Go to places where your heart calls you; notice different shimmering colors. Notice how the leaves on the trees may seem slightly different than usual; notice the feeling in the air; notice that the ground may be slightly different. Stop, pause, connect and feel to see if it is a portal. There are clues everywhere to be seen; symbols will show up all throughout Nature. You will begin to see faces and beings in rocks and on the bark of trees; they are there, if you just take the time to see them.

When you find a portal, always ask, "May I enter?" It is exceptionally important to ask the question, "May I enter?" It is not appropriate to simply assume that because you have discovered a portal that you can automatically go through. You must ask permission to be sure your vibration matches where you are attempting to go. It is respectful. Trying to force yourself through a portal where your vibration does not match would only cause more stress to the physical body, or you would not see the portal at all. So yes, the portals are appearing. You will not find them in any cities. You will find them in Nature. So, spend as much time as you can in Nature. We suggest specifically that you look for places where there are trees, for these very old spiritual beings— the trees of your world—have great access to being able to share where a portal might appear. So, connect with the trees, learn to speak with them, listen to your intuitive guidance and be guided by your heart. That's your map.

STEP FIVE:

WHERE IS YOUR CONSCIOUSNESS?

Today we will answer the question, "Where is your conscious-ness?" Many people have begun to believe that consciousness resides outside of the mind, and we have to applaud those who are awakening, saying, "Yes! This is true!" Humanity has long believed that consciousness is contained within the mind, even going so far as to say that it is a function of the brain. Many believe that when the brain is better understood, consciousness will be better understood. But that is not true, is it? Consciousness resides in everything! Your body is conscious. Your body has a consciousness that knows what it needs and how to regulate itself within the environment where it lives. Your heart has a consciousness. Your heart knows when you are reaching for unity, when you are trying to move away from separation, when you want to invite more love, and when you wish to eradicate all fears. That is the consciousness of the heart. You also have a spiritual consciousness, where you are awakening to recognize and understand that the third dimension is only one perspective of what you believe to be your reality. Your consciousness is not limited to the here and now as you perceive it in time. The magnitude of your consciousness is not reflected by time, which is only a third-dimensional construct created by humans. Our answer to "Where is your consciousness?" depends upon where you focus your intention, your curiosity, your understanding, your questions, and your desire for expansion. If you wish to expand your body awareness, you learn to listen more clearly to what your body wants and needs, and you honor that consciousness as wisdom. If you wish to explore communication with the plant kingdom, then you must recognize that each plant has consciousness and has its own needs for regulating within the changing energies. There is consciousness there; there is a continual communication. The same is true with the animal kingdom. Animals have consciousness also. They communicate; they have feelings; they have knowing; they have understanding, and they work more on instinct and intuition than they do by thinking. The consciousness of the animal kingdom is in some ways more in touch with the larger reality than is humanity's consciousness. To think of humanity as being the most "intelligent" form of consciousness gives too much credit to the mind, which is actually intended to be of service to consciousness that lives in the heart. But none of the above aspects of life explains exactly *what* consciousness is or *where* it is.

Consciousness is everywhere; even your car has consciousness. You can communicate with that consciousness by placing your hand on your vehicle and thanking it for transporting you safely. The car receives that communication as energy, and it functions better. If you are rude or dismissive to your car, hurrying it to perform without giving it time to warm up, your car will respond to being pushed. The consciousness of the car feels that you are not concerned about its wellbeing. A rock that you see on the path in front of you has consciousness too, knowing where it wishes to be in that moment and how it is evolving at its own pace. It is not something to simply be thrown or kicked aside. Pick up the rock and ask if you can help it go where it wishes to go or walk around it. Everything has consciousness, and it is all connected within a great webbing of light.

Consciousness is cosmic awareness. It is a knowing wisdom that comes from your trust in the Universe and an awareness that Nature's energy has intelligence. But consciousness can also be defined in much more clear terms, such as the simple understanding about not about taking sides or not judging someone else. Consciousness is about treating everyone with respect and kindness and always considering how your actions affect everyone else. Each of you is a spark of divine energy; how you use your energy defines your level of consciousness. Questions about consciousness cannot only be *what* or *where* questions. They must include *how* questions; they are questions about how to live your lives with regard for others and your environment. Consciousness includes living and treating others with respect, honor, kindness, acceptance, compassion, cooperation, peace, and love. Lack of consciousness results in thoughts and actions that are based on judgment, jealousy, rage, fear, greed, selfishness, and a desire to manipulate others or Nature.

Defining or seeking consciousness is not an intellectual pursuit, although your science would very much like to uncover the seat of consciousness and define the mystery of how consciousness evolves. However, regardless of the scientific perspective, consciousness cannot actually be found in the mind or in the part of the brain that does your thinking. True, deep awareness and understanding come from the heart. It is here that you understand how everything is connected and that you all are one. It is your mind that judges and separates, causing conflict, competition, and the urge to control others or Nature.

The heart discerns, accepts, and seeks harmony through exercising compassion. You will never find consciousness relying on the mind alone. A simple walk in the quiet of Nature can bring awareness, sensitivity, and empathy–principles that naturally raise your consciousness. True awareness and understanding only come when the mind is led by the heart.

To achieve higher consciousness, take responsibility for all of your choices, your actions, and your thoughts, which are potent energies! You experience an enlightened moment when you understand that killing anything for any reason is not acceptable. Consciousness expands when you realize the power within you and stop asking an outside force to save you. Taking responsibility to change the world you have co-created through your own choices brings an expansion of your consciousness.

On Earth, we see consciousness as living by the phrase *In Lak'ech* ("I am another yourself"). *In Lak'ech* is a principle of unity and comes with the understanding that what you do to others you also do to yourselves. You can use your emotions to guide you in bringing your consciousness to a higher level, where you experience a continual awareness of your thoughts, your actions, and your reactions. Cullen uses the below original quote to guide his life, and he has shared this way of viewing compassion with others since he was a very young man:

You cannot be in a state of compassion if you are in a state of reaction. Conversely, you cannot be in a state of reaction if you are in a state of compassion.

When your hearts guide your thoughts, you will begin to experience enlightened moments of recognizing that you are all one, that separation is an illusion, and that every aware perspective can be compassionately harmonized into the fabric of true consciousness. Consciousness is love.

We have taken you down to the minutia level of consciousness on this planet. Now we are going to take you in the opposite direction—to the consciousness of the Universe. You are part of the stars. You are communicating with us. We certainly have consciousness! How else could we translate the musical and mathematical tones of our language into your human language so that you can understand us? We are communicating through an expanded sense of consciousness. We use the libraries of words that this particular human language offers, accessing them through our connection to Pia and Cullen's brains. However, the consciousness comes from the heart connection, where our energy is merged with theirs. Then your energy can be synchronized with ours. Actually, the words do not matter as much as the energy that we are sharing. Sometimes when you hear us,[1] you interpret the energy of our message before you cognitively recognize the words. That is an expansion of consciousness. That is awakening to a larger aspect of who you are. You are not merely third-dimensional beings who are moving into a larger expansion of, perhaps, fifth dimensional experience, as so many believe. We have frequently told you that your evolution is not a linear progression, moving from lower dimensional consciousness into higher dimensional consciousness as you expand your awareness. Evolution is stepping beyond the boundaries of hierarchal linearity. It is moving your consciousness into a place where it is liquid, flexible, and able to be in *any* dimension (or all dimensions simultaneously) as you become aware of the possibilities. Your consciousness is becoming free-moving and expansive, moving beyond the confines of your limited perception of time, your limited perception of space, and even your perceptions of what you believe reality to be.

Some of you will begin (or have already begun) to have experiences that perhaps you cannot quite put into a regular linear perspective of normalcy. It may be a bit confusing to you. Or it may be exciting and exhilarating! Or you may be startled by your new experiences and not know what to do with them, asking yourselves, "What does this mean?" The energies are expanding now to allow humanity the option to grow at an accelerated rate. You now have the option of stepping into an even more fully realized consciousness, a consciousness that is more alive, more awake, and more aware than your accustomed perceptions. Even now your science says that the brain—which is not the seat of consciousness, as we have explained—is only understood to have a small percentage of known functions. The larger part of the brain remains mysterious to your scientists. There is no understanding (yet) of the use or function of the larger percentage of your brain matter, which is connected to your heart energy. That larger percentage of your brain is not even considered intelligent, or conscious, by your science. And yet, it is the undefined brain area connected to your heart energy that helps you to connect with us and other energies that science can neither define nor understand. You have within your brain this tiny little gland called the pineal, which is an opening, a portal, a gate of connectivity for understanding larger aspects of consciousness. You produce within your pineal a specific substance called Metatonin that gives you heightened awareness, heightened experiences, and a chance to grow in your understanding of how to communicate with others—your understanding of the larger realities outside the confines of third-dimensional thinking—and the understanding of concepts beyond what you may perceive in your everyday life. Metatonin is the active pineal gland secretion that dissolves the borders between third-dimensional consciousness and multidimensional consciousness. While the existence of this elixir of life has only very recently been discovered by your science, wise people have known about it for hundreds of years. Indian yogis call it amrita, a substance that provides bliss, vitality, wisdom, and connection. It is light. The pineal gland is there to help you perceive and use this light. It is there to help you understand connectivity. It is there to help you understand expansion. It is there to promote your opening to evolution.

We are speaking of this because it is coming into your medical and scientific awareness that your pineal glands have become calcified and may be unable to perform their (undefined by science) function. Many of your star sisters and brothers have been prodding you to do things to awaken and restore the functionality of your pineal gland. We have even previously given suggestions of supplements[2] that can assist the expansion of pineal utility.

There are many interstellar beings present to help you awaken your consciousness to the higher levels of awareness. They, like we, wish to help you learn to communicate as cosmic citizens so that when the question is asked, "Where is consciousness?" your answer will be, "Well, everywhere, of course!" Think of that! To move beyond believing that your consciousness resides only in your mind, or in your heart, or in your body to an understanding that your consciousness is *everywhere*. Every thought you have, every feeling, every choice you make radiates and affects everyone and everything else because your consciousness is everywhere. Everything is connected. You are not limited by focusing your attention on only one thing or one place at any given moment. The pineal gland is the part of your physical body that receives light. It conducts that light as information; it is related to how you communicate with the Universe. Sadly, we must point out to you things that are happening in your Earthly environment that are causing your pineal gland to struggle to perform its job. We are concerned about this and want to make you aware so that you can change it. This may be one reason why there are so many interstellar and interdimensional beings appearing to humans across the planet now. We wish to *get your attention* and help you understand that you have to make changes, *or your species will die.* Your consciousness will not die, but your experience and the experiment of Earth may be over, if you do not make these necessary and radical changes. That may be just fine too, for we do not judge you. You get to make the choice, of course. It is, after all, your species, and you are the ones in charge of your own evolution. We are just here to nudge you, to prod you in beneficial directions to point out opportunities, and alert you to possible outcomes of your choices. Because we have gone through this evolutionary process ourselves, we wish to show you the way so that you may benefit from our experience. That is our job—to support you, to be with you, to help you understand, and to help you make the choices that support your growth into what you wish to become: unified beings expressing love, joy, trust, compassion, and unity. We do this because we love you.

Your environment has been harmed greatly by many things. But the ones that are specifically harming your precious, tiny pineal gland—the portal to enlarging your consciousness, expanding your awareness, and communicating with other realms—are ones that you may have known are harmful to the body at the third-dimensional level. You may not have been aware that these toxic substances are specifically harmful to the pineal gland, to your etheric body, and to your spiritual evolution.[3] Even your science recognizes the harmful effects of all of these substances although your governments do not divulge this truth. These substances are:

Aluminum – is toxic to the brain, making it difficult for it to function correctly. It is also a major factor contributing to Alzheimer's disease;

Fluoride – assaults the pineal gland specifically through its toxic poisons. Many of your water systems and dental treatments use fluoride without understanding the harm to your overall health;

Glyphosate – is an assault to all levels of human health, including the pineal. It is being sprayed casually on your lawns and gardens as a weed killer all over the world. It is also intentionally sprayed on large areas of your food crops. The wind, manipulated through geochemical engineering, blow those toxins to areas that have not been intentionally sprayed, making it almost impossible to grow organic food, for all food is being dusted with this poison;

Bisphenol – is present in plastic bottles, inside food cans, in dental fillings and in thermal print paper used as your receipts. It poisons you, causing negative effects on your consciousness;

Geoengineering – spraying toxic metal particles from airplanes that cause physical and mental health problems, as well as affecting your weather; impacts your consciousness by shrinking your pineal gland;

Wi-Fi – is the most insidious toxin, and one that most of you use with great regularity. Wi-Fi EMF pollution harms your mind, your brain, and your evolving consciousness. The blue light produced from computers interferes with melatonin production, causing an assault on the pineal gland and all of the systems and organs it influences. Further, 5G's only purpose is to promote Artificial Intelligence (AI), the most dangerous enemy to your human consciousness.

We have always told you to balance your time in front of your computer or cell phone with an equal amount of time in Nature. Take a walk in the woods without your cellphone. Dip yourself into a stream. Immerse yourself in seawater. Hug or talk to a tree. Stroke a plant. Do things to rebalance yourselves through reconnecting to Nature. Any of these things that rebalance your physical body are more necessary than ever before. Your consciousness is everywhere, and if you do not wish it to be minimized into an experience that can only be perceived in third-dimensional terms through third-dimensional perceptions, or worse, surrendered to Artificial Intelligence (AI), you need to expand your consciousness by continually connecting with all life. Where is your consciousness? It is everywhere. It is in the food you grow and eat. It is in the thoughts you think. It is in the body that you either take care of or you push to over-perform. It is in the emotions that you either use to guide you to the changes you need to make, or allow to overwhelm you, filling you with anger, sadness, jealousy, greed, or fear. Remember, emotions are intended to point you in the direction of making changes within yourself. We do not wish to derail your progressive orientation toward an expansion of consciousness by frightening you with information about toxins that harm you. We point them out because it is necessary to have a balanced picture of the truth. You may understand because we have told you that you can work energetically to help disassemble chemtrails of poisons in the air. Some of you have been successfully practicing this for years, which awakens you to remembering your own power. However, you also need to practice removing toxins from your third-dimensional environment through physical actions, as well as by sending love consciously from your heart into these toxins that are permeating your planet. You need to actually use your minds, your speech, and your fingers to write letters, make telephone calls, and demand to stop these actions that are poisoning all life. Life on Earth will cease very shortly if these toxins are allowed to continue to contaminate your world. You may know that there is a great human voice speaking up globally about stopping 5G, since we first alerted you to its dangers long ago. This particular technology is a dangerous assault on your consciousness. There are many voices across the planet speaking up now to say, "No, we don't want it." And it may be stopped. But the protest against 5G can be accomplished by your third-dimensional protests against the dangers of 5G and by extending your consciousness to stop the assault. Some of you are finally recognizing and accepting that the attempt to implement 5G at a global level is an attempt to extinguish your own consciousness and instill Artificial Intelligence (AI). Your society is choosing to refuse to take a stand against a takeover by Artificial Intelligence, which will end the experiment of life on Earth. You need to change that *right now*.

You have the opportunity now, Dear Ones, to take your conscious awareness into a more expansive viewpoint. Take it beyond the idea of asking, "Where is my consciousness in this moment?" Take it beyond paying attention to your thoughts, your emotions, your body, or your meditation. All of these things are important, of course. But after you note where your consciousness is focused, expand your consciousness, reminding yourself that your consciousness is everywhere. Begin to expand your web of connection to all life on the planet and to all life in the Universe. Practice saying, "We are one; we are connected. We are bound through love. We are bound through unity. We may have different perspectives, but our consciousness shows us that we are all related."

You have spent so many years and lifetimes experiencing separation under the pall of fear of being different from others, thinking that those differences will allow someone else to harm you, compete with you, or get ahead of you. You have used those differences under a wall of separation that disconnects you from one another and from the Universe. You are now moving away from being under the spell and illusion of separation into the more expanded awareness of connection and unity. The more you focus your thoughts on "We are consciousness. We are connected. We are light. We are love," the more your awareness of your expanded consciousness will grow. It is important, for you are undergoing massive changes on the planet at this time, both individually and collectively as a species. You need to eliminate all remnants of fear. You need to eliminate fears and thoughts that if you die, you will cease to exist. You need to eliminate all elements of fear that tell you that you are not well, simply because you do not feel well. You are adapting and adjusting. Remind yourself that you are simply having a different conscious experience and that your consciousness is expanding beyond previous concepts of what it meant to "be well." Begin to think in terms of consciousness itself expressing as everything. Lend your energy to how it will unfold. Be sure that your conscious awareness is focused upon the energies of love and light. Remember the basic premise from which we began this Manual for Accelerated Evolution: *Everything* is energy. Therefore, we are energy; you are energy; everything is energy. If you want your consciousness to expand, focus upon the idea that your consciousness is also energy. Choose the higher vibrational signatures of love and light in every single moment as you pass through this chaotic opening to becoming something more than what you have been, something more than what you have dreamed of, as you step into the expanded consciousness as the New Humans.

QUESTION & ANSWERS
STEP 5

Can you speak to us about the difference between soul consciousness and body consciousness and how they struggle for dominance?

What you now perceive as a difference in soul consciousness or body consciousness was very different when all forms of consciousness were equally honored. When the body wisdom was more highly valued, people listened to the signs their bodies gave them to make corrections in their food, their sleep, or their reactions to stress. Healing used to be much more possible because body and soul consciousness were aligned. You do not have any recorded history about when humans were able to listen to their body wisdom in alignment with their spirits and their souls to perceive what their total consciousness was sharing.

There is a reason that your body consciousness is not as recognized as your soul consciousness is. Your body used to lead with just as much conscious wisdom as anything else that is part of you, including your soul. When the genders of this planet were respected equally for their qualities and gifts, body consciousness was highly attuned to needs of the present moment. Because body consciousness is wise, it is aware of what is needed in any given moment. Because the patriarchy has destroyed most of the balance that was in place for human consciousness when the matriarchy ruled thousands of years ago, body consciousness has been ignored, dismissed, or abused. With the invention of electric lights, humans began to push the body past its limits for rest, disregarding the body wisdom in favor of mental preferences. People began to disconnect from Nature's rhythms, staying up very late at night. When it was discovered that people could work with electric lights, night shifts were created as part of the new "normal." As people began to dismiss body wisdom about sleep, they began to experience more stress and anxiety, which many have tried to assuage through inappropriate eating, using sugar, caffeine, alcohol, and processed junk food to distract them from the imbalances they were feeling. Even though the body has never liked this type of abuse, body warnings were increasingly dismissed in favor of mental rationalization. None of this is listening to or respecting the wisdom of the body, and therefore, it does not support the evolution of the soul. Your collective focus on the importance of the mind has contributed to the dismissal of body consciousness, as well as heart wisdom, for that matter.

We encourage you to listen more to what the body consciousness does have to share, and as you are listening, ask the light to give you insight and understanding. Remember that the light of understanding can manifest in the body as well as in the soul. Both provide valuable information for your human form. When you pay attention to your intuition and make higher vibrational choices that honor all life, you are listening to your body awareness and wisdom. Your body will naturally feel more elevated and more raised in vibration when you are honoring all life through the choices you make about what you eat and when you sleep. Listening to your body encourages your body's contribution to your increasing awareness and your ability to make higher choices for soul growth.

Does body awareness precede us when we do things?

It depends on the individual attunement. Humans are changing vastly right now; sometimes your higher awareness will enter from body consciousness, sometimes through feeling states or intuition from your heart consciousness, and sometimes through your mental thoughts. It depends on where you focus your attention in the moment and how intentionally you break old patterns of focused awareness to create new and higher awareness.

Laarkmaa, could you just give us a brief talk on how our bodies are affected every time we send out love and light on a physical and cellular level?

That's a good question. Every time you send out love and light you infuse the cells of your body with love and light, which strengthens them. This helps your body combat other incoming toxins, fears, negative energies, or anything that is coming through you environmentally, from other people's lower vibrational thoughts, from challenging situations, or from other sources. However, as this is the time of great chaotic change, you will be noticing that your physical bodies are still experiencing symptoms of not being able to adjust as quickly as you would like. Obviously, the first remedy is to immediately send love and light into the body, not just out into the world, but into the body, so the body can adapt and adjust. That's important, but it's also important to learn to expand your consciousness beyond the concepts of "I am this third-dimensional person; I have a body; I have a mind; I have a spirit; I have feelings." Expand your ideas of consciousness beyond by saying, "I am expanding through my meditations, through my thoughts, through my speech, through my conscious choices. I am expanding beyond the limitations of what I have perceived as my consciousness. By doing this, your consciousness begins to grow.

Please, clarify a little bit how we perceive when our pineal gland is more active?

When your pineal gland is more active, you feel a sense of peace, and sometimes even a sense that everything is going to be okay. Perhaps you could be standing in the middle of a traumatic situation, and a rush of calm will come over you for no particular reason; you simply feel that everything is going to be okay. That is an indication that your pineal gland is being more active. There is a very delicate chemical balance between the chemicals melatonin and metatonin within your pineal gland[3]. Because of recent and current external assaults on your physical systems, the imbalance between these substances occurs more and more frequently. It is your job to try to maintain the proper balance so that you can receive greater instructions from the pineal gland, and from the other portions of your brain as well. It's important that all systems of the brain—what we call your five pack[4]— are interacting harmoniously so that you can function best here in the third dimension while simultaneously expanding your multi-dimensional awareness. The feelings you asked us to explain can best be described as feeling of a sort of peace settling upon your whole body and a sense of knowing that *everything is going to be okay* without understanding why or thinking about how that can be. Just a knowingness. That's the best way to recognize that your pineal gland is active. These spaces or moments do not generally last long, but they have a lasting effect of stabilizing your system. They will not stay activated long-term yet because of imbalances that are long overdue for correction. You are here to bring multidimensional awareness into this dimension. Bursts of peace from the pineal gland stabilize you and help you to remember and reconnect to your more expanded conscious awareness so that you can remember who you are and that you come from everywhere. Taking care of your pineal is important to support your task.

I was also wondering about other energies that seem to just arrive in the air. Are they also helping to harmonize our pineal glands?

Many of the energies that you feel of light, joy, peace, trust, and compassion are related to the pineal gland, but they are also related to the opening of your hearts. Their effect is not restricted only your brains, even when we speak of the mystical pineal. They also cause your hearts to expand in love, for through an expansion of love, you recognize and remember that you are connected to everything and everyone, and you ack⸍ yourselves as cosmic citizens. The energies arriving provide a delicate balancing within the human brain and heart. Remember, the pineal connects you to cosmic wisdom and opens you to the greatest force in the Universe—love.

How can we decalcify our pineal gland?

From a physiological point of view, there are some third-dimensional supplements that you can take, but the main ways to decalcify your pineal gland are avoiding the toxic substances we have named and to focus light into it. Sit in a meditative state, and beam light into the center of your head, where the pineal resides. Light is what the pineal needs, and light is also what the pineal offers to the world. The pineal is a portal bringing in light. Vitamin K2 in the form of K2-7 is a specific remedy for helping decalcify the pineal gland. Take it at night before sleep. Balance that by taking vitamin A in the morning. That combination is specifically helpful in decalcifying anything stuck around the pineal. Some people can take chlorella or spirulina (each individual must determine if that choice is right for her or him). Those green substances also help to break down calcification around the brain. We also recommend sea-buckthorn because it helps combat the radiation that's coming through when the Cosmic Rays are really strong on Earth, helping your entire body as well as the pineal to adjust to what's going on with the radiation. It helps your body adapt and adjust. There are other supplements that you can also take to help with apparent memory and cognitive decline. These are Bacopa Monnieri and Suma, a plant product from the rainforest. These plants help with cognition when you're feeling the effects of Cosmic Rays coming into your body. Bacopa Monnieri and Suma do not specifically address the pineal, but they do give your brain support when you're feeling confused.

Removing the toxic substances that we have listed is

exceedingly important. Supplements will do nothing if you continue to be poisoned by the things we have listed above. Also clearing out old traumas removes density and opens up space for the pineal to accept and radiate more light. The Trauma Clearing program that we offer is very good for helping to clear the way for the pineal to both receive and spread more light. Ultimately, you must change your beliefs and your habits to restore a healthy environment for the pineal gland. When your pineal is more open, you will also find that you experience bursts of light coming into your eyes when they are closed in the dark because the pineal gland is being activated. You may have that experience at random times, as your awareness expands, allowing you to see deepening and more shimmering colors around you. You may see waves of movement in the air as well, or waves of another being whose energy is present. You may see the artificiality of certain things such as the falseness of artificial light. Your higher functioning pineal provides a deepening awareness of reality. It gives you a journey of expansion. People experience it in different ways. Some may experience this growing awareness as liquid light, showing fluid movement of some sort. Light is the key factor and oftentimes the light that you will see first is the golden light of grace or the white light of truth.

You have told us often that many interstellar beings are here to help us to raise our consciousness. Is there anything that we can do to cultivate our relationship with these beings?

Yes, absolutely. Opening your heart and expanding your awareness and learning to extend your consciousness out instead of focusing only on the third dimension will enhance your ability to communicate with other beings. However, trust is important as well, for many people want to communicate with other beings while maintaining control of the communication. Recognize and understand that you are inviting only beings of love and light to communicate with you; allow them to communicate in their own way. Establish the boundary of love and light first, and then trust that only beings of love and light can communicate with you. Open your heart and say, "I am here; I am listening." You must also remove yourself from third-dimensional toxic influences, such as cell towers, city congestion, or many other things that interfere with your connection to Nature and your expanding awareness. Do all of these things while focusing on expanding your intuitive abilities, and you will be more able to communicate. The more you recognize, each of you, that you are all connected, that all life is connected, and that consciousness is in everything, the more you can communicate consciously with any other conscious beings as you wish.

Thank you, Dear Ones, for your very interesting questions, which provide evidence of your own expanding consciousness. We feel the energy of each of you is growing. We can say that your influence on the planet will also grow, and it will ripple out into the Universe. Do not focus on the fear within any situation or how it is described. Instead ask yourselves what else is there to see and what are its gifts?!

STEP SIX:

THE RETURN OF THE DIVINE FEMININE

W e have spoken to you about the principles of flexibility, flow, freedom, and abundance. And we have spoken to you about love and healing. We have spoken to you about many things that are important for accelerating your evolutionary journey. One of the things that is rarely addressed (except possibly in some women's circles) is the power of the Divine Feminine and the need for the return of honoring that power.

This planet has been separated into dualistic opposites through the thoughts that you think, rather than by your direct experiences. The split between male and female has been a division that has compromised your integrity as unified beings. What you may not realize, and we are here to tell you, is that you are androgynous beings. We have talked to you about your androgyny in previous books[1], and we have spoken to you about the power available with the return of the Divine Feminine. In gatherings, we have introduced you to our colleagues Mary Magdalene and the Great Mother Mary, who speak to you about the need for the return of the Divine Feminine. But what you have yet to fully realize, even though you understand the concept mentally, is that you are—all of you—regardless of gender, partially feminine and partially masculine. In your patriarchal cultures, the feminine aspect has been denied, dismissed, or ridiculed. The masculine is out of balance, and the feminine has been dismissed. You cannot survive by trying to do things exclusively in a masculine way. Cullen's phrase "Women in training to be Men" reflects a perfect image of how women have forgotten their feminine role and its gifts. If women forget the Divine Feminine within themselves, then certainly men will ignore it altogether. Men have forgotten their own feminine aspects, and women are ignoring or dismissing their feminine gifts as they compare and compete with men rather than cooperating by using their feminine talents. This choice to align solely with masculine aspects is causing women to not only compete with men, but to also compete with each other, which is completely against the nature of feminine energy, which is based on cooperation. This imbalance is increasing because there is such disregard for the feminine values of empathy, nurturance, and cooperation.

One of the things that absolutely must occur in this path of accelerated evolution is the recognition, honoring, and respect of the Divine feminine that is within each of you; it is awakening moment-by-moment as you raise your vibratory consciousness. The Divine Feminine includes all of the qualities we previously emphasized about flow, flexibility, abundance, and freedom. The Divine Feminine is always involved with justice and love. The Divine Feminine, which nurtures and upholds the truth, is out of balance because of your choice to align only with masculine principles. This alignment produces polar opposites creating separate viewpoints, rather than harmonizing viewpoints. Even these polar opposite viewpoints each still reflects masculine perspectives. The patriarchal rule has done that to humanity.[2] It is now time to recognize, return to, and live in all the nurturing, flowing, free qualities offered by the Divine Feminine. As you step more into the Liquid Time that exists now, the Divine Feminine will become more and more apparent in your daily life, guiding you through synchronous moment to synchronous moment in flow and freedom. Rather than your old paradigm of masculine focus upon a linear future, full of time-structured plans or a linear past often filled with longing for what was or what should have been, living in the present moment through Liquid Time will allow you to incorporate all aspects of the Divine Feminine through meeting the flow and freedom of each moment. It is the Divine Feminine that is helping you learn to examine, discern, and respond to whatever energy is present in every Now moment.

One of the things you are working towards and with which we wish to help you is the concept of how you integrate (or do not integrate) the opposites within yourselves. You are not doing a very good job of integrating opposites in your external third-dimensional world. When you begin to integrate both masculine and feminine energies within yourselves, you will have a deeper understanding of what it means to be androgynous. With that deeper understanding of merged feminine and masculine energies, where dualistic opposites work in harmony, androgyny, and unity, you can learn how to view opposites in your outer third-dimensional world. The principle of dynamic tension for growth operates here in your world, but you are not using it for your growth as it was intended. It has been used incorrectly for thousands and thousands of years as a force producing greater and greater separation, where each of you has aligned yourself with *this* or *that*, *male* or *female*, or *me* or *you*. Humans have assigned judgments of "right" or "wrong" to each of these opposites, rather than seeing that opposites are simply different perspectives that can be positively combined in unity. When you learn to use the dynamic tension that is present properly, you will begin to see how opposites push against one another for growth. You will see how they offset one another for expansion, and how through that expansion more creative possibilities come into your world. We explained the power and number of energies in *Pleiadian-Earth Energy Astrology—Charting the Spirals of Consciousness.*[3]

You have completely dismissed the idea of Universal energy of 3, creativity. In fact, you have either misunderstood or ignored all of the Universal energies that represent the Divine Feminine. Universal energy numbers are intended to be used together. The Universal energies of 3, 6, and 9 are specifically Divine Feminine energies: the energies of creativity, flow, and harmony. You do not seem to value these as important energies (or numbers) in and of themselves or use their power. We notice that you seem to focus upon certain masculine Universal energies almost exclusively, such as 1, 4, and 11, the energies of initiation, foundation (or tradition), and illumination. There is nothing inherently wrong with the masculine energies, but they are out of balance. Focusing on masculine energies exclusively without incorporating feminine energies leads to more and more imbalance, and imbalance by its very nature lowers your vibration. You need to focus more upon the energy of each number and discern what its gifts are for you. Begin to examine if each energy is offering the gifts of Divine Feminine or Divine Masculine; this way of using both is different from the current ways you use masculine energies almost exclusively. A melding together of the Divine Feminine and Divine Masculine is the only solution for regaining balance and equality in your very confused world.

One thing the Divine Feminine encourages most is the acceptance of the Divine Masculine, for the Divine Feminine encompasses all. The Divine Feminine loves all and accepts all. It offers the process of accepting the Divine Masculine as an essential part of the whole. Unlike the patriarchy, which has chosen to diminish the Divine Masculine into a lower vibrational usage of the Universal masculine energies, the Divine Feminine encourages us to put "Divine" back into masculine energies. For example, the Divine Masculine Universal energy of 1 is for starting things and new beginnings. It is assertive, but not aggressive. The popular warped use of Universal energy 1 has changed initiation into aggression, force, and controlled progress. The Divine Masculine no longer exists in your patriarchal culture (although it certainly exists within each of you who have worked to recognize, acknowledge, and honor who you are as androgynous beings). Instead, your culture uses masculine energy without its divinity, which further imbalances the relationship between genders. The Divine Feminine is doing everything it can to bring the divine aspect back into masculine energy for a balance of androgynous energy. You must work within yourselves to transform the dualistic opposite nature of who you are as masculine and feminine energies into a unified harmony that reflects both. You must also use the dynamic tension present in your third-dimensional world to push against each other in a way that encourages and supports growth, creativity, expansion, and unified harmony in the world.

Your feminine energies are also being used without their divinity. Are you using your creative potential to create with love? We don't see that you are at this time. We do not see that you are actually using your creative potential at all. We see you using your minds rather than your hearts to come up with what you believe to be creative ideas, which leaves out the very essence of the Divine Feminine 3 creative energy. Your creative endeavors are lacking because they do not come from the spontaneous and divine union of opposites. You are not creating high vibrational music or high vibrational art at this time. No wonder so much of your "creative endeavors" seem to be mere expressions of rage or grief. Your creativity also seems often to be linked with monetary gain through technology, rather than simply sharing your creative gifts to uplift others and society. You are not allowing your true creativity to come forth because you have dismissed, disregarded, or forgotten how to use the creative energy of the Divine Feminine.

Step back and focus on learning to be all that you can be.

Step back and focus on working to become a higher vibrational being. Focus on being light and being love at such a high degree that you begin to spontaneously marry and merge the opposites of the Divine Feminine and the Divine Masculine within you. Take on the androgynous aspects of a being of love. Stand up in all of your power because you know that you are a bright, shining light here to make a difference in the ascension path of this planet and in the ascension path for humanity. Allow, accept, and embrace the Divine Feminine, and ask yourself, "In what ways am I dismissing, ignoring, or not being awake and aware of the presence of the Divine Feminine in my life? In what ways can I ask and invite the Divine Feminine to show Herself to me? In what ways can I step away from my habitual, patriarchal, masculine habits, and step more into more balanced habits of the Divine Feminine? Am I creating with the power of Divine Feminine energy? Am I welcoming back the Divine Masculine's presence?" Use the Divine Feminine as She gives her gifts to all of humanity; accept those gifts with grace and gratitude, and step more fully into who you are. The Divine Feminine needs to be awakened in each one of you, and until you accomplish this, you will continue to struggle under the polarity of tension between opposites in the illusion of separation. The Divine Feminine is here to help you birth your Future Selves.

On the path of accelerated evolution, you must recognize that the old must die before the new can be born. The Divine Feminine embraces the full spiraling process of birthing the new in every moment, as the old dies away. There is a Hindu deity named Kali, who continually destroys in order for something new to be born. Recognize this energy and accept it as part of what is necessary and part of the accelerated evolution. The Buddhist deity Quan Yin, known as the goddess of compassion, brings the Divine Feminine energy of compassion into this process. The Divine Feminine energy of Mother Mary brings in the energy of grace, and the Divine Feminine energy of Mary Magdalene brings fierce love and justice with her presence. All of these various gifts of the Divine Feminine—the balance of death and rebirth, compassion, grace, love, and justice—are extremely needed at this time. You must choose to be part of the destruction of what no longer serves you, but you can achieve this with compassion and understanding. You must stop clinging to the old ways and traditions that have separated you from each other and from other forms of life. This separation supports the illusion that you have a right to choose who or what lives and who or what does not, what can be used for food and what cannot, or which country or religion is right and which is wrong. You do not have that right; those rights of life come from the Divine Feminine. All life is sacred, and each being has the right to choose. You, therefore, in accepting the Divine Feminine within you, must be willing to destroy all the old belief systems, all the old paradigm thoughts, judgments, and traditions, and all the old paradigm ways of misbehavior born from unfortunate choices made from fear. You must destroy everything that has been born out of fear, judgment, or separation, or anything that supports the continuance of such behaviors through competition or greed. The controlling nature of the patriarchy must simply come to an end.

Now is the time to put those things aside. Now is the time to be grateful for what is coming and for your own ability to participate in bringing in the new. Now is the time to be accepting, while also standing up for justice. This is the proper use of duality! Accept what is changing because it needs to change, and stand up for all the necessary changes, as the old that no longer serves you (and truly never did) dies away, making room for the birth that is coming. You are part of the birth process; you are all divine mothers, each and every one of you. But you must choose to give birth to the new. You must choose to become your Future Selves. If you asked a new mother (who may have screamed that

111

her birth pains were terrible) if she had a terrible experience, she would say, "Absolutely not," for she would have experienced a rush of peace once the birth was complete and she was holding her child. Enter into this birth process the same way, by not focusing upon fear-based thoughts about what is happening, but rather by focusing upon thoughts of expansion, connection, love, and light.

We invite you to make this choice now, and we accept you as our divine sisters and brothers who are stepping into a blazing form of light, as androgynous beings of love, filled with the combined energies of the Divine Feminine and the Divine Masculine.

QUESTIONS & ANSWERS
STEP 6

Laarkmaa, why has the Divine Feminine begun to resurface and come to public awareness at this time?

That is an excellent question. The Divine Feminine has begun to resurface now because the energies are available for humanity to open to its awareness for conscious evolution. The energies are here, and the Divine Feminine energy Herself is speaking to all who have Her energy awakened within them. As you become more and more awakened—and we are speaking primarily about the Light Bearers—you demand to have a life and create a world that is based more upon the Divine Feminine energies of nurturance, care, kindness, compassion, justice, and unconditional love. As the Divine Feminine begins to awaken in each of you, the Light Bearers, and you begin to demand these things, the rest of the world will have to pay attention to your demands because more and more of you who are awakening are saying, "This is how we wish to live." The reason it is happening now is simply because it is time for the evolutionary consciousness of those of you who have chosen to ascend with Earth to begin to accelerate the ascension process. It is time to move forward building a new foundation based upon the Divine Feminine principles of love, joy, trust, compassion, justice, and peace.

How can the Divine Feminine affect the natural balance of energies in the world at this time?

We have a saying that we have shared with you many times that *even the dark serves the light.* The Divine Feminine is aware that even the dark is part of the light and can show you how to invite the dark back into the light by extending compassion and love. The way this will affect the world is that things that normally are utilized by the dark will suddenly be redirected through the energy of the Divine Feminine. For example, the creation of the Internet was intentionally designed to control and spy on people. Yet during the period when you experienced a lockdown when powers were trying to control humanity more and more, those of you who were sequestered inside and were not even allowed to go out into Nature, chose to use the Internet to spread as many truths and as many uplifting vibrational things as you could. This is an example of the urge of the Divine Feminine to use nurturance and to apply justice to see the truth and work through unconditional love. It is a very good example of one way that the Divine Feminine is crying out for justice and balance that will ripple out into the world. Of course, after lockdown was over, the Divine Feminine urged you more and more to go out in Nature and to return to your natural state of intuitional awareness. As you open more and more to your intuition because of your realignment with Nature, you will begin to respond intuitively to every circumstance that arises on the planet. You will help the world to come back into balance because you are responding to your heart's wisdom from your intuition rather than from mental patterns and concepts that come from outdated beliefs and old thought patterns.

Thank you, that's a very wonderful answer. That makes sense. That will help all of us understand why the Divine Feminine is coming forward at this time.

Yes, excellent. We'd also like to say that as the Divine Feminine begins to make apparent what needs to happen, there will be an automatic invitation to the Divine Masculine to join the Divine Feminine in Unity. As we have already said, you have not been operating with the Divine Masculine energies. You've been operating under the lower vibrations of both masculine and feminine energies. As the Divine Feminine becomes stronger and stronger within each of you, there will be a point of change, and the Divine Masculine will be invited back into balance too. But the balance will only occur after the Divine Feminine has corrected the imbalance between masculine and feminine energies in general.

Laarkmaa, can the male gender surrender its need to control Nature and the female aspects in order to achieve harmony at this time?

Very excellent question. The male gender *can* surrender. *Will* it surrender is the more appropriate question. The collective will not wish to surrender anything that is familiar, and what is familiar at the current moment is a patriarchal structure. The patriarchal ideas of competition, greed, control, and manipulation that have infiltrated your species are lower vibrational energies of the masculine. There is such an overlay of fear at this time that it causes people to fear stepping out of what is familiar and into something unknown and new. So, *will* they willingly surrender all of those ideas, including "the women in training to be men," as Cullen says? Will they continue in the old patterns, or will they choose to step into new patterns? That will be determined by how much of the Divine Feminine energy demands that justice and truth be spoken so that everyone can hear the truth and then begin to make changes. This is why the Light Bearers have the job—all of you who are reading this book now—to speak the truth, and to do it with unconditional love and without judgment. As more and more of you begin to do this, patterns of fear that permeate the planet will be eliminated, encouraging you to become more curious about other ways to be and new ways to create through different kinds of thinking and acting.

Thank you, that's a full understanding of how this process is working today.

We thank you for these questions. They do help expand upon

what we have written in this chapter of the book. What is the next question?

Laarkmaa, how can each of us help to restore the wise balance of male and female energies within each of us?

Ah, another wonderful question. This question has to do with opening your heart. In order to restore the natural balance of male and female energies of the Divine Feminine and the Divine Masculine within each of you and to move closer to your natural state, which is androgynous, you must stop aligning with your conditioned ideas and thoughts about what it means to be male and what it means to be female. You have a cultural overlay that defines all feminine attributes as being the ones that are weaker and defining all masculine attributes as those that are stronger. This is completely erroneous! The Divine Feminine is absolutely as strong and powerful, perhaps even more so, than the Divine Masculine, particularly at this time as balance is being restored. The Divine Feminine knows to stand up for truth and justice. Therefore, you have to eradicate all of your erroneous beliefs that the Divine Feminine's qualities of nurturance, empathy, kindness, compassion, caring and caretaking, and generosity are weak and belong only to women. Particularly, you cannot ascribe intuition only to women. Doing this continues the separation into masculine and feminine energies, and it is false thinking, for men have all of these attributes within them also. You need to accept that the Divine Feminine is within each man as well as within each woman. It is not a weakness in them! Simultaneously, you must stop thinking that only men are aggressive, competitive, manipulative, greedy, and controlling because these attributes also exist within women. They are attributes of the lower masculine energy existing in both genders.

Aggression has replaced assertion. As the Divine Masculine vibration of assertion dropped away, it became masculine aggression. The same is true for control, which used to be contribution. Now contribution has turned into control through competition You have to realign the values that the masculine is portraying in both men and women who are thinking and believing in the lower vibrational expression of these masculine attributes. You have to look with your eyes wide open and discern that there are women who are acting in this way too. And then begin to recognize that much of humanity is acting and reacting in a pattern of misaligned masculine energy of the lower vibration caused by the patriarchal control that dominates the world today.

You can return to balance within each of you by beginning to accept the values that you feel make your hearts happy. When you give to someone in generosity, not because you think you should or because you feel you have to, that is awakening to the Divine Feminine's impulse to be generous. When you offer an idea to someone else cooperatively rather than competing with them, that is the Divine Feminine's overriding the masculine idea of competition. When you open your heart to discernment rather than judging, you are also inviting in more intuitional knowledge, which reflects the Divine Feminine's beginning to speak. When you judge one another, you are operating from reactive emotional and mental realms to something you have been trained to believe in duality through an oppressive patriarchy. So, instead of resorting to old thoughts and mental ideas, begin to open to your hearts' wisdom and listen to your intuition. Begin to think and act in a manner that makes your hearts feel glad and happy. This will help you to align more with harmony and to invite in the Divine Feminine energy. And as the Divine Feminine is once again honored and returned to Her place of balance within each of you, you will return to balance individually, and then you can reflect that balance collectively out into the world.

That is a very helpful and wise answer to a very important question; thank you.

Is it too late to achieve a balance of power and interrelationship between the genders?

Ah, from the third-dimensional perspective, you perceive a wide gap of separation between the genders. That is a great challenge lying before you. You have sayings like "Men will be men" and "Women are always weak". You have all these erroneous sayings that mean nothing. They are empty and meaningless. So, this is a great challenge at this time. However, because the Divine Feminine is speaking and being honored within your hearts once again, this challenge can only be perceived as an opportunity for growth. Therefore any time you perceive a challenge as an opportunity, it is not too late. It is never too late if you have awareness that change needs to occur. The moment that awareness comes into your consciousness, you are already beginning to make the change. You are already opening your hearts to listen to the Divine Feminine. And as you begin to listen to your hearts, you will also recognize that the Divine Masculine has also been dismissed and ignored.

There are many very wonderful parts of the Divine Masculine that bring you energies such as beginning new things, building stability, and bringing illumination. These are Divine Masculine impulses and yet they have not been honored in your patriarchal culture. They have been used incorrectly through aggression, competition, and force. When you begin to raise the vibration of the Divine Masculine into its true purpose and use its energies from a higher vibrational level, you are simultaneously increasing the awareness from both masculine and feminine perspectives. This will allow you to step out of the separation of duality and into duality's intended purpose: to use multiple perspectives to bring harmonious responses to life.

So, no, it is not too late. The very fact that the question was raised means the movement is in progress, and you are indeed healing the separation that has wounded you. You are moving into balance once again as you evolve into the New Humans. So, welcome the Divine Feminine in every way that you can as the next step in your evolutionary process.

Thank you, Laarkmaa, for that answer. That gives us trust and hope that it is not too late for us to achieve balance and harmony between all energies that exist, not only masculine and feminine but all of the energies that interact to make everything possible in this Universe. Thank you for such a detailed, helpful answer.

You are most welcome. We love each and every one of you, and we are thankful that you are reading this book so that you can begin to operate from the higher vibrational principles that live within your hearts. It is our purpose to have this help available for you so that you can accelerate your own evolution and join us as cosmic citizens, as you begin to understand more fully the energy that you truly are.

PREPARING FOR A DIFFERENT WORLD

We are excited to be helping you with your evolutionary journey!

Now we will speak about preparing for a different world. Here in the third dimension you have seen things from a certain angle all of your lives—your third-dimensional perspective, of course. You might think of that as seeing through rose-colored glasses or dark glasses that color your perspective according to your mood (or we would say, coloring your mood through your perspective!) You understand the concept of being able to see things from only one limited perspective. But we are not merely speaking of either seeing everything as being dark or seeing everything as rosy and wonderful. Humanity has been wearing a set of "familiarity" glasses that provides a consensus view, which causes you to have expectations. When you look at the world, you assume that everything will always be as it is, thinking, "This is the way it has always been, so this is the way it will always be." With your limited creativity, you do imagine better situations; however, you rarely move beyond what is familiar to you, even within those imaginings. Those interested in reading this book, however, are beginning to take off your "familiarity" glasses. You are beginning to peek out from underneath them and say, "Wow! Look at that!" or "Gee! Can you see this?" You are beginning to notice that there are other possibilities for being able to see a different reality. This is one way that you are preparing yourselves for a different world.

We want to talk to you about the meaning of the word *different*. Different does not mean better or worse; different means different. Hopefully, as you are all co-creators of divine sparks of light who can participate with what the changes are bringing, you will choose which vibration you wish to use in co-creating a different world. What is *different* going to mean for you, as you are stepping into another way of being human? You will begin to perceive everything differently. We will share two opposing scenarios: two opposite ways of perceiving the world. The first scenario shows a world operating at a higher vibrational level, where everyone is kind to one another, where you are transparent, honest, and full of integrity. The world you wish to create is one in which you do not have to hide behind a made-up image or facade of yourself because you are afraid you will not be liked or loved if you are simply yourselves. The idea that you can just be who you are comes from a place of unconditional love and ensures that you will always make high vibrational choices because you are always choosing for the highest good for all. This is the pathway towards community, unity, peace, and harmony. Can you imagine a world with all of these things in it? Can you imagine removing the separations that exist here in the third dimension—the separation that causes some to have and others to lack, the separation that causes controlling or being controlled, the separations that cause argument, discord, competition, judgment, and war? All of these things will fade into non-existence as you step out of your third-dimensional paradigm of seeing the world through the familiarity glasses you have used all of your lives on this planet. Everything changes when you change your vision and make use of a higher vibrational perspective. This vision of a different world makes your hearts light, makes you feel good, makes you sing and want to twirl around and hug one another, for you are happy! You are joyful! You are experiencing love, and you are remembering who you are and all that you can be together as the New Humans. This is the first (and preferred) scenario. We, of course, endorse this one!

The other scenario is born from your current experience of separation, judgment, competition, pain, and your expectations that you will continue to see more of those things all around you. Seeing this way does not mean that you will not reach the first described scenario. It means that you will have to do more work to change your vision, and you are going through and will continue to go through a bit of chaos as you change perspectives. We have been talking to you for years about the birth process and moving into this new reality that you are creating—this very, very different world. The process you are experiencing is chaotic because your current experience, comprised of energies of judging, controlling, competing, and separating, is in dynamic tension with the opposite energies of love, light, trust, joy, kindness, and communication from the heart, rather than from the mind. The birth process you are undergoing to create your new world and give birth to your Future Selves holds a great deal of conflict and tension between the old energies of discord that are dying away as the higher energies are arriving.

We are talking to you now to help you understand and accept that you can take off your glasses and see beyond what you expect when you stop clinging to familiar beliefs, fears, or traumas that have not yet been resolved. When you focus on questions such as, "Am I going to be safe? Will I have enough money? Will I be able to control my own life? Will I be free to do what I choose? Will I be completely controlled by others?" you are looking through the dark glasses of fear and separation. Your future will be determined by the individual choices you make and by the choices you make collectively in unity. However, as you take off the familiarity glasses and begin to see and experience the multiple possibilities of wonder and amazement that can be seen in multiple realities, your vision expands to show you the true, larger reality. As you step away from any fear, concern, or worry about letting go of this third-dimensional prison that has confined and conformed you through your belief systems for most of your lives (this third-dimensional prison that makes you work jobs that you do not enjoy, forces you to secure money to pay for your needs when everything should be provided freely and equally for all), you can begin to actually experience other possibilities. This third-dimensional prison is a limiting system of judging, comparing, and competing. This oppressive energy has made Earth a prison for you, and you have not been able to escape because of your unconscious investment in your belief systems. You are about to *break out of jail!* Isn't that wonderful?! You are about to be free. But have you ever seen a movie about a jailbreak that did not contain some chaos during the process of breaking free? In order to gain the freedoms that you are seeking, you must let go of the ideas, beliefs, and structures with which you are most familiar. Think about the many ways in which you are controlled by limiting beliefs. The principle one is your belief about money. You have been controlled by money for a very, very long time. Currently on your planet, if you want something, you have to pay for it. If you need things, you need money to pay for them; you have to work at various jobs to obtain the necessary money. As you are imagining and preparing for a different world, feel from your heart what it would mean to step into a moment where you think of what you need, and it is instantly available to you! Imagine walking up to another community member and telling her or him what you need, and you are met with the response, "Of course, I have that. Here you go." That is a very different world from the one you are living in that is controlled by money. So, a necessary part of the changes and chaos you will experience will be an equalization of your financial system. This change is necessary to provide abundance for all. Achieving this equalization means that the systems that are in power now must be brought crashing down. They will come to a halt. You already know that many of your world governments are printing money that has no value behind it. Governments make up the rules as they go, manipulating the availability of things you need. They print money as they need it to obtain their objectives, without regard for their citizens' needs or wellbeing. They do whatever they want to maintain their control of you. And you *believe* that this is the true reality. But the energies that are coming for the new world will not allow that any longer, and you are awakening to understand and claim your own power to equalize this imbalance and create abundance for all. Those current systems, by the very nature of their greed and corruption, will have to come down. Your job is to take off your glasses and step away from the fear that you will not be able to have what you need or provide for yourselves, your families, and your loved ones. Stop those familiar ways of looking at and thinking about the world. Begin to prompt yourself that it is going to change, and trust that together you can create something new, something that is much more potent, more fair, more equitable and more pleasing, and that actually benefits all of you rather than just the elite few who are in control. Take back your own power and begin to let go of your fears of what is going to happen when the monetary tables turn. They will come crashing down. We cannot give you specific timing because it is all based on the many choices that are made moment-by-moment. But we can tell you that the likelihood of the currency system of any country retaining its value and staying in control of its citizens is likely to fall apart, sooner rather than later. It will happen sometime. It may come in ripples, or it may come in waves, or it may come in one great big "boom" where everything falls at once.

To prepare for this, first practice *not* being in fear. Think that everything is going to be okay. Prepare by having some of what you need on hand, as we have suggested to you for a long time. Have enough clean water; have enough healthy food; have enough things to stay warm, such as blankets, coats, hats, and gloves; have candles and flashlights to provide external light. Be prepared by having everything on hand as you make your way into the transition to a different world. Scarcity of food may occur from disrupted supply lines, extreme weather changes, or social panic, so you should prepare for those possibilities. Also, practice being prepared by not ignoring the person walking across the street or the one calling out to you for help. Practice keeping your ears keenly attuned to those asking for help and your hearts open and available. Remember the spirit of *In Lak'ech,* that you *are* one another. Look for where help is needed; ask how you can be of service; share your gifts and whatever you have. This also is part of the preparation, and it is part of the process of moving toward unity and ascension.

In preparing for a different world, you also have to prepare for Earth changes and political changes. The political powers will continue to vie for control of the old paradigm; they are grasping to make that paradigm last. They sense that there is going to be a shift in the balance of powers and that there will be a massive struggle at the political level in which governments try to maintain positions of manipulation and control. But in the world for which you are preparing, *no one* is in control because the citizens are unified in making decisions for the highest good for all. During the birth of that eventuality, however, you will continue to go through chaos, and you will see it manifest through your various political leaders who feed you increasing amounts of propaganda in desperate attempts to manipulate how you think, feel, and respond to what is actually happening. Listen to your hearts rather than your news sources when you are told that something is not best for national security, or that another country is about to attack, or anything else that can be projected onto you to stir up fear. Remember that these assertions are attempts to keep you aligned with fear to promote what they want you to think and feel, and those thoughts are aligned to the old paradigm that is dying, not to the different world you are co-creating. This type of propaganda will also apply—and listen carefully—as your star sisters and brothers become more visible in your skies and as we begin to use energetic forces to help assure necessary energetic changes, adjustments, and balances while you yourselves make the choices of how you wish to proceed. We will be supporting those changes. As we help you begin to make these energetic changes, your politicians will become even more frightened, seeing situations through the familiar old paradigm glasses of fear and competition. They may tell you that your star sisters and brothers are here to harm you, take over your planet, or do something negative. We are not. We tell you as we always tell you, "Don't believe us (or them)", for we are only sharing our perspective. *Trust the wisdom in your own hearts.* Your hearts will tell you who is here to help you. Your hearts will tell you that the ships you see in the sky, the energies that you feel, the movement you see out of the corners of your eyes, the things you see moving in front of you that you cannot explain, all of these are appearing to your multidimensional vision. Your hearts will guide you, and your intuition will lead you to accept what is true and understand how these changes are moving you towards unity, kindness, peace, compassion, and a different world that you wish to create and build. This is how you need to respond to your third-dimensional political environments at this time.

With regard to Earth changes, you need to begin to attune yourselves more and more with Nature and away from the technologies that have captivated humanity for so long. At this point as a species you are absolutely addicted to your technological toys. They are not advanced technologies, as you believe them to be. They are addictive machines that do nothing to further your evolution. We do not mean to be unreasonable or unkind in telling you this, but you have thrown yourselves so far out of balance with Nature on your planet that you need to right that balance, both to keep yourselves safe and to proceed with your preparations for a different world. If you do not choose to do something different, together, in unity, about the way you interact with the existing technologies that are expanding every day, you may find yourselves in some very uncomfortable positions. We are talking here about runaway technologies and Artificial Intelligence (AI). Choose instead to integrate more with Nature, of which you are a part; *you are not machines.* Recognize that you are part of Nature. Learn to listen to Nature's warnings; trust and integrate Her advice for your wellbeing.

Earth is responding to a very long period of pollution brought about by human actions, as well as human interventions that disrupt Earth's weather. These interventions are harmful to the overall environmental system of sunshine, rain, and climate on your planet. Earth will not put up with these interventions much longer. She is already beginning to make movements that precede tremendous changes for the humans who have abused her. In addition to this, you are experiencing strong effects of a Solar Minimum and Cosmic Rays that are arriving on Earth from deep space; we will discuss this in more detail later. Know that the incoming Cosmic Rays along with the simultaneous manipulation of your weather are causing a complication for the evolution of the planet while also forcing you to change your perceptions so that you can align more closely with the incoming light. It is uncomfortable for you because the natural evolutionary process to move more toward light has been altered by the manipulation of your weather. You have two factors occurring at once. First, your sun is in a Solar Minimum. Earth's response to this is a weaker protective magnetosphere barrier, causing you to experience a greater impact from the Cosmic Rays that bring more radiation (light) to the planet. This is the evolutionary part that is natural. Secondly and simultaneously, controllers who are manipulating your weather are creating artificial weather that diminishes the protection of your magnetosphere even more, intensifying the effects of the radiation that you receive. These combined effects are chaotic and highly dangerous for all life on your planet!

You need to return to Nature. You need to rebalance what is out of balance so that you can right the situation on your evolving planet. You need to re-write the program; re-write the plan; step in and co-create; step in and prepare for a different world by being a participant in its creation. Step away from having your cell phones to your ears all the time or your Internet on all day long. Take an equal amount of time to be in Nature *without* the cell phone and *without* the Internet. This is a very good way to raise your vibration and prepare for what is coming. If you do not take conscious steps to do this, you may find yourselves thrust into a situation with no technology available at all as Nature re-writes the program for Earth. We are not trying to frighten you, but we are telling you the direction of movement that we see occurring on your planet—the possibilities and probabilities that are rising up to manifest because you have become so out of balance with Nature by allowing artificial technology to lead you and make your decisions for you. If you continue in this way, you will be completely under the influence and control of Artificial Intelligence (AI).

You must learn to lead from your hearts. You must learn to put aside your familiarity glasses and your familiar thoughts from the old paradigm, your old habits, and your old programs. Remember the old paradigm is based on a perception of linear time, an imagined future and a past history that does not exist. Time does not exist, Dear Ones. Some believe that looking at the past to try to learn is good; however, the exact same situation will never be repeated twice, so you cannot make plans for the future by looking at the past. The truth of this is proven every day by your making the same mistakes over and over because you do not engage with the energy of the moment to make your choices. The collective of your species is not learning. You (collectively) are repeating the same patterns that you write about in your history. You must help others understand that you can only recognize danger signals and change directions through making a new choice, rather than adhering to the same old choices. And as for the future, well, the future does not actually exist either. So why are you giving so much attention to technology that is supposed to bring you a better future? You think, "In the future, we will be able to accomplish this or that." But our question for you is, "What is happening to your Now while you are focused on all that future?" Where is your Now moment? If you are focused upon the future and the technologies you may develop, or if you are focused on the past and what has harmed you or caused you trauma, you are missing the present opportunity, the Now moment, and that is where your power is. Your power is in the Now moment. You must open your hearts, realign yourselves with your true nature and your intuition, which is connected both to this planet and to the stars and cosmos. Begin to listen for signs of what is necessary. This is how you will know when a change on the Earth is about to occur and how you can receive intuitive guidance about what those changes mean for you. You may receive messages that tell you to stay where you are to help with the changes as they occur, or you may receive messages that tell you to leave where you are for the best opportunity of your continued evolution. These are intuitive messages from open hearts; they can never be understood through the mind.

Your mind will always rationalize information and return your thoughts to the old loop. You cannot know the truth when you are stuck in your minds and in your technology, either planning for the future or clinging to the past. You cannot keep yourselves safe and free unless you step fully into the Now moment. Step in completely, and always hold the idea of working for the highest good of all.

These are our suggestions for you to prepare for a different world. We return to our opening statement in this chapter. Different does not mean better or worse. Different simply means different. How you manifest this different world and how you prepare for it has to do with how and what you are co-creating now, in your Now moment. It has to do with how you are returning to the balance of unity that is provided through Nature, which always has a balance of ebb and flow, in and out, just like your breath. Being in balance with Nature provides a way of listening and a way of speaking. Learn to listen to what the energies are telling you about how to respond, rather than halfway listening as you mentally decide what you want to say or do. Preparing means listening deeply; it means listening to understand, it means acting courageously and creatively from your hearts, and it means always considering the highest good for all. This is the preparation for the new world—a different world—and you will help decide how it is going to manifest. Remember, you do individually and collectively have a choice in how you decide to co-create your world.

QUESTIONS & ANSWERS
STEP 7

We have never been through an ascension before. Can you give us an idea of how our own ascensions are going to work with Earth's ascension?

You are experiencing a magnetosphere that allows more Cosmic Rays and more light to come in. You are going to feel more Earthquakes and more volcanic activity because the Earth will continue to go through more profound changes. And, of course, whatever humans are doing to manipulate Earth's weather will cause more raging storms, more devastating droughts, and more uncontrolled fires. Those who can see will understand that many of these things are part of the ascension process for Earth, whether natural or caused by humankind's mistakes. Those who look through old paradigm vision will view these things with fear, not knowing what you should do. For those of you who are choosing to ascend with the Earth, there will be a sense that you are simply going through changes yourselves as your planet goes through change. Some days you may look around, and nothing will look familiar at all, even though you are in a very familiar place, but it will feel "right." Sometimes you may sense you are suddenly in another dimension, even though you did not consciously try to travel to another dimension; you are simply just *there*. It is a bit difficult to explain in words until you experience it. The best we can offer is that this is something you have to live through, and you will not be able to recognize it until you are in the middle of it. When you are questioning everything because it is unfamiliar, then you will realize that you are in the middle of the ascension process—for yourselves and the Earth. As dimensions shift without your understanding how, you will experience a larger sense of what you call *"déjà vu."* We expect that many of you will have experiences of remembering situations and events, but asking yourselves, "How do I remember this? What is this memory about? Where and when did this happen?" Remember the concept of Liquid Time, because it is very relevant in this ascension process.

Does an increase in déjà vu experiences have something to do with the shifting of our reality?

Déjà vu has to do with losing your concept of time. It has to do with forgetting the idea that something has happened before or is going to happen in the future and realizing instead, that you are moving from one dimension to another in fluidity. It is stepping outside of time and stepping into the dimensions that are all around you. It very much has to do with multidimensional awareness. Pay attention to your déjà vu experiences and ask yourselves, "Where have I experienced this before? What is this connected to? What am I being shown? How can I integrate it into my experience in this moment? "As you do this, you will discover that you are able to access multidimensionality more easily because your perceptions are becoming more clear.

Can you tell us something about the impact of Solstices?

Solstices bring in new energy; we see them as celebrations. Winter Solstice celebrates the return of the light from the darkest time of the year. Summer Solstice celebrates the height of light's presence on Earth. Both solstices bring new energy and an increase in light. We notice that now on all Solstices, many people experience more light than usual. This is an indication that there is more light coming into the planet. Your planet is spinning on its axis and also wobbling a bit, which is indicative of its own lighter ascension process. Your magnetic North Pole is also shifting radically. Both the North and South Poles are finding a way for the light to return that is beneficial for the highest good for all. Solstices provide a pause for you to notice the light and the changes that are happening to your third-dimensional reality. They are perfect portal openings for shining light into the next Now moment, and the next Now moment, and the next Now moment, as you are preparing for a different world.

As we go through the ascension process, and at some point, reach a level of completion, will those who have not chosen to ascend with the Earth still be around us? Will they be around us throughout the entire process?

As the focus of your attention begins to change in your altering and elevating states of awareness, you will not notice if they are around you or not. And as they begin to go more deeply into the illusion, they will not notice you. In fact, that is already happening. Many of you have already noted and made comments that you can be somewhere, and others do not even see you, whether they walk right past you on the street, or whether they do not see your car. There is already an energetic separation occurring, so it doesn't really matter whether they are there or not. For them, the division will come from a lack of awareness of whether you are there, or not. Eventually, you will cease to see those who are no longer a part of your evolutionary path. You will not see them, and they will not see you; you will be living in two distinct worlds.

Quite a few previously unaware people are asking questions about different things that are happening on Earth now; they know something is changing, but they don't know what it is. Could you suggest something we can say to them? I tell them to send love and light to the Earth, but I don't know if there is anything else that I should be telling them.

Give them something physical they can do to make a difference. You may wish to look at the suggestions that we will provide about 5G in a later chapter of this book and give them some information on how to protest against it and against geochemical engineering.[1] They will not really understand what sending love and light can do to help change things. Although they may not be able to understand the concept of sending love and light as energy to make changes, you can suggest this as well if they seem open to it.

That's a great idea, thank you. I appreciate all the work that you are doing to help humanity; thank you.

You are very welcome.

I perceive that aggression and anger are rising quickly in children who have attention problems. Why is this getting worse at this time?

It is directly connected to EMF pollution and the sad reality that children are not engaged with Nature. They are engaged with technology, and their physical, mental, and emotional bodies are stressed by too much technology and too many electro-magnetic influences. All around the world, we see children stressed with the bombardment of EMF energies that are simply too much for their delicate systems to handle. It creates anxiety within them and a pressure that has no outlet. Their neurological systems cannot handle the speed of the technology that surrounds them. Mothers are giving infants cellphones to hold or play with, which harms them at a cellular and a vibrational level. Children in infancy are getting tablets to play with which, again, bombards their neurological systems with more images than they can comprehend, more sounds than they can adjust to. They are told in school that they must achieve this or that and given computers to work with; they are not taken into Nature. They are not taught to connect with Nature or with each other. They are reacting to too much input into their delicate systems, and so they are angry, they are frustrated, and they don't know how to cope with this. Society encourages parents to have all the latest technological tools for children to succeed and to prevent them from being left behind technologically. Society is teaching mind knowledge, while ignoring body wisdom or social eye contact and personal engagement.

Children intrinsically know that they need to move in order to learn. They learn best by playing. Play is an important part for childhood development and for balanced learning, as opposed to learning only at the mental level. Most children today are experiencing a deep imbalance because of societal demands for conformity and progress and because your environment is saturated with technological EMF fields that harm children (and adults) on every level. The younger the child, the more sensitive, and some children are naturally more sensitive than others anyway. These sensitivities cause an extreme imbalance because there is no relationship to Nature or even a simple awareness of breathing in and out, connecting through holding hands with another child, or eye contact. Things that are part of the basic human experience are being dismissed, as the children are trained to become robotic themselves. That's causing the primary problem.

During these rapid internal changes, do we still need to do third-dimensional things like having to go to our jobs, functioning in society amidst all those who are still asleep? What is our main job during this time?

As long as you are in the third dimension, you *do* still need to take care of third-dimensional responsibilities. You are not yet functioning fully in multidimensionality, so your third-dimensional responsibilities must still be met.

The best way that you can be of help is to extend compassion everywhere you go. Extend compassion, knowing that everybody is suffering in one way or another. Because they are confused, they do not understand what is happening to them. Those of you who have been working on your own and with us to raise your vibration know that a big shift is occurring right now. The greatest thing that you can do is to send out compassion everywhere you go, and at the same time monitor your own reactions so that when something happens around you (or within you), you respond rather than react in the old way. Does whatever is happening serve evolution? Ask what you can learn from any experience? Ask how you can make the experience positive, even if it is uncomfortable, and if you cannot make it comfortable, ask how you can help someone else? Ask how you can extend your compassion to make a situation better?

That's a very practical way to be love and light. If you're shining light on someone through your compassion, and you are opening your heart to respond with compassion (rather than reacting and focusing on your own pain or discomfort,) then you are being love; you are shining light. That is what is required at this time. Practice responding to everything, rather than reacting. Be love; shine light. That's your job.

While walking with a friend, we both suddenly found ourselves walking sideways, as if we had suddenly walked through some pocket of energy. Can you address that?

There are many energies arriving that are impacting all of you. Those who are sensitive will experience dizziness or feel off-balance, with racing hearts and feelings of sudden and deep fatigue. Let us paint you a picture. Imagine looking at your globe and seeing a blue haze all around the globe; that is the environment to which you are accustomed. Now imagine a child coming in with crayons and drawing a wavy line, about an inch wide across one side of the globe and stretching around to the other side. That is a picture equivalent to a wave of energy coming in that would be felt all the way around the globe at certain moments for certain people. But then the wavy line moves, and most people move back into their normal perceived third-dimensional reality. Imagine now that another child picks up a different crayon of a different color and draws another wave around that globe, coming from a different direction; as you see this, another group of people feel dizzy, imbalanced, tired, and are asking "What is happening?" This is a picture of what is happening on your planet, Dear Ones, as bands of energy and waveforms are coming in to help you understand and move into being in waveform in multidimensionality.

You are not going to be in human form, as you know it, forever. You will be able, if you choose and if you do all the things that we suggest, to ascend into Rainbow body form. But that does not mean that you will experience your physical bodies in the same way that you experience them now. Being in waveform means that you are fluid, flexible, able to move instantly, able to intend yourselves to be in one place or another. So, when you are affected by these waves of energy, simply remind yourselves that you are just having an evolutionary experience to which you are not yet accustomed. Let it pass, and then return to your normal balance, but take in the experience as an example of what it will be like to fly. Know that you are approaching complete freedom in a way you haven't experienced in your bodies. View the experience as positive and multidimensional, even if it is uncomfortable. It will happen more and more as you experience more signs of ascension. What you are experiencing is part of the ascension process, and you must learn to detach from your expectations of what the physical body will do for you and how it will perform. Instead, as you detach, begin to accept that you are a waveform. And as such, your reality and your structures of reality are going to change. They are already changing. Just know that you are not alone in your experience. When that wave comes, it touches others too, but those who are working with light and on the path to ascension will experience it as you described. Sometimes you may experience sudden awakenings from sleep, as if you are being jarred awake. These waves affect humans by jarring you out of your illusionary sleep state and third-dimensional physicality. They are awakening you to a new sense of multidimensionality.

Does moving into multidimensionality allow us to physically deal with the cold more easily?

Yes, to some degree it does, because you are stepping out of the dimension of duality. Here in the third dimension everything is expressed as opposites, like hot or cold. You are moving into multidimensionality where you will be able to view everything simply as an experience. As you do that, it becomes easier for you to physically deal with extremes because they will not be perceived any longer as extremes; they will simply be experiences. You won't feel changes in your environment as extremely as you have in the past. The more you move through multidimensional experiences, the less you are attached to your physical perceptions here in the third dimension.

I was wondering if you have any ideas about how we can help with the Earth changes? Are different Devas in charge of different areas on Earth? Can we get in touch with these Devas and work with them?

Speak directly to the Deva with which you wish to work. If you want to work with the clouds, for instance, say, "Governing body of the clouds, I'm sending you love and light, and I am here for your support." If you want to work with the trees, do the same thing. If you want to work with the Earth Herself, again do the same thing. With the water, do the same thing. The best way you can provide your support is by connecting to the element of Earth with which you wish to connect by sending your love, light, and appreciation. Your love, light, and gratitude are the very best support you can offer. It does not need to be specific; it also can be generalized by saying, "I'm here pouring all of my love and light into you, Earth, water, trees, or sky." Do not try to make something specific go away or make something happen with your thoughts alone. Simply keep your hearts open, offer gratitude, love, and light, and take conscious actions to change things.

I'm trying to understand the upper realms and how to be here at the same time. My awareness is becoming sharper, and I'm observing things I've never seen before. Everything is changing. What can you say about that?

Everything *is* changing. As you do your own spiritual work and go more deeply into your own explorations, you will find your own unique way to see the world. You will understand that everything is changing, and you will become more accepting that these changes are for the higher good. You stop attaching to your beliefs about the way you think things *should be*. Truth can flow to you from many different directions, expressing the same thing in different ways. Each aspect of the truth is coming to you as a form of *we*, which is the energy of unity. So, yes, things are changing, and they are changing very rapidly, which is why we are giving you this information now to help you take advantage of the energies coming to Earth for human evolution. Whether they feel good or whether they feel uncomfortable, the idea is to take advantage of their gifts at all levels to accelerate your own evolution. This helps you, and it also helps the planet to evolve and ascend.

I have noticed that during periods that appear chaotic, if I slow myself down and just observe dispassionately, I realize that chaos is seemingly very orchestrated or very intentional, and the end results are actually manifested throughout it. So, it is not really chaos when you really slow down and take time to observe. I am wondering if this is a moment where controlling our thoughts or observing the importance of our thoughts is what manifests the end results, or is there an orchestrator?

That is an amazing question! Thank you very much. We will answer it in two ways. First of all, you contribute 50% to what is being created or manifested. While the universe presents other influences to orchestrate changes, these changes only represent 50% of the equation because of the power of your choices. What you and your species choose to do goes into the collective choice, making up the other 50% of what is manifested. And remember, within that 50% of human choices, those of you who carry more light and are living from love have more influence in the ultimate collective choice than those who are asleep, for your higher vibration carries more power. It becomes much more important that each of you who is reading this is actually involved in making choices from that slowed down, dispassionate place, for the highest good for all. We are speaking to you about preparing for a different world for that very reason. Just because you may perceive chaos from an old third-dimensional perspective does not mean that chaos is something to be afraid of. You mentioned moving into chaos slowly. We respond to you by saying that when you slow your thoughts and your responses to look at what is happening simply as an observer, as you suggested, you are indeed participating because those thoughts from a non-emotional and detached viewpoint intermingle with what is happening to help co-create the outcome. So it is *very* important. Being in that slow space, or even a meditative space, or even walking in Nature, all of these things are very important to help you prepare.

Now, about the perception of chaos, we remind you that chaos by its very nature means "out of order." But we see an implicate order within all chaos. Chaos is only the process of change. You participate with the process through your thoughts, feelings, and actions. You will come through the chaos into a new order until the next chaotic period arises. Slow yourselves down to participate with whatever is happening in a conscious and higher vibratory way. Slowing down is important. Although chaos has order, it is also malleable and changeable. You may see that everything around you is changing, and perhaps you cannot see the order, but when you slow down enough to distance yourself from what is happening and objectify your experience, you may perceive the flow of change and can participate in making the changes beneficial for the highest good of all.

When we see movement or lights from the corner of our eyes, is there anything that we can do to interact with those energies, or should we just notice them?

Open your hearts, remove any fear, and appropriate interaction will happen spontaneously and automatically when the moment is right. All you need to do is to keep preparing for a different world and know that it may bring some things you haven't been able to see with your familiarity glasses on. Actively communicate with any and all energies coming from love and light that you notice around you, and with practice, you will most likely receive a response. It's an exciting time!

STEP EIGHT:

MOVING FORWARD & PREPARING TO BE YOU!

W e are excited because change is at hand! You are on an accelerating evolutionary path, which is why we began this Manual. We wish to help you understand how to move through the changes in a beneficial, profitable way, for the highest good for all, guiding you to live in a way that is good for everyone where every single person can profit from whatever occurs. We do not mean financial profit. We mean abundance of spirit, of soul, and of heart, providing for all of your needs so that you can focus on being the divine sparks of light and beings of love that you are! As we explain now about moving forward and preparing to be you, we will revisit some previously explained concepts, adding in new ones, giving you a more complete picture of how to move forward in each Now moment. You may wonder what "preparing to be you" means. Perhaps you think you already know who you are. But we remind you that you are only one aspect of your total self; your spirit, your mind, your feeling state, and your physical body are different aspects that form a part of your third-dimensional personality. The total you is your consciousness that incorporates all of these aspects and your multidimensional selves. And who are you preparing to become? What does it mean to prepare to become you, to be you? We've been telling you for years that your only purpose is to be light and to be love: to shine light into the dark and be as loving as you can. We have spoken about unconditional love, and we have also spoken about healing and the fact that you cannot truly heal until you know how to practice unconditional love. Unconditional love is love without judgment or agenda; it is love that is so full of joy, it just ripples out of your heart towards everyone you meet and makes your light shine everywhere you go. So, you see, you are so much more than third-dimensional physical beings in these human bodies. That is only part of who you are. And, you are not just a personality that defines itself as a mother, a father, a brother, a sister, a worker, a boss, a daughter, or a son; you are none of these things only. These are roles that you play as you move through your challenges, learning your lessons, and learning to manage consciousness. We will speak more about the role of your families soon. For now, consider how much more you could learn more if you were to open to each experience that comes to you without judgment of that experience. You learn by choosing in the Now moment every single thought, action, and behavior that you wish to be a part of yourself. Choosing those things in the Now moment helps you to become the highest version of yourself. You raise your vibration when you let go of the density of negative thinking and heavy thoughts, like worry, and uncomfortable emotions whose signals you have not been able to understand and things that you believe because you've been taught or because they are based on your experience. The energies that are arriving help you to erase all of these old paradigm thoughts, feelings, and behaviors. Your job is to be a co-pilot in letting them go as you maneuver into the new reality and as you steer towards becoming who you are. Yes, we mean a co-pilot. We remind you that the Universe has 50% say in what occurs, and your collective, as a species, has a 50% ability to co-create your reality through the power of choice. Your choices, your thoughts, your feelings, your tones, how you express yourself, the actions that you take, and everything that you do is co-creatively designing the reality that you will step into in the next Now moment. Everyone who is reading this wants to be a being of light, a being of love. Each one of you wants what is the highest good for all. Each of you is striving for the highest levels of consciousnes—to be aware, to be kind, considerate, compassionate, cooperative, loving, and peaceful. All of these are elements of your becoming your Future Selves. When we wrote the book *Remembering Who We Are,* we told you and are telling you again now, that you really do need to remember who you are. You are the ones who need to do the remembering. In that book we gave you some guidelines[1] to help you understand the true nature of reality, to help you understand the foundations of your consciousness: love, joy, trust, and compassion. Your reality is not based solely on earth, water, fire and air. These are elements on this planet, but they are not the foundation of the larger reality.

Everything is based on energy, as you know. And the reality of the larger foundation is based on the energy of your natural feeling states—those things that offer you moment-by-moment opportunities to be compassionate, to be loving, to be joyful, trusting the entire time that everything is working as it should. Your job is to do your part by staying centered in your hearts, raising your vibrations, and shining the light that you are through the love that is in your heart.

Emotions are signposts that signal when you are out of balance[2], giving you the option to make necessary changes and make higher vibratory choices. And most emotions arise from experiences and traumas you have had in childhood and have not cleared during your life experience. You carry those emotions into your adult lives because you have been trained to think and react in certain ways.

Your families provide the most challenging things that you experience while trying to raise your vibration and stay centered

145

in your hearts. The reason you experience such challenges is that you do not understand the *purpose* of your families. Your families are your training ground, and you are placed in your families to learn how to use the emotional signals you receive being around them to *change yourselves!* Now we will share the real reasons for having a third-dimensional family and how you can use your emotions more positively to understand more thoroughly why your families have been a place for your emotional growth. It is time for you to let go of old beliefs and old structures that hold you together under a false sense of loyalty to your families. You need to learn to appreciate them for what they have offered you in learning, and then change the relationship—or move on. Oh, yes, this is a very touchy subject. You love your families, and they drive you crazy at the same time. We want to explain more in-depth exactly what the purpose of a family is. How are you to interact? How are you not to interact? What is your responsibility, and what is not your responsibility? As we have suggested, your family is your training ground. Your family is where you land when you first arrive on Earth. Your family is ready and willing to enact an agenda to help you develop in all the ways you have not yet developed during your parallel lives. Remember, there are no past lives nor future lives from our perspective; everything happens at once. Your parallel lives are happening simultaneously in other dimensions. In those parallel lives, you are living out other story lines with other challenges in other families. When you choose to come to Earth, you come with a specific purpose. That purpose is aligned with your Universal energy[3]. This is the one particular energy you choose to bring from the thirteen cosmic energies to guide you in how you share your gifts on Earth. It is part of your personality. Your purpose also includes a decision to investigate one of twenty Earth energies by allowing it to express through your personality. Your job is to learn to understand that energy and work to bring it from its lowest vibration to its highest vibration, and then to join it into the collective, like a part of a beautiful quilt. Your job is to perfect your part of the quilt and add it into the whole.

We always tell you your true purpose is being love and being light. However, that simple purpose does not define in detail what you are to do or how to do it as a personality. When you know what your Earth energy is and what your Universal energy is[4], you have a better idea of how to align yourself with your purpose and carry out your mission. You come to Earth with a particular alignment, and you land in a particular family. That family is going to trigger you in all kinds of ways, allowing you to practice moving from lower vibrational reactions to higher vibrational responses. In our previous sharing, we have told you that when you have an emotional reaction—something that is frustrating, or makes you angry, sad, jealous, or afraid, anything that makes you extremely agitated, or unhappy—that emotion is a signal, a signpost that you yourself need to change. You are responsible for changing the situation. In regard to family triggers that cause emotions to surface, look at those emotions as very clear signals that you are being guided to change something about yourself. Either you need to change the way you are reacting or responding, or you need to change your perspective about your loyalty to that particular family member or why you feel responsible for or dedicated to this particular family. In other words, you need to disengage from the training ground and recognize your first responsibility is to yourself and your own necessary evolutionary growth. Sometimes these changes require that you no longer participate in the same way with the family or participate with them at all. However, it is a clear signal that something needs to change. That is why your families trigger you in so many ways; they trigger you until you remember how to transcend the particular triggers and take responsibility for your own wellbeing. Sometimes the transcendence comes by simply accepting the family member as he or she is, and not reacting at all. Other times the transcendence comes in forming a new relationship with the family member so that you no longer relate as a child, a mother, a sister, a brother, a father; you simply become friends. And sometimes the transcendence is the recognition that the family member, or perhaps the entire family, has served its purpose, and you no longer need to be associated with the family at all. There are multiple ways that you can transcend old patterns in regard to your family, but all of them have to do with your transcending the training ground—graduating, getting out of school, and becoming free.

Unfortunately, you have been taught by your societies and your oldest cultures that your highest loyalty should be to your family. Sayings such as "Blood is thicker than water" (which is a ridiculous saying because blood plasma is exactly the same composition as sea water) instill the false idea that your blood relationships are more important than any other relationships. We wish to dispel that idea and help you to realize and understand the truth. You communicate with one another through water.[5] You connect through water. All of you share the same water, and you all share similarities in your makeup. You should not be more loyal to or responsible for any particular blood family than you are for any other of your human sisters and brothers, for you are all part of the same family. You are part of the same water; all are connected. The purpose of the family is simply to serve as your training ground for growth and evolution.

That means, Dear Ones, that when you figure out that you no longer need to be in the same kind of relationship with your families, you have several options:

1. convert the relationship to one of friendship;

2. walk away from the relationship altogether with gratitude; or

3. stay stuck in the same old patterns that cause you frustration, anger, or sadness.

The good news is that you have choices—and that is true freedom! The greatest loyalty you need to have is loyalty to the truth, and the truth lives in your heart. It is your heart that is associated with Source and with the highest consciousness and the highest vibration of all that is. If you find yourselves overwhelmed by your family, stop and ask, "How am I supposed to interact and still take care of myself?" Remember that if you evolve through taking care of yourself, that action will naturally radiate more light out into the world, including to your family.

Other than mothers and fathers who have small children, you are not responsible for your family members. Children are the responsibility of adults, but once the child is grown, that responsibility ends. Everything at that point becomes a karmic choice for each family member as each member continues his or her own pattern of growth. You have been taught that you are not allowed to abandon your family and that you must be responsible for those who cannot take care of themselves. We say, "No." That is not true. But you are required to be kind and compassionate; you are required to assist when it is your heart's desire and when you feel it is appropriate. But you are not required to feel overwhelmed and dragged down in your own evolutionary process by taking responsibility for someone or some situation that is not yours. All parents should plan and make arrangements for the time in their lives when they will need assistance, not rely on their children to care for them. If the parent has not done that, it is not the responsibility of the child to care for the parent, although your society tells you that it is. Your heart may dictate that you wish to help, and that is fine if it is your heart's choice. But it is not a duty, nor is it an obligation. Your parents brought you into the world, and you are responsible for the children you bring into the world up until the age when they are grown. We want you to spend some serious time searching your hearts, not just your minds, about what you *feel* about your families. Ask yourself, "Where are the challenges, and how do I transcend them?" What type of transcendence is best for me and for the highest good for all? Use your families as the training grounds for which they were intended, for that is their gift to you. Your gift to them is to be grateful and continue your own development and growth, which is what they intended for you when you were brought into the family. It is the highest form of respect to give to others (mostly family), the space and opportunity for their own growth without your interfering as if you are their master or savior.

We also want you to know that there is another aspect to family, and that is your true spiritual family—that is each and every one of you reading this book. You are connected energetically. You are connected as the Light Bearers of the world. You also are connected with us, for we are your spiritual family too. So you have multiple levels of understanding and perceiving family, and you have multiple ways of being able to adjust and adapt to what family means to you, and how, with all the love in your hearts, you can better apply family relationships in your own life.

Now that you understand how your families have influenced you and the choices you can make about those relationships, we return to the idea that you are moving towards a new foundation. We will address the effects of the light and higher vibratory frequencies you are receiving. Some questions may arise about what these changes mean for your physical bodies or what happens to Earth. Well, Earth is ascending, as most of you know. You're moving towards a New Earth, and we have talked to you many, many times about what will happen on this planet[6]. We sometimes refer to it as the Cosmic Pop. Others have referred to it as The Event or The Shift, and we have told you that it is not necessarily *one* event or Cosmic Pop that will occur. There will be many such events strung together in Now moment after Now moment after Now moment as the planet moves through Her ascension process, giving you multiple opportunities to change with the planet. We have also told you that the choice point has been made. Everyone on the planet has (consciously or unconsciously) already determined if they wish to continue on this path of ascension or if they wish to cling to the old reality of the third-dimensional illusion. This is why so many of you are suffering physical, mental, and emotional "symptoms" of change and a sense of aloneness; the collective is not feeling many of these symptoms. We will talk more about that later. Everyone who is choosing to read our words has made the choice to ascend with the Earth. And yet, you do not know exactly what that looks like or exactly what that means. We've spoken in earlier chapters about the light body, your etheric form, which is the blueprint for your physical body. We have explained to you how when you merge your Light body together with your physical form, you create a Rainbow body, a different form of physicality where your consciousness manifests at a higher vibrational rate. We have given you guidelines of how to ascend into the Rainbow body form. And now, we are going to give you some specifics to dispel some of the illusions or misconceptions you may have been holding concerning your evolution and ascension process.

You are not simply going to ascend into this perfect body leaving your hair and fingernails behind, although that also has been an ascension process for a few on your planet. Ascension is a process. At this time and with theses energies, ascension into Rainbow body occurs by achieving a higher and higher vibratory rate, changing your form as you elevate your vibration. So, in each moment, each choice you make raises your vibration to a higher state or lowers it. You are learning to make choices from your hearts, to link with your sisters and brothers on Earth, in ngdom, the Animal Kingdom, and the Interstellar Kingdoms. Each time you make a choice that raises ....tion, you are moving towards becoming your Future Selves. You are becoming the real you!

The ascension process also involves stepping into multi-dimensional reality. Most of you are still focused upon your third-dimensional reality, while having *some* multidimensional experiences. These experiences may reflect the fourth dimension, which you perceive as time and we perceive as *movement*, the fifth dimension, the eighth, the ninth, the twelfth, the eleventh. There are many, many different dimensions. Many of you may not be able to identify where you are; you just know that something very, very different and unusual is happening. Yet you are being "trained" by some to focus only upon moving into the fifth dimension, like the next step up a ladder. We want to open your consciousness to perceive that setting a rigid, hierarchal goal for the next linear dimension is not realistic; it is limited. There are multiple dimensions awaiting your awareness and experience! Many of you have been reporting lately a feeling that you are somewhat fluid (which is an awareness of your wave form), or you're having strange electrical pains in your bodies (which indicates a change in your power and abilities), or you're feeling like you don't know what's happening, and you can't control your bodies very well here in this dimension (evidence that you are becoming more aware of other dimensions). Many of you have been reporting that you just don't have any mental powers anymore (a sign that you are learning to let your hearts guide you), you cannot remember (because what you have been focusing on is not particularly memorable or no longer needed), that you cannot think, and that your cognitive functions seem to be disappearing. The incoming energies are erasing your overly active mental faculties. You volunteered to participate with this evolutionary step as you co-create a world that is based on wisdom from the heart. You don't need your minds as much.

You are in the transition phase right now where you may forget a lot, and you may need to rely upon each other to remember what is important. But this process moves you towards unity, where you must learn and recognize that you are not solitary individual beings who do everything by yourselves any longer. You are instead, beginning to recognize that you are linked together. What you cannot do, someone else can do. It is part of the process of moving towards unity and helping you to leave the illusion of separation that dominated for so long on this planet. And so, as you move more and more towards unity, we'll give you some things you can practice to help you understand how to work with this.

First of all, we want to tell you that when you need something, can't find something, have forgotten something, need some sort of healing, or need someone to help you with something, realize that whatever you are seeking individually will affect others as well. In unity, someone will always be able to provide whatever you need. This is why we opened this manual with telling you to begin to think in terms of "we" rather than "I." We suggest that in those moments when you need something, begin to realize that as a species you are a collective, and while each person in that collective has individual choice, together you can achieve more. When you truly have a genuine need that will harm no one and will benefit the highest good for all, why don't you try telepathically reaching out to the collective of all the Light Bearers on the planet to help you fulfill that need? Just try it in a meditative state. Practice it. This creates more synchronistic flow in your lives and may produce an unexpected and surprising answer to your needs. You are aligning yourselves in the way that we, Laarkmaa, work, seeing ourselves as One of Six, and Six of One[7] in unity. This practice promotes and enhances your telepathic communication abilities. As you begin to do this, you will begin ll the flow of abundance we spoke about earlier. You are stepping forward into recognizing what it is truly like to live in a more integrated way in unity as your Future Selves.

Many people have wished for years to start communities, and we have told you that true communities on this planet will not occur until a higher level of consciousness is attained. So, your first spark, your first point of entry for being able to join together in community comes from what we are sharing with you now. You must learn to be transparent, honest, open-hearted, seeing yourselves in the spirit of *In Lak'ech* ("I am another Yourself"). This is what we call being an *Authentic Human.* And as an Authentic Human working in unity, this portion of the collective "you" in this moment could use a little help learning how to flow together and support each other. Work with it. Practice it. Now we will return to the topic of multidimensionality that you are increasingly experiencing.

The experiences you have of the electricity in your bodies or strange pains that you cannot explain, or other symptoms we have previously discussed are the effects of the vibration of your cellular structure becoming lighter and lighter. You are moving out of your carbon-based form into a crystalline-based form that is of a higher vibration, accelerating your process of evolution toward ascension into Rainbow body. Each time you have one of these experiences, it is an indication that you are becoming lighter. So, don't ignore that! Don't eat junk to distract or comfort yourselves because you do not feel well. Instead honor your experiences and say to yourselves, "Wow, this is amazing!" Feed your bodies the most healthful food[8] and water so that you contribute to co-creating the beautiful Rainbow body you wish to achieve by nourishing *these* bodies with what your higher vibrational light bodies are directing you to eat and drink. This also applies with your mental bodies. If you see something distressing, immediately send light to it; then if suitable and necessary you can help; being helpful is often appropriate. Once you have done whatever you could to change the situation, dismiss it, trusting that everything is unfolding in the way that it should for a greater purpose. See the truth of what is happening and trust the process. These attitudes and actions are powerful! They will help you! As you are moving through this ascension process and having multidimensional experiences, you will also begin to notice that many people are leaving the planet. Earth will shake off many humans to regain natural balance. We remind you that you have chosen to be here at this time. You did not make the choice to join all those who do not want to be in the ascension process. Your path has already been determined by your High Self Angel and the choices you make moment-by-moment to raise your vibration.

We now want to address the difference between what happens to those who are not on the path of ascension to Rainbow body and what happens to those who are on the path of ascension by death. There is a very different process for each. You are all one collective species. But just as a tiger and a bear are both part of the Animal Kingdom, they also have differences. Likewise, the choices made by those who do not wish to move towards the New Earth have a different path from those of you who are carrying light and wish to ascend with the planet to form the New Earth. Those who choose to leave the planet will go into a safe holding place that we call the Golden Trough of Light. They will die out of their physical forms, but their consciousness will be transported safely to this holding ground, and they will stay in that holding ground for a long time until the right opportunity emerges again somewhere in the Universe for them to emerge and continue their evolutionary work on the karmic wheel in a new life as they continue their lessons and their learning. It will not be this planet, for Earth is ascending to become the New Earth. But it will seem familiar to them and will help them continue to grow as they evolve at their own chosen rate. When these changes happen, do not be sad for all of those who (according to their own choices) appear to be harmed, hurt, or die. Instead, recognize that they made this choice some time ago and that they are moved now for the period of rest within the Golden Trough of Light where they will wait and be held safely and securely until they are ready to move forward on the karmic wheel of lessons and learning once again. Now, we want to speak about the ascension process for those of you who are here now and have made a different evolutionary choice.

Most of you have an illusion or a false belief that you will simply step out of this physical body into a new physical body, or that this physical body will suddenly get an upgrade and you will be able to instantly ascend with the Earth on clouds or in fire, or whatever you may be imagining. What *actually* happens as you move into your Future Selves is that the cells of your body become so full of light that you vibrate at a different level and speed. The process to reach that place is uncomfortable in your current physical forms, but the vibration will continue. In order to complete your ascension process, you must reach the point where you have incorporated into yourself the ability to have a peaceful heart, the ability to be compassionate in *all* circumstances, and the ability for your love to be non-judgmental and completely unconditional. You will be transparent, with nothing to hide. You will continually make choices for the highest good for all. Through integrating all of these abilities into yourself, you will become an Authentic Human. When you are living in that peaceful state almost continually, you will be ready to complete the ascension process. You will be of a high enough vibration to be able to achieve that. What happens at that point is that you will radiate so much joy, so much peace, so much trust, and so much love from your heart that these energies reflect immediately into your etheric body or your light body. Your light body, at that point, begins to heal from all the infractions that it has experienced through your poor, less evolved choices, such as eating harmful foods with sugar or having negative thoughts when you are angry or judging yourself or someone else. All the things that have harmed your light body will begin to heal because you are no longer in that vibratory space. You will be in a higher vibratory space, feeling, thinking, and acting with higher vibrational energy. Now you will be able to heal your light body, which is the blueprint of your physical body, completely through the energy of unconditional love. You will be able to watch and participate as your etheric form, your light body, creates for you a new physical form. We have been asked questions such as, "Will I have hair? Will I look like I did when I was younger? Will I be male? Will I be female? "You will be able to determine through your higher consciousness what form you would like to take. If you wish to take your current form, you will take your current form, but it will be healed, whole, beautiful, and lighter, the way it is intended to be, the way it was before you had so many toxic thoughts, feelings, and physical poisons on Earth that corroded it and made it so dense. You will be in your Rainbow body form. If you choose to appear as we do, as waveforms of energy who shapeshift into any form that we choose, you will be able to do that also. You will be made from the spectrum of light of the Rainbow. And when you move into your Rainbow body, you will have the ability to move back and forth to this planet or to other places in the Universe at will. You will go where your heart directs you, always for the highest good of all, because your highest wish is to be of ultimate service.

Now, let's say that you are a married couple, and let's say both partners of the couple are working with the light, and both individuals of the couple are moving through the ascension process. That does not mean that your High Self Angels will take each of you at the same time, for you are still individuals in expression. One of you may precede the other. Although it will be a short separation, it may be that one moves through one portal moment of opening, and the other moves through another portal moment of opening. We are telling you this because when you look around at Light Bearers who are ascending, we want you to be aware of what you will see. If you look through your multidimensional eyes, you will see the energy of consciousness as it departs, and you will know that your partner has moved into a new form. Continuing to focus through your third eye, you may be able to see them where they are, as they are. However, if you are distraught, distressed, and seeing through your third-dimensional vision, where feelings of grief and loss take over, your third-dimensional perspective will show you a shell of a body. But it will not be like the body of those who die and are buried or cremated after their consciousness has moved to the Golden Trough of Light. The shell of one who is ascending into Rainbow body will be thinner and more fragile, and it will disintegrate more quickly. So, we want you to not be shocked and alarmed that a partial physical body still remains. You need to be prepared for this change. You will not attain a Rainbow body in one, two, three simple steps. It's a *process* as the person moves to the New Earth. You, as potent contributors using your power of choice, can help to manifest how that process is completed. That's important for you to know. Take a breath in, assimilate everything that you know already and what you have just read. Check in with your own hearts about what you have chosen on the path to ascend with the New Earth. The process you are experiencing is somewhat chaotic from the third-dimensional perspective, but chaos is just bringing order in a different way—implicate order that is not bound by space, time, or expectations. Chaos brings forth whatever *needs* to arise, and you are able to participate as you step more and more into the Future You, the real you. You also participate by slowing yourselves down and seeing the chaos through the eyes of objectivity and the eyes of unconditional love. The higher the vibration you achieve, the more you will be able to see where you can send light and how you can be of service. Rather than being distressed by whatever third-dimensional perspectives may appear as part of the illusion of separation, put on your multidimensional glasses for a broader perspective. Use your multidimensional vision, and you will begin to see everything that is happening through a more elevated perspective.

When outer influences such as the Cosmic weather impact you, go into a quiet meditative state, deep into your heart, and touch into the love that is there and all the wisdom that your hearts hold for you. Go into meditation with a single request, "Let me be love and light; let me be love and light; let me be love and light." Let that be your mantra until you dissolve into a meditative state without words, thoughts, or feelings to support your understanding of what is happening to you now in the ascension process. Spend some time connecting with the new light energies that are here to support and nurture you as you move forward through the chaos, finding and reaching the order that is unfolding. Feel the significance of every energetic change. *The Pleiadian-Earth Energy Calendar*[9] is a very valuable tool to help you regulate to the energies. Move away from using time to organize your lives, and step into what you perceive as chaos by observing energies and learning how to successfully navigate them. Your role in being able to participate as co-creators of the new reality during these changes is vastly important, as you ascend into the real you—an Authentic Human in a Rainbow body.

QUESTIONS & ANSWERS
STEP 8

Regarding responsibility to family, I assume that your comment extends to a much larger family, including all life on Earth—plant life, animal life and all life?

Not exactly. Of course, all plant life, animal life, and all humans are part of your family. But they are not all your training ground, as is your original human family. You have a different kind of responsibility with your larger Earth family than with your family of origin. Your responsibility to the larger family, which includes all life on Earth, whether human, animal, or plant, is simply to treat it by using the Golden Rule: "Be to others as you would like them to be to you." That is your responsibility to all of life. You have to respect and treat each human family member and members of other kingdoms as you would like to be treated yourselves. Consider your choice of food. If you wish to be treated kindly and compassionately yourself, do not make a choice that involves killing an animal for your food. Killing in any form is not in alignment with the highest good of all. If you wish to be treated kindly by others, be kind to plants by being gentle with them and making sure you do not tread on them unnecessarily when you are walking in Nature. Simply appreciate them, and move to walk beside them, side by side, or take their gifts of food with gratitude and nurture their continued growth. When you grasp this with your larger spiritual family, it will be easier to apply these rules to your family of origin as well.

As far as transcending the bonds of family from our training period, please give us some clarity to know when we have transcended the relationship. Would that be when there is no longer any anxiety related to the thought of that family member? What is the process to know that we have truly transcended our training ground?

When you are no longer upset by them. When you are no longer upset in any way even when you think of them, then you have transcended it. Also, when you take a physical action to make a choice to either no longer associate with the family member or to associate with them from a non-reactive place. That is your choice. Both are a measure of transcendence. But basically, the ultimate measure for transcendence is *when you are no longer triggered at all,* for the purpose of a family is to trigger you in the ways that cause you to grow. Sometimes that takes on the form of "I need more self-esteem," so the family member (or members) will put you down or belittle you. Sometimes the trigger has to do with learning how to trust and who to trust. In this case the family member (or members) may betray or abandon you. Sometimes the trigger is the need to defend yourself, or to learn how to intuit when danger is present so that you can avoid it. In this case, the family member (or members) will do things that encourage you to learn when danger is present and how to avoid it. But all of these are just examples of what you yourself, as a soul, have come here to learn and improve upon in your skill sets, things you must learn to work around, rather than being upset by them. However, if the family has been toxic or abusive, then your transcendence will include your no longer having any interaction with them, and you will most likely choose not to be in their presence or environment. You will disconnect from that abusive and toxic family. If the family is simply pushing buttons to trigger you in smaller ways, you may choose to transcend the family training ground by being objective and non-reactive, and then changing the nature of the relationship, taking it from a child-parent or sister-brother relationship to one of friendship, if that is possible.

Typically separating from family occurs when something has pushed the family member away, which usually has a lot of loaded emotions. Once the situation or emotions have been resolved, what is the requirement for moving forward? Is it just something you know because you are no longer triggered? Is there a factor where you are not triggered simply because you no longer interact, or is the triggering truly gone?

There is a difference between avoiding a trigger by not having anything to do with the family and being non-reactive to a trigger. If one is simply avoiding the family and there is an underlying fear that the trigger will be pushed again in the presence of the family, then the person is not done with the trigger. However, if the trigger is something that no longer threatens you or makes you uncomfortable, and you simply decide not to be around the family member anymore, that is a sign of evolution. You are finished. Most triggers that cause a family separation do come because someone pushed the trigger a little too hard, and the injured party finally got the lesson, realizing that he or she must stand up and say no, walk away, or say that the treatment is not acceptable, demonstrating his or her strength or power by a non-reactive response of saying no. That is what is being learned. If the person learns that lesson and is no longer feeing the threat or the potential of threat from the family member, then that person has a choice to make.

You may re-engage in the family of origin, using your new power and strength by simply saying, "This is not acceptable" every time the person tries to push a trigger again. Or you can say, "I'm finished with this. I thank my family for what they've taught me, and I have no need to be around them again." The key point to differentiate is determining whether there is an underlying fear that *if* you are around them again, you will be triggered. If that is the case, you have some personal work to do. You do not have to do your personal work by choosing to continue within your family or origin, however. You may reach a point where you can learn about the trigger from an outside influence that reminds you of the original trigger in your family of origin. Either way, you must reach a point where you are no longer unsettled by the idea of being triggered in that particular manner.

How do we proceed to stopping talking with or seeing the people in our family with whom we are no longer resonant without hurting them?

There is a key point in your question. You are not responsible for other people's feelings. Each person is responsible for his or her own feelings, including you! In a situation where it is for the highest good of all to transform the relationship by stopping communication, then you must find a way to do it with compassion and kindness. That is your job. It's not your job to take care of the other person's feelings. Your job is to be true to your heart and do what is best for the highest good of all. If someone is complaining that a particular relationship is causing them stress, nightmares, and great deal of harm, then we would ask, "Why continue in this relationship? Why do you make that choice? Why would you want to do that?" Ultimately, every choice that you make is yours. You cannot listen to someone else about what choices to make, but the choices you *do* make need to be done for the highest good of all with compassion and kindness.

What is your perspective on forgiveness (or lack of forgiveness) in family relationships?

Well, we would say never look for forgiveness from someone else. Forgiveness is never for the other person, anyway. When you forgive someone for what they've done (or have not done), you move into objectivity and acceptance of who they are, and there is no longer any judgment or blame. Ultimately that means that there is no need for forgiveness because you accept the other person as they are, whether you continue in relationship with him or her or not. So, forgiveness is not about the other person. It is not something you do *for* or give *to* another person. Forgiveness is about what you do for *yourself.* It's about detaching from the emotional trigger of what an incident or series of incidents has caused or detaching from what the person has done or not done. It's about detaching from the situation and saying, "Well, I see who this person is, and I accept who they are." It does not mean you have to interact or engage with them, but you have to accept the truth of who they are. Again, forgiveness is never something that you give to the other person. Forgiveness is all for *you.* It's to put you in a place of peace and objective acceptance so that you can move forward in your own life. It may be hard, but understand this: even when a person asks for forgiveness, he or she is asking for permission to forgive themselves. They are seeking a way to look at whatever it is that they've done (or not done) objectively, without judgment, so that they can find the way to do things differently next time. And as always, the forgiveness is about them, not about you. Try to remember that.

Sometimes we find ourselves in relationships with people who don't share our spiritual beliefs, but there is an agreement of love and of support within the relationship, and it is not causing triggers. What is your perspective on this type of relationship where both people are really living from their hearts even though they have different beliefs about how the world functions or about spirituality?

It is a completely individual thing, Dear One. Obviously, people can negotiate and decide that they love someone, and the other person loves them without having exact shared influences and opinions. That is absolutely possible. However, many times people surrender into a situation they've been in for a long time, knowing that there is no resonance and knowing that is not helping them to evolve in any way, but it is *easier* to stay in the relationship than to leave. Spiritual growth is not about doing what is easy. In each relationship, the partners need to address the essential question, "Am I choosing to stay in this relationship because it is easy, or am I choosing to be with this person because there is deep love and acceptance, and we are both growing?" People in relationship often evolve at different rates, at a faster or slower pace of growth. Sometimes there is not a match between them any longer, and at other times their growth is more well matched. It is a very individual question of the heart.

Are some of us catalysts for others to clear their shadows? I notice that as I have a clear vision of where we want to go in our evolution, situations show up that seem to compete with my vision.

Yes, indeed, sometimes when you become more and more clear and you are reflecting more and more light, more darkness *can* come toward you because it wants your light. But that is only part of the explanation. Sometimes things that keep going wrong, which you clearly recognize are not in flow, are a signal that you should be focusing your energy somewhere else. Sometimes it is not the best intention to stay wherever the problem is because what is not in flow is *not* your responsibility. This is where you can be a catalyst for others to change, but only by handing their responsibility back to them, not by trying to fix it yourself. You must respect them enough to allow them their own choices and responsibilities. Check with your heart and ask if you are receiving signals to change situations and use your energy somewhere else, or if you are to remain because you can actually see that you are making a positive difference. If you see challenges decreasing, situations changing with flow for the better, and people opening their hearts, then your presence is acting as a catalyst for positive change. But if you feel like you are falling into a hole and everything is collapsing around you, with more and more problems or situations arriving, the Universe is redirecting you because you are not in alignment with that particular situation or person any longer; you are in alignment with higher vibrational beings. In that case, you should allow your heart to lead you to higher vibrational situations and people. This can apply to a community, a job, a marriage, a family; it can apply to anything. The key to your understanding and clarity about what needs to occur must be matched by actions that support what you see so clearly. That is not always an easy thing to do. There are many contradictions and restrictions right now. And the dark does not know that it wants the light, but it does. This causes chaos. With the confusing values your societies have thrust upon you, you do not always know how to make the choice to leave a situation that no longer fits your growth. Each situation must be evaluated by your heart, which knows when it is time to leave, even if you do not yet know where to go or how. Just keep listening to your heart.

When you think you are doing everything right and challenges continue to occur, it can be that the dark, in its wanting your light, is making you stronger through its interference and challenges, or it can be that the Universe is positioning you to go somewhere else or in a different direction. Only your heart can lead you to the answers. Listen to your heart and be willing to make changes. Understand what we have long said, the highest and best loyalty is loyalty to the truth, not loyalty to a promise or commitment you made that no longer fits your evolving circumstances, not loyalty to a person who no longer resonates with you, not loyalty to anything except the truth. So, make your commitments over and over again every day. Begin each day noticing what your commitments are, and act through those commitments. At the end of the day, evaluate if your commitments and loyalty should remain constant or change. This is not a light exercise of changing commitment through your changing moods or emotions; it is a deeper and deeper look at the truth and how you are aligned with the truth and allowing your heart to lead you. Meditate in the quiet. Integrate your thoughts about your feelings. When you awaken the next morning, ask yourself, "Where do I wish to place my commitment today?" and then commit for the whole day. At the end of the day evaluate again, asking, "Is my loyalty to this commitment still in the right place and has it served its purpose, or do I need to move my loyalty somewhere else more in alignment with the truth I am recognizing?" Often concepts about which you are clear are not ready to be implemented because other people involved do not share your clarity about unity, oneness, light, higher vibrational thinking, highest good for all, solutions, and a refusal to judge or blame anyone or anything. Align yourself with people who wish to work in those vibratory frameworks using those terms and understandings, and you will find the flow that you seek. Be willing to share even with those who do not have those under-standings and give them a chance; if they do not take that chance, and the opportunity to embrace a higher perspective, take your beautiful gifts into a place or situation that is more in alignment with who you are. Always remember that you can never change anyone else. Change has to come from the inside; however, you can be a catalyst for changes in someone else through teaching by example and handing them back their own responsibilities. These are the only ways to contribute to someone else's growth.

Can animals or plants act as triggers for emotions to help us learn?

You can actually learn from them, but generally speaking when an animal or plant triggers an emotion, if you trace that emotion backwards, you will find that its origins usually came from a human. Sometimes a trigger can come from an incident with an animal, like a child's being bitten by a dog or scratched by a cat when it was young. That is a type of trigger that can be easily cleared. But most things that are triggered by animals have to do with situations in which you have been treated unfairly by other humans, thus causing insecurity. But certainly, you can learn from animal triggers just like you can learn from triggers with the human family. It's a very good point, thank you for sharing it.

What can we expect in this time of transition from a third-dimensional body to a multidimensional body? What are the symptoms, and what will the transition look like in the final stages?

Expect nothing. Expectations are based upon old paradigms of thought and old belief systems. If you are going to expect something, expect *change*; expect excitement; expect confusion; expect awe and amazement and abundance and lightness and laughter that just rolls out of you! But if you choose to focus on expectations rather than allowing the changes to unfold, you can also expect that everything will feel *different*. You may feel dizzy, as if you are walking out of balance; you may hear what we call "Earth noise" that is so loud that you cannot think, a buzzing or humming or low level vibration in your ears or a constant white background noise from the changes in Schumann Resonance frequencies on your planet. What some of you call "Space noise" and we call "Earth noise" is the sound of Earth's moving through the ascension process. It will become louder and louder as you also move through the ascension process. Those of you who are sensitive will hear this, and it will be *different*. Sometimes it will be more intense than others. You may have bodily responses to eating and eliminating that indicate that you need to nourish yourselves in other ways, such as living on love, light, and water, as we have suggested for years[10]. You can expect the unexpected; anything that you would have previously categorized as "normal" will change as a new normal arrives. What you have previously perceived as illness or imbalance will soon be perceived as simple ascension symptoms, changing you from a dense carbon-based form into a lighter crystalline form.

We have told you that this is a positive change, so be objective when you feel these uncomfortable symptoms rather than categorizing them as "illness." Just live through it. Ascension is a process. The only thing we can provide for your guidance is to tell you that you will have to live it to understand it. Humanity has never before undergone a transition where you ascended with the planet. All previous catastrophic experiences on Earth have almost completely eliminated humanity in the catastrophe, leaving only a few to survive. This is a completely different experience. It is not the same as death; it is the same as lightness, perhaps a bit like moving into a dream state where you know your experience is real, but you cannot orient to where you are. You may feel glad that you are "there", but you won't understand exactly where "there" is! This is all part of the transition process.

As far as the final stages—there are no final stages; everything is a process. What you perceive as final is what you see when someone dies. That person leaves their body; they are dead; it is final from the third-dimensional perspective. But even that is not accurate, for in truth, only the body goes away. That person's consciousness continues to live. The consciousness of those departing now either goes into the Golden Trough of Light to await another opportunity to learn on the karmic wheel, or it goes with the new form you create by merging your etheric (light) body with your physical form to create a Rainbow body to ascend with the Earth. Those who made the decision to leave with the Earth will not appear dead to those left behind; the human shell will be much lighter and will disappear much more quickly as the new Rainbow form shows up. You will see yourselves as lighter and lighter as you move through this process. There is no final position. Everything in the Universe is constantly changing, guided by the Universal energy of 3, creativity, constantly expanding into something else. As you expand into Rainbow body you will be asking yourself questions like, "How am I expanding? Where am I going? What am I learning? What would I like to experience? Where do I want to be? How do I want to flow with what comes next?" All of those concepts will become much more powerful for you, but for now they are simple ideas that live in your mind but not in your experience.

You can expect that your physical bodies will not perform in the ways that they have previously, nor will your minds perform as you are accustomed. It is a good idea while going through this process to create a buddy system so that you can remind one another of things that need to be done or remembered. You can expect a bit of the Mandela Effect[11] to happen. More specifically, many dimensions will converge at one moment, so that one person may experience the moment in one way, and another person will have a completely different experience. Do not argue about which view is right; both are! Thinking in unity requires that you acknowledge that there can be two rights, rather than a right and a wrong. Recognize that you are experiencing different dimensional perspectives and be grateful for the opportunity to broaden your perspective and understanding.

Do not look for a final result, but instead, enjoy the ride; enjoy the process. Have gratitude that you have chosen to take this ride, to be in this process, to ascend in these auspicious times. We think that you will see many things you did not expect in these changing times. These changes can be seen as an exercise in keeping you flexible and helping you to learn to flow. As you learn to flow with outer third-dimensional circumstances, you also learn to flow outside your dense, carbon-based physical form and to shapeshift into other forms, using your Rainbow body to manifest what shape is required for when and where you are. All of these things are steps in the ascension process. If you ask this question again in two months' time, and then again in six months' time, each time you ask it, you will be asking from another perspective, having more depth of understanding of what you are learning by living through the process. If we explain as you go, it will make more sense to you.

You have said that "grounding" is not necessary anymore as we move into more etheric forms. How do we reset and regain our balance from these varying intense physical symptoms?

We would tell you to continue to spend as much time as you can in Nature because Nature is calming to you, but don't feel like you have to "ground" yourself into the Earth. Instead appreciate that you *are* Nature. In doing so, you allow yourself to be flexible on this planet, you allow yourself to move more into a feeling of lightness, a feeling that you belong, but that feeling is not so heavy. It's a shift in attitude somewhat. "Grounding" is something that you have been taught to do when you feel unstable or imbalanced. To correct an imbalance or adjust to a new energy, spend time in Nature or take a salt bath. These things help to calm you and support your physical body, but they are not grounding per se, they are *naturing*. Let's create that term: "Naturing!" Become more involved in Nature and realize that you are a part of Nature, as well as a part of the stars. And when you feel a little different, a little weird, maybe a little not quite normal, remind yourself that you must be experiencing another dimension, and that's okay. Just accept it as part of what you are instead of immediately rushing to the kitchen to eat some "grounding" food or running outdoors to put your feet on the ground to "ground" yourself. Those techniques are not necessary any longer. What's necessary now is to recognize that everything that happens is simply part of the experience of changing. As you change, you can remember who you are and take your cosmic position in the Universe.

I understand; we are all of these things. We are the transparency of matter, where things are becoming more etheric and less solid; at the same time, we have these muscle cramps that are debilitating. It feels like we are being pulled in two different directions at once, but your perspective really helps, so thank you so much.

That feeling of being pulled in two different directions is part of the pull of duality in the dynamic tension that pushes you to evolve. We understand that it is most challenging, but it will pass, as everything else that each of you has gone through does. It will pass. Take the symptoms of whatever you are experiencing and ask how you can use it to your benefit? Ask what the experience is showing you. Perhaps it is teaching you how to uncramp your thoughts or your beliefs a little bit and move into another direction. Perhaps it is simply telling you to slow down so you can experience a different realm. Perhaps it is encouraging you to explore your experience from another dimension. There are multiple things that it could mean, but each person has to figure that out for him or herself.

Well, we are very lucky to have you as friends, Laarkmaa. So, thank you so much for this.

You are welcome.

I have a few dietary questions about foods that may no longer be beneficial to those of us who are transitioning? Are mushrooms good for us?

Mushrooms are a type of fungus, a very damp food for the body. It may not be beneficial for the human system in crystalline form. Learn to stop and ask your body if a specific food is beneficial or not beneficial as you move through the ascension process. Stop and think about what it means to take fungus into your body. You don't want fungus over-operating within your system. If you have fungus overgrowth, such as candida or athlete's foot, you take an anti-fungal medication to get rid of it. So, it makes logical sense that eating a fungus could be contradictory to your health at this time. Each person must weigh that and figure out what foods feel appropriate for you. You do not need fungus in your human body form at all for proper nutrition.

It is a damp and heavy material, and you are trying to move to a light and fluid position with your body. So, you need to calculate and consider if that's a good idea for you. It is not as detrimental to you as eating meat or sugar, but you would need to consider if it's truly appropriate for you any longer.

What about tomatoes and peppers?

Peppers, tomatoes, and eggplant have never been beneficial for the human body. They are of the nightshade family, which makes them challenging for the human system. They cause stiffness in your joints and muscles, and they can even lead to conditions like arthritis. Peppers, tomatoes, and eggplant are not beneficial for humans, nor is corn, especially corn that has been altered with GMO material. Potatoes, which are also a night-shade vegetable, can be beneficial on occasion because they have something in them that helps eliminate negative viruses from the body. But they should not be eaten as a staple every day or even more than once a week.

Other things that are not good for you are gluten (as in wheat or other grains), alcohol, and caffeine. Spinach should never be eaten raw because of its enzymatic activity, nor should Iceberg lettuce be eaten at all. These things are detrimental to the human system. Most processed foods are not good for you. You need simple food. Basmati rice is a simple food, and it is good for you, but do not use it simply as a filler. It is beneficial in this time of change to eat less grain or even rice. Gluten is not good for the human system at all and is even worse now that most gluten products are affected with gene-altering chemicals produced by Monsanto (now acquired by Bayer). Do not eat foods that are laced with chemicals like glyphosate. You want to eat organic foods as much as you can because they are pure, and they are lighter. You want a balanced diet of rainbow colors. You probably want to include more hempseed in your diet because it contains all the amino acids, which support the transition the body is going through. All of these things should be helpful for you. This reminder is to help humans know what to do within your bodies.

Thank you so much for your wonderful wisdom, information, and energy. I've been feeling like I'm going through a major transformation for the past few days, as you said, moving step by step. And I've been able to send healing light to parts of my body that are out of balance. I am just so grateful for the wonderful energy that you, Pia, and Cullen provide for all of us and as a community, sending love and sending peace into the Earth.

You are learning that you are an amazing being. You are learning what the power of trust and the power of your own light can do to change your circumstances. So, we thank you for sharing your experiences because they help others to learn what power they hold to make changes in their lives. Send peace into your heart first and then out into the world. That way it will be magnified every time you send it.

You have mentioned that as we raise our frequency and vibration, we will be able to leave this dimension and to go into other higher dimensions to bring back information. Can you tell us more about how to raise our vibration enough to do that?

The best way to raise your vibration is to practice kindness and compassion in every single circumstance. Try to tune out any reactive old patterns that you may have and instead immediately catch and correct yourselves, remembering that only compassion and kindness operate at the higher levels. Be grateful for what each experience offers you. As you do these things, your vibration automatically goes up. When your vibration goes up, you are able to travel into other dimensions more easily. You may want to spend time in a meditative state, instilling kindness and compassion as a first response. Say or sing to yourself," I am kindness. I am compassion. I give kindness. I give compassion. I receive kindness. I receive compassion. I am grateful." Use a mantra like this, and then go into a deep quiet space where no thoughts exist to instill those qualities into yourself. That's a very good way to help raise your vibration.

What will we experience going into the higher dimensions?

That is a question that will have to be explored as you experience it. It's not something you can prepare for except by doing what we have suggested above. Raise your vibration, and you will be very pleasantly delighted with the experience. We cannot define it for you because that would put it in a box and would disallow your freedom to experience it in your own way.

I know you've addressed this over the years many times, but can you say anything else about various ways to help us go through this process without fear or even terror?

Work on your fear now. Don't wait until bigger changes come. You will perceive these changes as terrible if you are in a state of fear. Many people will be frightened of what's happening. But when you work on expanding your consciousness now, and you work to eliminate all of your fear, you will begin to see that whatever is happening has a purpose, and you will experience it as a joyful opportunity, not something to be afraid of. If you want to embrace these changes without being afraid, you have to eliminate your fear *now*, not wait until later. There is fear even within your question. You are already fearful of what these changes mean and what they are going to look like. Work on that individually. Learn to understand that your perspective affects everything. It's all experience, and how you perceive each experience determines what you will feel. If you perceive something as terrible and you are frightened of what that's going to mean for *you,* your experience will be terrible. If you see something that on first glance appears terrible, but you immediately understand that it is necessary for evolution, the terribleness of it drops away because you have no fear. You step into the wonder of it, saying to yourself, "Great, we've been waiting for this to happen, so we can manifest a new reality. Finally, it's here. Yippie! I get to participate!" So, our answer for you and anyone else who has this concern is to change your focus. You are here to expand beyond what your third-dimensional perspectives and choices have been. You are here to expand into a cosmic awareness of who you are as larger and more awakened and aware citizens. So, if you have remaining fears and concerns, work with them. If you are afraid of dying, ask yourself what you are afraid of, and then look beyond it. If you are afraid that you may not have enough money to eat, ask yourself, "Do I not trust that the Universe will provide, as long as I do my part?" Ask yourself where these fears are coming from, and work with your own fears individually. Many of you may need trauma clearings[12] because you are attached to or addicted to certain fears within your system. We would suggest that you do whatever you can to free yourselves from the traumas that are still holding you back. Welcome each challenge as an opportunity to grow and expand.

In my dreams I get visits from people on the other side that I have not seen in a long time. It seems their visits are becoming clearer and they bring more information. Is that happening because we are raising our frequency and vibration?

This is a direct example of opening to multidimensionality. This is an example of you doing your work to prepare for a different world. That's exactly right. Many people are experiencing this and, yes, it is happening because you are opening to multidimensionality.

When I interact with other Light Bearers, I feel nurtured with a heightened sense of connectedness. You have told us that we are islands of light strategically positioned around the planet. I'm wondering if there are more opportunities for Light Bearers to come together physically as we evolve?

The probability is that you will begin to see movement of like-spirited, like-hearted people coming together more and more in various places during this time of change. Some will move by intentional choice because you are led to find each other. Some will come together through circumstance because circumstances on the Earth have pushed you to find each other, but the likelihood is that, indeed, more and more of you will be coming together soon. We appreciate every single one of you who is here, connecting as you are evolving and changing together.

You have told us that we do not really understand what love is. Would you please expand on what love is?

Yes. Love is the essence of light, and light is the essence of love. Love is the absence of doubt, the absence of fear, and the absence of questions that come from a place of fear. It is the place of brightness that brings forth feelings of gratitude, truth, acceptance, and joy. This is what we call unconditional love. You cannot approach healing without a deeper understanding of love. You perceive love on this planet as something that you give or take. You give love and expect love to be given back. You take love and expect it to be given in return. You see love as something that is to be reciprocated, and if it is not, your heart is broken. But that is not true love. True love is having so much light, joy, and gladness in your heart that you simply cannot help sharing it, so you share that light wherever you go. There may be a special person in your life that you share love in an intimate way, as one expression of love, but that is only one form of love. Unconditional love requires that everyone you encounter receives love radiating out as great compassion, acceptance, and understanding—every person, every animal, every rock, every tree on the planet—knowing that each has a goodness about it, no matter how you may perceive the outer personality. Your love allows you to know that each person is on his or her path of evolution according to their choices, even though those choices may not match yours or may not be for the highest good for all. You can discern that difference, but you do not need to judge it. When you are living from a place of unconditional love, you send out the vibrations of loving acceptance and light. Those vibrations cannot be misinterpreted because they are so simple and so pure. Love is evolution. Evolution is love. Unconditional love is the key to evolution (the word *love* is even contained in the word *evolution,* even though the order of the letters is different). Therefore, to evolve, one must experience unconditional love. You may first experience unconditional love in in a glimpse, in a moment of clarity, or for one particular person, but as you evolve, that unconditional love becomes so much a part of you that you shine it on everyone you meet. That is true evolution. Having that kind of love brings so much joy to your heart, that your vibration is raised at a cellular level so that you can accomplish true healing. When you raise your cellular vibration by continually keeping joy in your heart, love radiates out from that place of joy; love simply overflows because you are joyful. You cannot force the experience of unconditional love; you must simply allow it through your attitudes of compassion and gratitude. Find something that brings joy to your heart, then turn your love outwards towards others to expand it. Others will experience unconditional love from you when you do that. Radiate love from yourself through the higher version of love in your cellular being as you express attitudes of gratitude and joy, and that will take you more quickly and happily into a place of unconditional love, which the true essence of who you are and the true reason

178

of why you are here. You are here to be love and to shine light out into everything so that the darkness is enlightened. Then the darkness can remember what has been forgotten and see the light. When you send love, you are sending light. When you send light, you are sending love. When you do that, you are evolving. When you are evolving, you are healing.

How should we deal with the dark? I know you have said that this cosmic drama is playing out because of how the dark energies are manipulated. How are they manipulated and why?

Dark energies are stimulated and feed upon negative thoughts. If you have a fear, an emotion that is negative, or anger that is unresolved, a sadness, a grief, or any of those emotional states, and you are simultaneously thinking thoughts of judgment and blame, then you are stimulating and feeding the dark energies. Dark energies have forgotten— just like so many people on Earth have forgotten—that they are part of the whole, that they are part of the light. And so therefore, in this dualistic environment dark energies fight to gain control because duality on Earth has become a field of competition, manipulation, and control. In that field, the dark says, "I want to be first; I want to control." The dark then takes in and feeds upon any negative energy, building its power. Then it begins to stimulate, manipulate, and control in other ways. The light energy, on the other hand, does not act in an aggressive way. The light energy is more subtle and more lasting. The light energy is a powerful energy of love. You can radiate love from your heart to any place where you perceive the darkness has been agitated. That gentleness of the light and potency of the light begins to permeate the darkness, reminding the dark to awaken and remember that it, too, is part of the light. And it does not have to misbehave so.

Your best course of action is to focus upon being light, being love at all times and sending that vibration out into the world.

As each of you do this, that light and higher vibrational energy is penetrating the dark at multiple levels, layers, and places all across the planet. Gently, but powerfully, it awakens the dark to remember to stop trying to control, stop trying to manipulate, stop trying to harm, stop trying to block. It invites the dark to awaken and remember. Awaken and remember. Humans are referred to as being asleep because they make poor choices, sometimes dark choices, but the dark itself is also asleep. It is in a place of *forgetting*, even though it is part of Source too; it is part of the light. It has simply forgotten who it is and through its actions has made itself be something that is now abhorred by all who are working with opposite energies. We say, "Do not abhor the dark." Instead, send it love and welcome it back into the energy of the light. Does that help?

Yes, but I want to understand at a deeper layer. I want to understand what you are referring to as dark energy— its primordial nature before there is spin put on it. We tend to see the dark as the opposite of light, and therefore bad, so we work to bring in more light. Then all of a sudden, we became more susceptible to negativity. What is the pure essence of the dark versus the light? They seem to both be potent energies, right? I'm trying to better understand its essential nature prior to the dark forgetting that it was part of the whole. I don't know if "dark" is even a good description of it. Perhaps it's a term we used because of the lack of better understanding of its essence. The sense that I have is that there is a powerful way to work with the dark energy at the higher vibratory levels.

On this planet of duality, the energy of duality was always intended to show you different perspectives so that you could add those perspectives together and create a more harmonious whole. In such a use of duality, the primordial essence of the dark, which you asked to understand, would be like gazing at the dark of the night. The essential nature of the dark is quiet and peaceful. Darkness can provide a place of repose, a place of emptiness and waiting, knowing that anything can fill that space. Darkness can be a place of holding energy and potential. That is the essential energy of the dark. However, as an energy full of emptiness and potential, the essential energy of the dark became filled with negative intentions, negative thoughts, confused ideas based on fear and separation, and belief systems that included competition and control. The essence of the dark was corrupted—co-opted you might say. The energy that was there was filled and shaped it into something malevolent and something that is not benign. But that is the forgetting. That is how the dark forgot who it was. It's much like looking at someone who is a murderer; when that murderer was a child, he or she was joyful, normal, and playful. Something happened to him or her along the way; he or she was attacked or abandoned or hurt and became retaliatory, thinking, "I'm going to hurt back." Something like this story is the way that the dark was transformed and changed. Now it is your job as Light Bearers to shine the light back into the dark and help it find its way back Home. Once it realizes that its gifts are part of the whole and it does not have to compete to be loved (just like humanity), once it recognizes its own place in the harmonious whole and its own primordial state with its own beautiful gifts and talents, it will regain its state of emptiness, quiet, and waiting. We hope that this more in-depth answer helps you understand.

STEP NINE:

COSMIC WEATHER & THE EFFECTS OF LIGHT

Accelerated Opportunities & Responsibilities

Currently humanity seems to be stuck in a loop of behavior patterns reflecting the lower vibrational thoughts that you collectively think, which are reflected in governmental, educational, and religious controls. And yet, those of you reading this book are part of a group that is here to bring more light into the planet as the planet ascends. It is important that you learn about the higher frequencies we will be discussing below: the higher spikes in the Schumann Resonance frequency, the higher spikes in the Schumann Resonance amplitude, and incoming Cosmic Rays[1]. As you discover how they can impact you, it is important that you do not blame them for how you are feeling physically or emotionally. Rather, accept them with gratitude and take greater responsibility as Light Bearers to know that with the presence of more Cosmic Rays and a higher Schumann Resonance more light is entering the atmosphere. Your job is to raise your own frequencies to match these incoming energies. Accept the transfer of the higher light and higher energies into yourselves with grace, gratitude, and love. Send your appreciation and high vibrational unconditional love back into the planet and beyond. This is the way to have a fair and equal exchange of energy that allows the light coming toward you to raise your vibration, as you raise your own vibration to match the light that you truly are. You are experiencing a unique opportunity now of having these solar and cosmic events impact and affect you in a way that brings either great challenge or great opportunity, according to your perspective. From a lower vibratory response, you can complain about how everything is not working and how you don't feel good, not taking any responsibility to acknowledge and work with the gift of these energies, *or* you can raise your vibration to create an opportunity from each challenge.

Energy and life always cycle, and because of this, you will not experience a high Schumann Resonance spike continually on an everyday basis. But the general levels of frequency and amplitude are increasing, as your own consciousness is rising. These random spikes in energy are helping you to evolve. Again, you are experiencing an increase in spikes in amplitude while the frequency may or may not remain stable *and* increased spikes in higher vibrational frequency. Both spikes serve the sole purpose of raising your own vibration to match these energies, accelerating your evolution to match the Earth's ascension process, and raising your vibration to match the vibration Cullen calls your Future Selves.

With an increase in Cosmic Rays coming into your magnetosphere because of the Solar Minimum, you have even more radiation, or light, coming into the cells of your bodies, causing you more and more physical symptoms. We guide you to *not* focus on the symptoms, but instead focus upon the spiritual gift, and remember that you are consciousness itself. By using this spiritual gift, allowing more light into the cells of your being, and continually making choices for the highest good of all, you will—moment by moment—raise yourselves to be more in alignment with the ascension process that allows you to enter into Rainbow body form, as described earlier in this book.

The Outer Effects of Light

We want to explain the frequencies and vibratory changes you are undergoing in terms of the inner and the outer experiences of light, discussing both the Schumann Resonance and incoming Cosmic Rays. The Schumann Resonance is the resonant frequency of Earth's electromagnetic field. And it is increasing. The Schumann Resonance is a register showing energy transfers from one place to another. When you experience a 7.83 Hz resonance with the Earth, you experience calmness, for that frequency transfers a sense of peaceful tranquility into your awareness, causing you to feel that you have no need to worry about anything. This is the frequency that resonates with your Theta brain waves. That 7.83 Hz frequency has supported humans on this planet for a long time. We, Laarkmaa, and the Universe support you as you move to adapt to these higher frequencies. We know you will be more fulfilled and more able to step into your true selves when you are able to step beyond your current range of experience between 7.83 Hz Theta to 8—12 Hz Alpha, and 12—40 Hz Beta frequencies, into the 40–-100 Hz Gamma frequencies that unfortunately, you only experience infrequently at the present time. These amazing higher Gamma frequencies coming to the planet are appearing in larger and larger spikes, taking you beyond your accustomed range of frequencies. This increase in pulsing higher energies into the planet will continue. The higher the frequency you experience, the higher your consciousness becomes. You are receiving increasing spikes of the Gamma range energy, as well as the more uncomfortable high Beta energy spikes, so you will begin to acclimate to the higher ranges and begin to understand, or feel, that you are incorporating more light into your cells. You will begin to understand that the Schumann Resonance brings higher frequency and the Cosmic Rays bring you light so that you can experience a greater awareness of the connection between your own light and powerful *cosmic* light. You can then begin to transform your bodies from the carbon-based forms they have been into the crystalline forms of lighter density and higher vibration. You will not need to nourish your new forms with food in the same way. You will not need to do as many physical things. You will be more interested in being in the Now moment, rather than accomplishing things as you previously have. You will feel increasingly less lonely, less separate, and more and more fulfilled, as you connect more with others. You will experience unity more directly as you live in the spirit of *In Lak'ech* (I am another yourself) guided by *Ahimsa* (Do no harm). These are characteristics that thrive in the Gamma brain wave frequency, elevating you to the highest version of yourselves. Those of you who are working with the high Beta spikes of energy to acclimate yourselves and prepare for the coming Gamma ray resonance will become more aligned with the Gamma ray spikes as they arrive. At this point, we will congratulate you, for you will have gone through a new type of birth process that your species has never done before, similar to moving from a caterpillar through the metamorphosing process of being in a chrysalis state to finally emerging as a beautiful butterfly, ready to spread its wings to fly freely anywhere you wish. In other words, you will have achieved a Rainbow body!

As we, Laarkmaa, scan new information from humans around the world who are beginning to understand, we feel it worthy of and necessary to share with you the following quote from Derek Knauss[2]. This information summarizes what we will explore more in-depth, helping you to both understand what is occurring on your planet and how to work with it. You may find some repetition between this article and our explanations; however, we hope that the entirety of this information supports your deeper awareness and understanding about your Cosmic Weather.

You're Not Dying –
It's the Schumann Resonance!

By now, there isn't one person on Earth that has not felt some kind of weird and unexplained physical symptom that makes them feel uncomfortable. Many do not understand why this is occurring, and some go to their doctor to find that there is nothing wrong with them. In turn, doctors are realizing that there seems to be a phenomenon of unexplained "psychosomatic" occurrences. There is scientific evidence that something is happening on the planet that is shaking the apple cart up at this time, and this evidence is from a Russian website that tracks the Schumann Resonance.

The Schumann Resonance is a global electromagnetic resonance named by physicist Winfried Otto Schumann who predicted it mathematically in 1952. The official description from Wikipedia is:

"The Schumann resonances (SR) are a set of spectrum peaks in the field spectrum. Schumann resonances are global electromagnetic resonances, generated and excited by lightning discharges in the cavity formed by the Earth's surface and the ionosphere."

As you can see, the Wikipedia explanation says that we have had a whole lot of lightning lately if you read the charts that I am about to show you. Regardless of whether what is happening on the planet is indeed causing more "lightning" or whether it is causing the equipment to pick up extremely low frequency (ELF) portion of the Earth's electromagnetic or something else, the scientific evidence proves that something is disturbing or spiking the electromagnetic frequency on the planet.

For thousands of years the Schumann resonance has been measured at 7.83 hertz or within shallow spikes of this depending on how many storms are on the planet at the time. The Russian website is one of the only public sites that releases the daily data on the current Schumann fluctuations. The reasons for this are unclear but seem to point at the control of keeping the data from the public eye.

As a spiritual being merged with a human body, we also merged with the consciousness and energetic makeup of Earth when we were born into a human body. To stay in sync with the planetary composition and frequencies, the human body has an auto correct system that can re-calibrate to the environment when needed. When the auric field of a human is not in sync, however, it is difficult for the emotional, mental, spiritual, and etheric bodies to sync with the physical body and the frequency of Earth. At the same time, a burst in frequency of Earth's magnetic frequencies can jostle any energetic blockages in the auric field that can cause the physical body to stay at a low or stagnant ELF (extremely low frequency). Bursts of higher frequencies are a good thing for clearing of the auric field of the human, as long as it is done in moderation. For instance, if a person were to be electrocuted from a household electrical outlet, they may have a better chance at recovering than being struck by lightning.

The spiritual and metaphysical explanation of raising the frequency of the physical body is the higher the frequency, the less dense reality the human will be experiencing. The goal is to transform the dense, controlling reality we are experiencing in a way that unifies humanity in a love based higher consciousness while still existing in the physical body. This can only be achieved by releasing the energetic blocks of the past and of childhood that keep one stuck in creating a recurring illusion of denseness and disease in the physical reality. This will allow the physical body to vibrate harmoniously with the planetary frequency and to have a healthy energy flow within the body, which prevents aging and disease.

If a human is stuck in old patterning and beliefs, or perhaps is lulled by complacency into a low frequency, then a burst of frequency can do one of two things. If the person has raised their consciousness enough to realize something is happening and is able to have an open mind and an open heart, then the person will begin to absorb these frequencies as much and as fast as their mind and spirit allows them to. Absorbing these frequencies causes the water in the body to begin to vibrate at the frequency of the spike. This could cause many uncomfortable symptoms, but in the end, it is also a testament that something is really happening to our planet and to our consciousness.

A few of the most common symptoms of these spikes in electro-magnetic frequency are:

- *Hot flashes – as the body vibrates faster it generates heat*

- *Blurred vision*

- *Vertigo (dizziness)*

- *Irregular or skipped heartbeat*

- *Unexplained pains that may linger to be acknowledged or may mysteriously come and go*

- *Ringing in one or both ears – High pitched frequencies, harmonic tones, and/or sometimes temporary deafening*

- *Mood swings as emotional blocks come up to be resolved*

- *Extreme fatigue or extreme energy bursts depending on the kind of frequency experienced at the time and how the individual is dealing with it*

- *Increased intuition, a sense of knowing or remembering things that guide you through difficulties, and increased sixth sense abilities (beyond touch, taste, feel, hearing, and sight)*

- *Nausea*

- *Flu-like symptoms*
- *Problems with bowels*
- *Extreme hunger or lack of hunger – different than usual*
- *Anxiety and increased fight or flight mode in the body*

As you can see, if some of these negatively affected symptoms persist without the person doing things to help the body acclimate, it certainly could feel like the body would begin to exhibit more evidence of shutting down and may make you feel as if you are dying. In fact, it is purging in order to be able to acclimate, very similar to how it deals with flu or viruses. If a person is completely unconscious and is not a caring, compassionate human (or is not a souled human at all) then these frequencies will irritate and disturb and will most likely not be integrated.

Thus these types of people will stay at a low frequency and will not benefit from the incoming waves of energy. It could even begin to cause their physical body to shut down because it will not be able to stay manifest in harmony with the planet's frequency. Unfortunately some people are not handling this well physically and we are seeing people "leaving" at this time (dying). There is certainly no judgment in this, as some people did not choose to go through this shift in frequency or simply did not have enough energy left to handle it, and no one ever really "dies" anyway.

They simply move to another frequency outside of the constraints of the physical body and go where they need to in order to continue on their journey.

There are many ways to help yourself adjust to the energies, but here are a few of the most common:

- *Meditation – not the kind of meditation to connect with astral beings or to have out of body experiences. Peace, pause, and breath meditation and focusing on energy flow works best, and open eye meditation is also good.*

- *Grounding or Earthing – Bare feet on the ground, spending time in nature, sea salt baths, swimming, eating grounding foods.*

- *Asking your higher being (higher self/Source/Guidance team) to assist you in acclimation, especially if you are suffering.*

- *Drink plenty of pure water! No fluoride*

- *Rest – the body has an uncanny ability to do much of its re-setting while it is asleep or lying still.*

- *Loving yourself and caring for the body.*

- *Gentle exercise – moving the energy to release blockages and encourage proper energy flow.*

- *Whole foods — as opposed to processed or GMO foods.*

- *Massage*

- *Listen to your body and do what feels right to make it comfortable.*

Those who are sensitive to energy have been able to correlate when they are feeling something really different, and look up the chart to see if a "wave" is occurring. On the left axis you will see the hertz and on the lower axis you will see the time of day in UTC +7. The top axis shows the date. The green shows what I assume are normal pulses of electromagnetic frequency. A "white out" has been shown to correlate with thousands of people being able to feel the fluctuation in their physical bodies. The wider the band of the white out, the longer the wave is consistently hitting. Frequency means how many wave cycles happen in a second. 1 Hz means 1 cycle per second, 40 Hz means 40 cycles per second. Amplitude is the size of the vibration, how big the wave is, and the chart shows the frequency variation in Hz and the amplitude using the white color. We can deduce logically that large white color bursts in electromagnetic frequencies and for long periods of time are going to affect our physical bodies! These blasts of energy frequency help humanity to awaken from the spell that a low frequency can keep a person stuck in. We can all think back to a time in our lives where we found ourselves hypnotized through entertainment or even through slaving at a job we hated for the need for money out of survival.

Many people, including of course those reading this article, have realized that there is something really wrong with what is occurring on the planet at this time. It is these people who are being affected through waves of energy or vibration, light, and sound that will help them break free of the chaos and unhappiness they may find themselves in. On a "Matrix" level, there is 1% of the people on this planet who would like to control the 99% of people on the planet. They do not have the consciousness or ability to move through these up-shifts in frequency like someone who is awake, aware, and has made a conscious <u>choice</u> not to be under the control system. Eventually, those who raise their physical body frequency to their higher consciousness will be able to outwit, outsmart and outplay those who wish to control them on many levels.

New understandings, abilities, and higher dimensional connections will occur to the individuals who are able to adjust. As the frequency continues to blast, rest, then blast, we are slowly (but lately at an accelerated rate) connecting the physical to higher dimensions, densities, and consciousnesses that are beyond those who have controlled humans for a very long time on the planet. The up-shifts in frequency also help people to awaken.

This article is a simplified explanation of the Schumann Resonance fluctuation showing a correlation with the way the human body has been experiencing this while examining the scientific proof in increase of frequency through charts found on a Russian website. It is intended to help alleviate the fear of the shift and changes that are occurring by providing logical conclusions. It is not intended to keep anyone from seeking medical attention nor is it a complete explanation of the bigger picture of why it is occurring and where the waves of energy are coming from. Please use your own discernment and do your own research to understand more about this phenomenon, and please share far and wide so that those who are having difficulties can use the techniques described in this article to alleviate their adjustment symptoms. Finally, in the practice of questioning everything in our reality, here is a note for the doubters. It at least helps us to realize that we need to take care of ourselves in a more holistic way and that we can share information with each other that helps us feel like we are not alone or that our symptoms are not psychosomatic.

Many people started consciously working with these energetic frequencies years ago and have reported on what has worked best for them to be able to feel better. These people, including myself, no longer suffer when huge waves hit, as we have tried many things and compared notes with each other.

—*Derek Knauss*

Until humans created radio waves and EMFs, which disturb Earth's natural rhythms, the Schumann Resonance was consistently near 7.83 Hz. Humans have actually contributed to the current imbalance in the Schumann Resonance by creating all of the EMF waves that alter the natural frequencies on your planet; you have disturbed the normal balance of Earth's energetic balance by developing all of the technologies that you depend on, created by your simplistic and archaic science. Additionally, you contribute to the frequency of the Schumann Resonance with the thoughts you think. You are being pushed to accelerate your own evolution to match the higher frequencies of the Schumann Resonance, which is a rather uncomfortable, but necessary process. Obviously, you must adapt to survive and evolve.

At the same time that the Schumann Resonance is increasing, the interaction of solar winds with your magnetic field is allowing more Cosmic Rays to enter Earth's environment, bringing more radiation to all life on Earth. You are experiencing changes in frequency through the increased Schumann Resonance and simultaneously an increase in light from the Cosmic Rays. We perceive this as an opportunity to bring more light into your cells while simultaneously raising your vibration. From the outer experience of light, the Schumann Resonance shows spikes of energy in the Earth's magnetic field. These random spikes in energy are helping you to evolve, bringing more light by changing the frequency of your vibration. From our perspective, light and high vibration are synonymous. Because the Schumann Resonance was discovered at a time when it was consistently measured at about 7.83 Hz in vibration, your scientists designed the measurement scale with a high of 40 Hz. The Schumann Resonance has stayed at 7.83—7.85 Hz for most of humanity's existence, which is deeply in tune with Nature and your experience of calm, relaxation, and meditative states, or Theta and Alpha brain waves as you measure them. We will discuss the correlation of your brain waves with the Schumann Resonance in a moment. Beginning in 2014 and continuing in 2016, the Schumann Resonance began to spike at higher frequencies that caused you to feel higher energies that you did not register as normal. Now the Schumann Resonance is on occasion registering spikes that are off the charts, at an indeterminable measurement, reaching higher than 40. These spikes are continuing to increase.

We want to discuss what effect this change has on you. The resonance between 12—25 Hz is the low Beta brain wave range–the range you are most accustomed to feeling in your waking state. We do not mean one who is "awakened;" we mean one who is literally not asleep at night but is going about everyday life. You are most comfortable being active in the low Beta wave range of 12—25 Hz; you are interested in what you are doing, and you move about your life in a way in which you are accustomed. But when the Beta waves spike into a higher range between 25—40 Hz, you experience feelings of overwhelm, anxiety, depression, anger, grief, and intense emotions that you may not understand. You may feel that your emotions have become "unglued." Also, at the higher Beta wave range frequencies you may feel extreme physical distress. These are the symptoms that you are now feeling as the Schumann Resonance spikes regularly into the high Beta wave range, and sometimes into the Gamma range of 40—100 Hz. As we have told you, these are ascension symptoms, related to your accessing more light. They include extreme nausea, upset digestion, inability to sleep or disrupted sleep, migraine-type headaches, dizziness, and a general fatigue or malaise that causes you to feel like you just can't get motivated or you don't know how to summon enough energy to do your usual work. These high Beta and Gamma waves can also and often cause a decrease in your memory.

Does any of this sound familiar to you? Most likely everyone who is reading this has experienced some level of this type of distress. The higher brain waves that some humans do access on occasion are called Gamma brain waves, in which you may experience occasional heart-based insights. These are the wavelengths that cause you to feel bursts of unexpected joy and love for everything and everyone. They bring the deep experiences of connection to everything and to Source and the feeling that you are one with a tree you are hugging or admiring. This is the gamma wave frequency, which ranges from 40—100 Hz. It induces a greater sense of awareness, compassion, and unconditional love. Most likely, each of you reading this has experienced this brain wave activity in some burst during your life. But now your Sun is experiencing a Solar Minimum and moving toward a Grand Solar Minimum, as your magneto-sphere is allowing more intense Cosmic Rays to penetrate your atmosphere, which then cause more lightning, which acceler-ates the frequency of the Schumann Resonance causing higher spikes of energy. This means that you are accessing more light and more energy.

We have been telling you that you are receiving more light, and not to consider it as irradiation that makes you sick. Instead, see this light as illuminating you to make you whole. The Schumann Resonance is showing a higher vibrational Earth. Since you have chosen to ascend with the planet, isn't it natural that you, too, would need to adjust to a higher vibratory rate of being? It is nothing to fear. You are not dying; you are simply experiencing ascension symptoms that are quite uncomfortable. You feel physical distress and disorientation; you can't remember things; you can't think clearly; you are foggy; your stomach may be upset, or your digestion may be disturbed; you have unexpected waves of nausea; you find that you tire easily and feel fatigued. And you have bursts of joy, connection, and uncon-ditional love! All of these symptoms are indicating that your physical, mental, and emotional elements are adjusting to the higher vibratory rate of new energies. That is what is happening to you. We know that it is uncomfortable; we see the distress that you are experiencing. But we are here to assure you that are you growing and are on track for accelerating your own evolution.

If you focus upon being light and sending light, you will begin to mitigate your symptoms. They will begin to lessen because you are going to be acclimating to the incoming higher waves that radiate at the higher Gamma frequency—the radia-tion frequency that you receive when you are in deep, profound meditation or in a cosmic experience of awareness of connection to all that is. Or when you are experiencing deep, unconditional love, or when your heart is touched with the deepest compassion. Humanity is waking up and achieving this on a daily basis. Yet you may look around and wonder why some appear not to be suffering as you are. You may ask why they are not having as an uncomfortable experience as you are. You may recall that in an earlier chapter we explained that not all who are with you on the Earth plane have chosen to ascend with the planet. They do not appear to be suffering because they did not choose to have their forms elevated into crystalline light bodies that join with your etheric form to create a Rainbow body that can emanate all the rays of light that exist in the Universe. They did not choose to go through this process that allows them to share all these rays of light and to shapeshift at will, as we do, or that allows them to travel at will, wherever they want to go in a moment's thought. No, they did not make that choice. Why? Because they do not believe it is possible. They are stuck in a third-dimensional mindset that clings to what your scientists tell them is possible and what is not. Therefore, they choose to live and die, returning somewhere else to continue their lessons, evolving very slowly at their own chosen rate.

You, however, have chosen to ascend with the planet. You have chosen to work to attain a Rainbow body. You have chosen an accelerated rate of evolution to become your Future Selves. You have made this choice, and we are here to walk beside you, guiding you and making suggestions all along the way to make the ascension process more beneficial and easier to bear. Until that grand moment we call the Cosmic Pop, or little Cosmic Pops that happen along the way, be assured that you can trust in the process; you can trust that you are exactly where you are supposed to be and that everything is occurring exactly as it should in the manner that it should. We do understand that it is uncomfortable. We assure you that we do understand that. We have been through our own evolutionary process, and while not exactly like yours, we promise that it was uncomfortable. We can also promise you that it has been *well worth it!*

We want to give you something to look forward to during the challenges now; we want to let you know that the suffering you are experiencing is on purpose—a birth process taking you into higher states of consciousness and an awakened state of being, as you move into liquid light.

The Inner Effects of Light

We have been speaking about the outer effects of light. Now we will speak about the inner effects. The largest inner effect of being infused with more light is that you drop away from emotional reactivity. If someone cannot see who you truly are, if they judge you incorrectly or project their own anger or frustrations onto you, you will simply look at them, reflect the energy back to them (because it is not yours,) and send them compassion, over and over again. You will not be affected because you will have a greater sense of the light that you are. At the same time, when you see someone who is struggling and you know that they are suffering, you will automatically, with compassion in your heart, extend your light to them. This means that more and more, you will begin to act as the light beings that you are, and you will move closer to unity. You will begin to remember and understand that you are expressions of energy that can and do change in every moment. Your changes affect one another with every thought you think and every positive action you take because you are connected.

There are several ways you can work with these times of ups and downs—the physical, mental, and emotional swings between cosmic highs and lows that leave you wondering what you are doing here. Your higher selves know *exactly* what you are doing here. As you become more and more conscious, you will begin to acclimate with that knowing and trusting, and you will be glad that you have persevered in order to be here at this time of incredible transformation. Ways to work with the intense frequencies of light include:

- Every morning when you awaken, spend as much time as you can sending light into every cell of your body. Your cells are acclimating to the increasing light in full recognition that all strands of your DNA are awakening. As your cells hold more light and your DNA awakens, you will experience yourselves more and more as multidimensional beings, incorporating all of your experiences from other dimensions into this conscious moment. So, pour light into yourselves—into all of your cells, into all of your thoughts, into all of your feelings, into everything. Just spend time saying, "Give me more light please. Thank you. Please give me even more light. Thank you." Take the light in.

- After some period of time when you feel saturated, begin to send the light outwards. Send it to your beloveds, your family, and your community. Send it to the world. Send it to the people who disrupt harmony in their political and govern- mental roles because they are confused. Send it to the masses, even though they have made the choice not to ascend with the planet. Send light outward, everywhere you can. Start in your own environment with your own family, and then continue to radiate it outwards. Send light. And then send more. And then send even more. And then come back to yourself and notice how you feel. Notice that you will actually feel a little bit lighter. And we mean that in terms of vibration as well as in terms of the light that is radiating from you.

These are things that you can do to help yourself adjust. Remember, the high frequencies that are coming in from the higher Schumann Resonance spikes and from the increased Cosmic Rays are both transforming your cells and your DNA. You have twelve strands of DNA. We have told you that before.[3] Only two have been recognized by your science, but the other ten strands, which currently sit as a cosmic soup within you, are all beginning to awaken. That also has to do with your feeling disoriented and a bit unlike your old selves. You *are* unlike your old selves, for you are becoming your Future Selves.

Expanded Understanding of Resonance Transfer

We have one final thing to share about resonance: the Schumann Resonance is a transfer of energy, a spike of energy within the Earth's magnetic field, and it can be transferred to you; we have been speaking about how you receive these transfers of high Beta energy or Gamma energy, and how these transfers press themselves upon you at a cellular level (physically), a mental level, and an emotional level.

But guess what? Transfers go both ways; they do not only work in one direction. Your scholars have recently discovered something we have always known: humans, when acting on a collective level, can affect the structure of the magnetic field of Earth. Not only do you feel the increase of the vibration of the frequency of the Earth's magnetic field, but the Earth also responds to an increase in your magnetic field. If you are experiencing feelings of love, joy, trust, and compassion, your vibrational frequency goes up and radiates outwards into Earth and space. If you allow yourselves to dwell in feelings of sadness, frustration, anger, jealousy, or fear, your vibration drops to an abysmal level that impacts not only your physical, mental, emotional, and spiritual selves, but also impacts the vibration of the Earth's magnetic field. As you can see, what you feel makes a difference, so we encourage you to choose your feelings and your thoughts from a higher vibratory range. You are responsible for transferring positive high vibrational energy back to the Earth, Gaia. The positive energy that you experience from a Gamma energy spike and infusion allows you to quite naturally, automatically transfer back to the Earth in unconditional love, compassion, and grace. You do that quite naturally. At the same time, an awareness of what kind of energy you are transferring when you react to a high Beta wave spike—when you are feeling tired, dizzy, have a headache, don't feel like you can go on because you feel too sick to survive—is necessary to prevent your transferring negative and unconscious expressions of what you are experiencing, which have a negative impact on the Earth. This is why for so long we have reinforced the idea that *what you think makes a difference.* The thoughts that you think matter; they are *energy,* and they make a difference. Allow yourself to acknowledge that you are not feeling your best, but then express your gratitude that you can recognize by the symptoms you are feeling that you are doing your work and you are, indeed, transcending old ways of being. Be grateful that you are being shown that you are ascending with the Earth. To change the vibration of what you are experiencing, change your thoughts to gratitude. As you change your thoughts in that manner, you send out a higher frequency to the Earth, which can then invite in more of the Gamma waves that promote ascension. If you are feeling these things, you are succeeding in your quest to evolve.

There is no doubt that you are changing, along with your world. To face these enormous changes with trust and excitement, you absolutely need to learn to accept the physical, mental, and emotional differences you are experiencing with trust and gratitude. It is important to stop judging yourselves or falling into old patterns of thinking that you are sick or dying. You are ascending—a process that takes you from the dense carbon-based physicality that you have always believed to be your essential selves into the liquid crystalline waveforms that you truly are.

You are waveforms of consciousness, not merely static, unchanging particles of a third-dimensional body.

You are here on Earth at this time because you make a difference. You are here to evolve. You are here because there is much to do. You have a job and the responsibility to be light and to send light into the world. Doing this will free you, sooner than later. You will be able to move to your Future Selves in Rainbow body form in the Cosmos, and then you can choose your next assignment, where and how you want to be, and with whom you want to connect. It is all very promising and exciting! You are still at a point where you can make a tremendous difference, and if you follow our suggestions, you will be much more comfortable in this time of chaos and transition. We trust that our talking about light in this way has brought more light in your awareness, brought more light into your hearts, and brought lighter energy into your vibration. Think on these things and let them sink into you, and you will begin to experience this reality and feel the truth of what we are sharing . We will soon be able to invite you to join us in celebration!

QUESTIONS & ANSWERS
STEP 9

Laarkmaa, could you comment on anything we may need to be aware of with the transformation of the Earth and the Sun?

Oh, everything, absolutely everything! There is much acceleration on the movement of your planet. What you refer to as The Ring of Fire when referring to a particular range of volcanic activity is activating in a large way. Historically, Solar Minimums have always correlated with higher Earthquake and volcanic activity, causing food shortages from the lack of sunlight. And now in the United States, there are specific places that we've warned about for years that are beginning to become quite active with Earthquakes or volcanoes. That is around Bandon, Oregon and then branching up and down from there towards Vancouver and down towards Los Angeles and east across the country in the United States to your supervolcano Yellowstone and beyond to Missouri and Tennessee, following the New Madrid fault line. The Ring of Fire is showing much action in Hawaii and in South America also. In the southern hemisphere, Tonga. Vanuatu, Fiji, and New Zealand are experiencing increasing Earthquake magnitude. Earthquakes and volcanoes are more active in other parts of the world as well, and they are getting larger and more powerful. There is Earthquake activity that moves from Japan, across to Iran and Turkey, to Europe—through Greece, Italy, up into Switzerland, and through Portugal. Russia is also experiencing increased Earth activity. There is no place that is not being affected. So, you need to be aware of everything around you. You need to tune into your intuition and ask yourselves, "Where do I need to be at this moment? What's happening with the Earth? How can I be a part of this for the evolution of all and for all of us to move into higher levels of awareness?"

Earth changes are also a part of the awakening of humanity. New land masses are appearing, which are actually ancient land masses appearing once again on the planet. They are coming to the surface now as volcanic eruptions happen. Old islands will perhaps sink to the bottom of the sea as new ones rise because this is their time to be part of the Earth's surface. Changes are happening all over. And it's not something that you can necessarily run away from, declaring that you just don't want to be there. It's something that you need to tune in to and ask, "What's happening? How can I help and where is the best place for me to be at any given moment?" Understand that the vibrations of the Earth are producing an accelerated rate of change, as are your own vibrations. We don't make predictions and we don't usually give timelines, but we did tell you that in 2020 everything would accelerate quite a bit. You have already begun to see this in many different forms, including weather changes, volcanic changes, Earthquake changes, governmental changes and lockdowns, awakening humanity's changes—all kinds of changes. We can only tell you to be aware of everything! Pay attention to your own intuition moment-by-moment, day by day, learning how to respond to *whatever* is happening rather than reacting in fear. Your intuition is at the heart of your evolution and your source for survival. It is your source of joy; it is your source of knowing how to be of service. Say every day, "I am listening. What do I need to know? What do I need to hear? Where do I need to be and how can I help?"

I'm so thankful and grateful for this information you have shared because I am dealing with a lot of off-balanced energy as I walk. I try to shift my focus, and it seems to shift a little bit, but it is a challenge for me, even though I know that I can get through it.

You will, indeed, get through it. The Solar Minimum is predicted by your scientists to increase the Cosmic Ray activity.

We don't work in time or count calendar days, but we want you to be aware that what you are experiencing may feel somewhat worse for a while, and then, as you adjust to the new energies, you will begin to feel more resilient. So, redirect your energy and move through it with trust and grace. Perhaps by doing fewer projects and being less responsible in the outer world while being more responsible in the inner world will help you to manage and move through this transition more easily.

I thank you so much for the information, and I am really happy that you brought up the high Beta waves because I have experienced all the symptoms of lethargy, dizziness, and a sense of time slowing down, but I have also experienced really high vibrations that seem to be speeding things up. It felt like my body was on major caffeine without the side effects of caffeine because it was not jittery. I seemed to be operating so fast, it was almost impossible to focus or do anything. So, my question to you is when we reach those spaces of really high Beta frequencies, what do you suggest we can do so that we can function in the world?

Yes, you are indeed feeling this way because the cells of your body are sped up. They are activated and that affects your emotions and your mental thoughts, as well as the physical body itself. It is also the high Beta state that causes an inability to sleep or to have disruptive sleep. When you are experiencing these symptoms, acknowledge that whatever you may be experiencing is temporary. The Cosmic Weather is absolutely affecting you. Begin to alter your thoughts by being grateful that you are moving through this, and see if you can find someone to partner with to share your tasks. You can help each other with responsibilities, which lightens the load for both of you. Carpool, share grocery shopping, cook for one another, care for each other's children. These measures encourage you to reach out to form a larger sense of community. In whatever ways you can, partner with one or two other people and say, "Let's do this together," and see if you can share your responsibilities in community.

You may also experience sleep interference at night. Just breathe deeply and just spend time intentionally taking in light and saying, "Please give me more Light. Thank you," and then sending light back into the world as you exhale. Also, during sleepless periods at night, you can ask for grace saying, "Please, give me grace to help me moderate this as I adjust to it." Doing those things at night over and over again like a mantra will keep your mind somewhat calm and will help to rest and restore your body, even if you do not fall into a sleep space.

If you find you are experiencing a prolonged high Beta state, you may experience so much fatigue that you feel you can hardly make it. Just trust that your body is adapting and will be all right. Don't think that you are in a decline or something is wrong with you. See it as a positive and evolutionary cosmic influence. Remember this—Not everybody feels these symptoms. Not everybody has the nausea or the inability to sleep or the dizziness, or the headaches, or the mental confusion. Not everybody feels this; if you are feeling it, it is the sign that you have done your work. It is the sign that you are progressing on your path for evolution. It is a sign that you are indeed ascending, and that is what you have chosen. So, be grateful for that rather than saying, "I wish it weren't like this." Look at others around you and realize that their experience may be very different from yours because they have not chosen the path to ascend with the Earth. Eventually they will have to go through the same process, but at a future time. Look around you with gratitude and wonder. If you are feeling these symptoms, congratulate yourself, for you have graduated, and you are now working at a higher level in the ascension process.

I can't think any longer. I can't follow a line of thoughts sometimes for more than 5—10 seconds, and I forget what I'm doing; I don't know where I am; I don't even know what day of the week it is. I think I might be experiencing Dementia or Alzheimer's. It just feels like I have lost it. Are other people experiencing the same thing during these changing energies?

We would say that most of you are going to experience similar things in various forms as these higher energies arrive, but you haven't "lost it", as you say; you are "gaining it." Some of you are experiencing not being able to think or remember because your minds are simply adjusting to following your heart. Remember, you have been trained in cultures all over the world that the mind comes first, and if you have any time later, you can open your heart. We have been telling you for some time that this is out of balance. You have to let the heart lead, for the heart's wisdom is intuitive and is your direct connection to Source. Your heart knows what needs to be done in the right timing with anything and everything and everyone. So, you are simply going through an adjustment period during which your heart will be taking over and leading your thoughts. Try not to let it distress you too much. Make use of notes; write down what you need to remember to do. Recognize that you are being affected by the incoming energies that cause you not to be able to think as usual, but you will get through it because this is not a permanent change. It's a temporary change. It's something you have to endure for a while, but it does not mean you are never going to be able to function fully again. It means you'll be learning to function differently. This is something that people are experiencing from sixteen to eighty. It has nothing to do with Alzheimer's or age dementia. It has to do with the energies that are coming in and your adjustment to the light and the release of what no longer serves you. So, team up with someone and have them work with you saying, "This is a temporary thing, I know," but work with it the best you can together. We love you, all of you, and we don't want you to suffer. We want you to know that what you experience as suffering is temporary. It's not forever. Also, remember, while you are going through these intense high Beta rays until the Gamma rays are here more frequently, remember that when you fly at altitude you are closer to the magnetosphere, and you receive more Cosmic Rays. More Cosmic Rays will impact your memory; they will impact your brain; they will impact your physical body. Choose your flight times carefully and limit them unless they are absolutely necessary. Use protective devices[4] to eliminate some of the outer influences so that your body can be safe. This will prevent such intense experiences and symptoms.

Many of you are also feeling a variety of intense heart symptoms. Part of the reason for this is that you are opening the heart chakra, moving more into alignment with unity. There was a similar wave of heart openings many years ago, and there is another wave of heart openings now. The increased Cosmic Rays are also impacting heart issues. The Kp Index, which is the index that measures the level of Cosmic Rays coming into Earth, is often very, very low, which indicates that there is little protective barrier for the planet. This means you are receiving ultra-radiation from the Cosmic Rays. This causes the heart to beat unevenly; it is causing difficulties balancing and adjusting. Additionally, increased EMFs—particularly 5G—also impact your hearts, causing irregularities and sometimes even cardiac arrest. Some people are more sensitive to these heart issues than others. Do not approach these heart issues with fear, but do what you can physically to stop 5G on your planet, and trust that the increased light from the Cosmic Rays is aligning your body more with the energies that are coming into Earth at this time. Listen very carefully to what options are available for treating your heart. Make decisions based on what your heart says, not what anyone around you recommends, nor what anyone who is afraid to lose you says; listen to your heart and ask yourself, "Is this option the best one for me? Is this what I should do?"

Assess whether there are external 5G EMFs where you live that are affecting you, and do something about it. If you need to move, move. If you require a medical procedure, do not be afraid, but instead go into it trusting that whatever is happening is happening for you to align your body more with the energies that are coming into Earth at this time, and you will know how to proceed. If you require surgery, set a date to talk with us through Pia and Cullen; we can help you choose auspicious timing or help you verify that you are proceeding correctly. Please ask for help when necessary.

The opening of the heart chakra moves you closer and closer into the ascension process to your Rainbow body form. Trust the process, and do not be afraid; allow your heart to lead the way and tell you what is best. We do suggest that anyone who is experiencing these heart symptoms or any severe symptoms that have to do with Cosmic Rays not fly very much when the Kp Index is low, for that accelerates the energy and can put more strain upon the heart.

I've been experiencing the body symptoms of ascension for a long time simply as what they are—just a temporary upgrading and shifting of the body in a good way. However, it is interesting to watch other people who are now starting to experience these symptoms react with a negative viewpoint about it.

Yes, they will begin to understand as they experience it, and you cannot help them to understand the truth until they're ready to see it from their own perspective. We have often told you that it is the Light Bearers who will be helping those who do not understand at crucial times, saying, "Here is what you need to do; here is how you do it, let me help." You will be helping others to understand the shift from one form of reality into another. Your job always is to send light, no matter what the circumstances. Some will die. And as they do, your job is to send light, rather than grieving. Trust that they are leaving the planet at the appropriate time for them because they wish to go into a holding pattern while these changes occur. Some will die because they are ready for the next assignment, and they will go through whatever is required for them. And those who have been working to raise their vibrations to become liquid crystalline bodies will be offered the opportunity to move into Rainbow bodies. As your appetites decrease, as you become less aware of what is physically uncomfortable and more aware in each moment of the joy in your heart, there will be times that you may even be able to look down at your hand and see it as almost translucent. You will almost be able to see right through it, or look at one another and see dots or waves of energy, instead of the physical form you used to see. These observations are indications of an increased vibratory rate that is helping you to step into your new physical form as a liquid crystalline human.

With respect to our moving into Rainbow body, which is the merging of the etheric and the physical, please give us your insight on activities we can do to help the process of moving into our light bodies. What does the light body require for sustenance?

We need to clarify for you. Your light body exists now; it always has. It is the blueprint for your physical form. The thoughts that you project into your light body and the field around you are reflected back to create what you experience as your physical form. You are moving from a dense carbon-based form into a liquid crystalline physical form. This is a lighter form of the body, but it is still a physical form. When you achieve that liquid crystalline form, you will merge with your light body form, allowing you to move into Rainbow body. In the Rainbow body, you will be able to go back and forth between your etheric light form that can travel anywhere and your liquid crystalline form, which you will use on the planet. You will have the opportunity to use your Rainbow body as a place of merging and moving back and forth, as you choose. You are asking how to promote these changes now; this requires a greater focus on the liquid crystalline body form. There are several things that you can do to encourage this, but two are most important:

- Engage with water and remember that you *are* water. This helps you to understand your own fluidity and your ability to shift forms. We have spoken for many years about the importance of water and how water is used as a form of communication[5]. You need to revisit your concepts about the water that you are and try to be more fluid in your thinking, in your movements, in your reactions, responses, and in every-thing that you do. Work on being fluid.

- Work on being transparent, so that you reflect clearly the essence of who you are as a being of light. Honesty, integrity, and truthfulness are part of being transparent. When you are able to clearly reflect who you are as a being of light, and when you can be flexible with whatever the energies require, you will be much closer to attaining that liquid crystalline body form, which is a step toward attaining Rainbow body. The diet you choose, the conversations you have, the way you spend your time, all of these things are helping you to move beyond your current and previous experience of density. One thing that can help you is swimming, which can show you how to be more fluid and remind you that you are water. Another thing that can help you is breathing exercises, so that you can remember not to hold on to your breath (or anything else.) Allow your breath to flow in and out, and allow your experi-ences to bring to you what you need in the moment and take from what you no longer need; you are creating more adapt-ability and flexibility. These are two specific practices that you can do. Anything that helps you move in a fluid manner, such as Cranio-Sacral technique experienced with a practitioner who understands that everything is connected can help you activate the fluid content in your body, or practices such as Continuum Movement[6], where you practice being fluid and allowing your body to move spontaneously, or Tai Chi, where you move fluidly through the air. These are some practices that can replace your less flexible, habitual ways of being in the world. As you practice, begin to think more flexibly until you feel yourself beginning to change, from the inside out.

I would like to ask a question concerning the Kp Index. I realize that lately it's very low, and I perceive that I do not have much energy to do things, and I am a bit more disorientated. How can we support our systems to be stable and to create our own energy field as being part of the Earth?

The first thing you need to understand in looking at the Kp Index is that you are not in control of the Cosmic Rays that are arriving. What is in your control is writing to your governments across the world to tell them to stop 5G and the geochemical engineering that is weakening your magnetosphere at a time of Solar Minimum, causing a greater impact on you from the Cosmic Rays. When the Cosmic Rays are naturally coming in more heavily, geoengineering inhibits Earth's magnetosphere from protecting you from excess cosmic radiation. Other than making political statements, you can recognize and accept that when the Kp Index is down, you are not going to have a normal range of energy; you are not going to feel inspired; you may have trouble thinking or even be confused and cloudy. Give your body time to adapt to the new energies. Stop doing and just be. Take this time to understand that you are altering and becoming a *being* rather than a *doing*. Schedule your work with as much flexibility as you can, working on days when you feel the energy is present and resting on days when the energy is not present. That may be difficult for those who have regular jobs, but try to arrange such a schedule with your employer to allow you to work more on days when your energy is high and less on your days when your energy is lower. Your bodies are going through temporary adjustments, so preserve your energy during the transformation by being prudent with it in each moment.

For digestive distress try a bit of aloe vera every day to keep your stomach calm and coated with a healing substance. Also, be sure to drink four ounces of water once an hour to prevent dehydration in these more intense energies. Avoid external light for a period of time if your eyes are causing you challenges. If you are having vertigo or difficulty hearing (or hearing too much Earth noise), remember to tune out extraneous noise in your environment and spend extra time in Nature, in meditation, and listening to your hearts.

If you are not sleeping, which is a pattern for so many of you lately, recognize that this too is changing because you are recharging your body in a different way. Meditate or send out light. You can recharge your body with higher vibrational thoughts, rather than regenerating in an unconscious state of sleep. This is important! For all the other issues that may come up when the Kp Index is low, look at them as simply experiences. All of these things are changing for your evolution and for your highest good. So, trust the healing process. Give your bodies time to adapt to the new Cosmic Weather and the increase in light. Trust that you have the power to heal within you. Trust that everything is for the highest good and that you can ask for outside help from Pleiadian star dust and from one another at any time you need a little extra support. It's a challenging time, but you are up to it because it is precisely why you came to Earth. You came to transcend all the challenges and to simply send light, no matter what is going on in you or around you. Just be the love that you are and that will help you heal and adjust.

You have mentioned previously that you perceive a possibility for a Grand Solar Minimum on Earth. Do you still see that as a realistic possibility?

Yes, we very much do. The Sun goes through regular cycles of activity that include Solar Maximums and Solar Minimums. However, humans are exacerbating the intensity of the effects of a Grand Solar minimum because of the geochemical engineering by those who think they know what is best for Mother Earth; that is going to cause some adverse reactions that your scientists do not expect. This question is not just about the Solar Minimum that the Earth is most naturally experiencing; it is also about what your scientists and those who wish to control Nature are trying to do with limited understanding of their actions. There have been decisions made to spray particulates commonly used to make pesticides as well as other toxic metals into the air to cause clouds to block the amount of solar warmth that can come through to the planet, disregarding the natural cycles of the sun and the present Solar Minimum. No one is even thinking about what these particulates do when they're landing in your atmosphere, poisoning the plants, poisoning the water, and poisoning life on Earth. They are seeing only half of the equation when they make their choices. So, there will be some uncomfortable repercussions if they persist with geochemical engineering under the misguided and alleged attempt to prevent Global Warming. The Solar Minimum is definitely both increasing and lasting longer, and the interference from ignorant governmental decision making is increasing the likelihood that the current Solar Minimum may, indeed, reach proportions on a scale with a Grand Solar Minimum. Your planet has experienced its worst winters in some places and unprecedented warm winters in others because of higher volatility as the solar cycle changes. We are noticing that the cold every year is moving farther and farther south from where it used to be, and that those

214

of you who are experiencing warmth are experiencing ‹
heat in the summers, as this change in weather patter﹈
As cycles change, volatility is increased. People tend to confuse
short bursts of extreme weather with a long-time trend. However,
we do see an increasing trend toward a grand Solar Minimum
as a definite possibility, enhanced by unnecessary attempts to
prevent an imagined Global Warming event.

*It is particularly helpful for me to understand that while the radiation
from Cosmic Rays is increasing all around us, it actually doesn't have to
be harmful, and it actually can help us become more crystalline. I think
that is really wonderful. It helps us not to worry or feel uncomfortable
and to just accept the energetic changes.*

Well, worrying about something never helps. Let us be clear.
When we say, "Use the energy coming in from the Cosmic Rays
because of the Solar Minimum," we are not referring to the same
thing as the irradiation that is occurring because of 5G technology. We are not saying, "Oh, just turn the 5G into something
positive, it's going to bring us more light." Let us be *very clear*
about that. 5G causes real physiological and mental damage.
So, you need to remain aware, and you need to send light to all
those who are trying to implement that particular technology
as it is capable of eradicating all life on Earth, and you need to
physically do whatever you can to stop it! But, in terms of the
Cosmic Rays that are occurring because of the Solar Minimum,
you can consider the increased radiation as a positive thing to
support your growth. Fear and worry will not help, but you do
need to know the difference, and you do need to pay attention.
You cannot just believe that you can send light and convert the
energy of 5G into something beneficial. That kind of thinking
by itself will not change physical reality. But by doing your part
to mail letters, sign petitions, joining groups who are against
5G, and telling your government officials that you object, can

change the reality of further developments of these dangerous technologies; sending light and positive thoughts is a powerful exercise, but is not meant to stand alone. You must take physical action as well. Use the power of your third-dimensional voice to protest the presence of 5G satellites, and make choices not to use any technology that is based on or connected to 5G.

Can you say more about how we can tell the differences between the normal solar and the cosmic energies that come in and the additional radiation we receive from 5G, wireless, or smart phones? Are there any more ways that we can distinguish between these impacts on humanity?

When you feel the effects of Cosmic Rays or the higher Schumann Resonance, you may have disorientation, you may feel hot, you may have different physiological symptoms that come and go in waves. The physical body does not know what to do with the extra light and higher frequencies that you are receiving, so you may also experience muscle contractions, bone aches, shivering, nausea, headaches, and all manner of things as your physical body tries to adjust. You will experience many of the exact same symptoms from 5G pollution. The difference is that 5G and EMF symptoms don't come and go. They stay and build on each other until you become critically ill; you don't adjust. One way to distinguish the effect between the two is to measure if you are feeling symptoms specifically when the Kp Index is low (0 or 1) or the Schumann Resonance is high. Another way to distinguish is if you are feeling increasingly ill regard-less of the Cosmic Weather. Investigate if 5G is around you or near you. The intentional human placement of 5G all over your planet in conjunction with these cosmic effects makes it diffi-cult to determine if you are feeling EMF sickness, which lowers your immune system, causing many of you to become ill in one way or another, or if you are feeling symptoms as your bodies adjust to the higher frequencies of new Cosmic Weather. If the symptoms are continuous, you are experiencing EMF poisoning. Symptoms such as migraine headaches, heart irregularities, stomach distress, or any number of other symptoms that make you feel ill, may be the effect of more irradiation from Cosmic Rays while you are simultaneously bombarded with 5G irradiation. The more 5G equipment that is placed in space and the more antennae around your homes and businesses, the more everyone will become weaker and sicken. There is a distinct difference even though the symptoms are similar. Be aware of everything in your environment. Your bodies need a chance to adapt naturally to the changing Cosmic Weather, and that is impossible when you are simultaneously affected by intentional and continual 5G assaults. You will adjust naturally, if you are able to completely eliminate the 5G poisoning.

I've noticed over the years that the clouds have changed; they appear wispier. I am curious about "cloud bursts" where the clouds appear to be flowing away from a central point. Is this happening because of higher energies coming in or is it from man-made technological intervention?

Most of what you describe is from the geochemical engineering that is interfering with your planet's natural cloud structures and patterns. You can also see more lightning, which impacts the cloud formations, and therefore you will certainly notice a difference in the clouds. You are witnessing how much things are out of balance when you see these changes in your clouds. Chemtrails are quite prevalent now, particularly over cities. The wispiness you see is the residual energy left after a particular cloud has been manipulated. It then migrates to a less populated area of the sky.

Apparently, telecoms have been collecting subsidies to pay for fiber optics and giving us 5G instead. Is there a way to expose such abuse and a potential to bankrupt big telecom's 5G agenda because of their misappropriation of funds? Is this a potential pathway to end 5G?

articipation of the collective in exposing such abuse ... refusing to participate with 5G technologies creates a very, very big possibility of ending it. Because humanity all over the world has begun to speak up, there is more possibility to use your mass voice to make a difference. Each of you can do something to make a difference. At the time of writing this book, a 50% chance existed to reject 5G and overcome its deleterious effects. However, on the other side, those who are in the process of launching more satellites to promote 5G are doing so quickly before they are closed down by your voices. So, you're already being impacted and harmed by 5G, and you have seen the effects of this as it has lowered your immune systems and made you more susceptible to various imbalances, including particular symptoms that appear to mimic viruses.

Those who are fighting for 5G are determined to complete their agenda to end life on this planet and to install Artificial Intelligence (AI). They feel themselves protected because they separate themselves and feel themselves not a part of humanity, which is absolutely ridiculous and is not true. However, they still fight for this misunderstood and inappropriate goal. It would be best if you continue to do whatever you can collectively, all of you, to stop 5G by standing up and saying, "No, we will not allow this." 5G is the biggest threat to life you have ever experienced on this planet. When you step out and start using your voice to say, "No!" you are also awakening your power of choice. You are awaking that divine spark of light and the power within you that has a 50% impact on what happens in your world. You are awakening to the power of who you are and remembering that you can co-create the next Now moment. This is a test, or a battle, that has two purposes—to stop the annihilation of life on Earth and to promote your own powerful evolution as a species.

What is your perspective on what humans have diagnosed as ADHD. What is it, and what do you think causes it?

Attention Deficit Hyperactivity Disorder, or ADHD, is seen mostly in children, although it is even occurring in adults recently as well. This condition results from an EMF overload on your human neurological systems. As we have discussed earlier, there is far too much EMF activity, radio waves, TV signaling, and all kinds of signaling waves in your atmosphere for the human body to handle. Additionally, humans are becoming more and more detached from Nature, which worsens the effects of too many EMF waves in your bodies, causing hyperactivity of your neurological systems, which then causes an inability to pay attention for an extended period of time or to be able to absorb all the data and information that is projected towards you. A human cannot stay still, pay attention, or absorb mental ideas when the system is already trying to deal with an overload of electromagnetic information. Many, many children and some adults are suffering from this syndrome because you are simply overloaded with EMF or other electrical waves in your atmosphere.

We do not necessarily see this condition in the same way your medical or educational communities do, however. We certainly don't feel that it should be treated with drugs. Drugging children rather than immersing them in the balancing effects of Nature only complicates the problem. Many adults choose to give drugs to a hyperactive child to calm him or her down, but those drugs also diminish the child's creative abilities. A better solution is to take the child into Nature, where the physical system can discharge some of the overstimulation. Nature makes the needed adjustments. Children and adults today experience a constant streaming of data, overloading your neurons. It's a wonder that all of you are not experiencing this hyperactive syndrome, especially since so many people are out of balance with Nature. Under the influence of artificial lighting, both adults and children stay awake at night past the natural time they should go to sleep, which does not allow the body proper rest and regeneration. When humans get up tired in the morning from lack of proper rest, adults drug themselves with caffeine, and children are often given cereal with food coloring and sugar, an even worse drug. Drugging yourselves in this manner and going against the rhythms of Nature puts each of you at risk for ADHD.

If we live in cold climate, especially during wintertime how do we spend adequate time in Nature?

Bundle up and go outside for short periods, not for very long, but frequently. You can bring Nature inside your home also if it's too cold for you to go outside. Create a nature-based place within your home, where there are lots of plants and where you do not allow any Wi-Fi or cellphone use at all. Create a place in the home that is full of living plants and beauty, Nature.

Is it possible to set the intention that the 5G is surrounded with white light and actually deactivate the 5G components around the world? Is this possible?

Well, anything is possible. But we have to tell you that there are more energies who are sending intentions for 5G to rule the world and replace human consciousness with 5G than there are people who are awake, aware, and are *accomplished* at using intentions to change what is happening. The plan of those who seek to control humanity is to replace you with an artificial robotic type consciousness. 5G is not about cellphone usage. It is about controlling humanity through the Internet of Things, which is part of the hidden agenda of promoting Artificial Intelligence (AI). The Internet of Things can communicate back and forth without human interaction at all. So, there is already a battle of non-consciousness that's working to eliminate consciousness through 5G technology.

While it is *possible* to be able to disassemble 5G, it wi more than simply sending it light. It will necessitate taking physical actions of participating to make political changes by saying, "We will not allow this." Once the satellites are in place around the planet, those high intensity beams of energy will affect your cognition, your emotions, and your physical cells. You will not be able to focus on sending light (or on anything else) under the influence of 5G. You will be irradiated and experience cell death. Whatever is the weakest point in your body, the cell death will begin to occur there. Your bodies are already challenged by the need to adjust to the intense light coming in from Cosmic Weather. Human placed 5G satellites will *completely* overwhelm you with high EMFs, causing you to become ill and die. This situation requires more than just "sending white light." You have to be aware that you are facing a very real third-dimensional enemy and you have to employ both third-dimensional tactics of writing letters of strong protests, making telephone calls, and showing up in specific places to protest what is being done. Take back your governments, *and* use the multidimensional way of sending love and light, saying, "We refuse this technology." Do not try to change it by simply sending light; you need to be clear in voicing that you will not accept it. Tell your presidents and prime ministers, your parliaments and congresses, your state leaders, your city leaders, your kings and queens, your cell phone companies, and at your employers that support 5G. All across the planet, you need to stand up and say, "We do not want this technology, we will not stand for it." AND THEN STOP BUYING OR USING IT.

While your conscious intention can help to change the situation, doing that alone will not be enough. Do what it is necessary to reject the current environment of too many EMF waves. The first step, of course, is to severely limit your use of cellphones and Internet technology yourself. If you are not using the things that they wish to use to control you, they can't control you as easily. The more you detach from this manner of communication, the more the message gets out there that their attempts to disempower you are not going to work. Absolutely continue to use the multidimensional approach of sending light to surround the 5G technology wherever the satellites are. But do not rely upon this alone. You are in a great battle against those humans who wish to control this planet. They intend to eliminate your species by sending you 5G energy that is harmful to all life and replacing your ability to work as their slaves with robotics. When you speak out, you will find yourselves in opposition to the leaders of your governments. Ask yourselves, "Is it worth being in conflict with the beliefs of my employer and risking my job to save my life? Is it worth a step of this magnitude to save all life on this planet?" If you don't start taking strong steps to stop 5G, then you will be acquiescing to what's happening by *choosing to do nothing*. You will be putting yourselves in the position of thinking that you cannot do anything about it. Just think, if enough people had the courage to say, "No, I won't participate in this" and walked out of their jobs, think of the magnitude of change that would happen just from everyone banding together. Ask yourselves if your lives or your children's live are worth fighting for? Do you really want a job at any cost—even if the job is killing you, your children, all your pets, all the trees, and all the bees or birds in the air? Will you continue working in these jobs even if you know this to be true? Will you continue working in such circumstances and just allow life to be extinguished? Ask yourself if you are willing to give up devices that you perceive make your life easier, or would you rather die than give them up? It is a very simple question and decision to make. Those are the questions your heart must ask. Our purpose is to inspire you to recognize the strength you have within. You do not have to continue being victims of a cycle that seems bigger than you are. It is not. It seems that way, but that's only your perception. As you join together, as you band together and make different choices, you create a different future, but you have to take the actions individually and collectively. Thank you for your question. It was vital.

Thank you, Laarkmaa. That answer resonated through my body. As you were speaking, I was overcome with this sense that we literally have to do this to save our planet and our life.

You have encouraged us to connect with Nature. Often in our environment there are cell towers almost everywhere. What are the implications of the presence of these towers when we try to connect with Nature?

We have a lot to say about that. The placement of many, many cell towers is an intentional dumbing down of humanity. It's a process intended to addict humans to cellphones that are held at their heads, causing irradiating damage to their pineal glands and other portions of their brains. It is an intentional ploy to detach you from Nature so that you do not recognize the power you have within you. If we could wave a magic wand across humanity, we would eliminate *all* cell towers and anything connected to this EMF frequency and tell you, "Humans, you need to get back to Nature. You need to understand your relationship with Nature. You need to listen to your hearts and how they are connected to the Cosmos." Choosing to live in a city because of a job is not a heart-based choice; it is a choice usually based on tradition or circumstances in which you have allowed someone else to tell you what to do or based on a history of what you have believed to be best. We would suggest that everyone who is capable, find a way to move out of a city, do not live in a city in these times. The changes will be too great, and you will find yourselves crushed more and more by the magnitude of cell towers and the implementation of 5G all around in the cities, which are the first places that they will impact. They will use cities first to reach the maximum number of people, and the more they dumb down people—and we understand that we are using a very colloquial term—the more they interfere with the human intelligence that arises from the consciousness within your *hearts* and your conscious connections to yourselves as Universal citizens. They disengage your awareness and ability to know who you are; then they win in the process of making you slaves, so that you do whatever they say, or you die.

It's very simple. We do not support city life. We understand this to be a powerful statement, but you did ask, and we are sharing it because we know all of you want to know. Now each of you living in a city may stop and consider—is this your best choice? Ask yourself, "What is my reason for being here? If I truly cannot leave the city, how can I include more Nature in my life?" Perhaps inviting Nature into your home can help combat the negative energies of the cities. Use everything you can. Use the power within you to find ways to move to where your heart tells you to be.

Magnificent changes are coming to the planet. You are a part of these changes, and to fully participate, you must use your hearts' guidance to tell you where you need to be and how you can serve and participate with the changes that are happening. It's a time of great opportunity, but the opportunity will pass if you don't use your power and your choice to do something different. The salvation of your species is in making different and better choices. Thank you for your question. We are trying to help humanity step up and recognize who you are. You are expanded consciousness. You exist everywhere. You are not confined to this planet. However, if you don't take care of the environment where you are in third-dimensional consciousness, your choices will ripple out and affect your entire experience of consciousness, either shutting down your awareness completely or detaching you from it so you cannot contact your hearts' wisdom.

Are there a lot of things going on now that we do not know about?
We have been telling you about what is happening both in your atmosphere and in your magnetosphere. Some of your scientists are beginning to share that information with humanity. But your governments do not want you to know the whole truth, and some scientists report things that are in alignment with your governments' agendas rather than the truth. Learn to discern the difference between false "facts" and the real truth. Pay attention to what is happening. This is your world. Look at what's happening all around you—truly open your eyes! Do what you can to stop the geochemical engineering. Absolutely stand up against 5G, which is poisoning you. Do what you can to adjust to the changing Schumann Resonance, as you match your vibration to the higher frequencies. All of these things are impacting you.

There is much fake news and manipulation in your world at this time. There are those who are putting 5G satellites into space and installing cell towers in your cities and towns and doing other things in space and on Earth, and they wish you to believe certain things about what's going on that may or may not be fully disclosed as the truth. Your lockdown was more about keeping you ignorant than keeping you safe. So, we would suggest that when you watch or read information you receive, determine who is producing it; what is the source? Where is the information coming from? What money supports providing this information, and what agenda is behind it? Then ask if the information resonates with the truth in your heart, or does it sound like propaganda from someone trying to convince you of something. You have been conditioned to believe that your governments care for you. *They do not.* Take care of yourselves by paying attention, taking responsibility, and standing up for the truth. Use your hearts and your voices.

All the work that you all have done to stop 5G has made a difference, but not enough of a difference. Those who seek to control you will continue to try. You must continue to stand up and take back your power. And remember that transference of energies matters. When you are worried or afraid, those negative thoughts and emotions are transmitted as lower vibrational energy. When you are trusting, powerful, grateful, and living in grace, you are transmitting higher vibrational energy. When you work with your power by saying, "No, we will not accept 5G!" you are transmitting a very strong message, not out of fear but from your power. Know that as you listen to your hearts and use your power, you will recognize more and more just how you can make a difference. This is one reason we've told you for so long to monitor your thoughts and your feelings, and choose higher vibrational ones because it matters. It changes things.

That certainly helps, thank you very much. We know that there is light at the end of the tunnel.

Yes, there is definitely light at the end of the tunnel. There is light even *in* the tunnel. You are the light, each one of you. Remember that you are the light.

My particular symptoms have been showing up in my digestion; I'd like to understand the effects of the Cosmic Weather on our digestion more deeply.

All of you who are sensitive will have varying periods of time when you have conflicting symptoms of nausea, hunger, and of not being interested in food at all. Your bodies are adjusting to the idea that they can be nourished by light instead of being nourished by food, so your bodies do not know whether they are hungry or whether they are nauseated when the waves of energy arrive or change. They are simply adjusting. In terms of food, the lighter your diet, the better it is. Of course, we have always said not to eat food that carries the energy of death from animals that have been killed. That type of diet is not aligned with the highest good for all, and therefore, it is not of an appropriate vibration for the ascension process of entering into a Rainbow body. We assume most of you know that by now, for we have said it for so long. Also, as you know, we have suggested that you eliminate all sugar because sugar cuts holes in your light body and disconnects you from your higher powers. We have told you that alcohol and caffeine are destabilizers that keep you from being in rhythm with Earth and promoting unnatural rhythms of waking and sleeping. These are the most important things for you to avoid. Additionally, in terms of moving toward ascension and a Rainbow body, it would be better at this stage to begin to eliminate grains and begin to live on vegetables, fruit, and a limited amount of protein, whether that protein is hempseed or some kind of soaked beans. If you eat beans, we suggest that you soak them overnight, drain the water off, rinse them again several times, and then cook them to make sure that all lectins, which are difficult to digest, are removed. This is the diet that you are moving towards. Begin to incorporate more raw food, particularly in warmer weather. Plan for more salads and fruits with the appropriate amount of protein, as you need it. Our Diet for Ascension provides guidelines to help you[7].

The most important thing for your diet now during the infusion of light you are receiving is to be sure that you are taking in enough pure water. We suggest you drink four ounces of water every hour from the time you wake up until about five or six in the evening. You need to be more hydrated now than ever before because your bodies are receiving all this extra light; therefore, hydration is extremely important. You are electromagnetic beings; you need water to be part of the electrical (light) portion of your makeup, as you move toward living on love, light, and water.

I am so grateful for your support because your advice always comes just when we need it. Thank you. Last night I felt very strong symptoms and I started to be concerned—maybe even alarmed. Then I realized that these are ascension symptoms; that's all they are; it's nothing serious. I started to breathe deeply and to be grateful. I calmed down and relaxed. I really felt a lot better, and I actually had a good sleep. So, I followed your advice, and it really helped. I am very grateful.

Thank you, Dear One. We appreciate that very much.

Thank you very much for your messages. A couple of days ago I experienced extremes of Gamma rays as I was lying in the bed closing my eyes. I was completely one with the Universe. I was merging with the stars; I was part of waterfalls. It was so incredible for about half an hour of experiencing bliss and a state of being one with everything. The following days when I had more ascension symptoms, I was able to handle them much better, and now you have explained that they will come more often, I'm very glad. Thank you for lifting me up in this way.

Thank you for sharing your experience. We anticipate we'll be hearing many more stories like this. So, thank you for sharing your experience.

I want to thank you all so much. I have been practicing sending love and light, and it has helped so much. I am very grateful.

You are very welcome.

Hi, Laarkmaa. Even though you say you do not make predictions, everything you have said previously is happening now. We really appreciate that difference in perspective as we shift into a different vibration. There are times when it is even hard to breathe, and we have your objective reminder that this was something that was always coming, and we knew it was coming. Here we are, and it is happening, and we are breathing through it. As a group who has been listening to you for some time, we are very calm and serene, and we are breathing through it and enjoying the ride, so to speak. Thank you for your perspective and your help to get through these very interesting times.

Thank you for your respect and appreciation. The reason we do not make predictions is because you do have the power of human choice. If we were to make predictions, it would indicate that we do not honor your power of choice. So therefore, we simply share our larger perspective so that you can remember, and through that remembering, hopefully you will make higher vibratory choices to align with the possibilities that are ever present. Together we can step into each moment in a way that respects the highest good for all. Remember, we are you, just as you are we. We are your spiritual brothers and sisters, just as you are our spiritual sisters and brothers.

STEP TEN:
MANIFESTATION!

W e, Laarkmaa, your Pleiadian star sisters and brothers are
continually evaluating how humanity is resolving your
evolutionary challenges. There is no judgment in this type of
evaluation; we simply look for the places where you are stuck
and may need assistance, and we provide another perspective so
that you can move forward with more ease. We do this because
we love you.

About fifteen years ago while living high in the mountains of
Colorado, Pia and Cullen were experiencing a snowstorm. The
world was very quiet and blanketed with snow. We told Pia and
Cullen that what the world needed was a two-week snowstorm
where everything would be quiet. People could go inside to do
their inner work and spend time with those they loved and their
family in order to recognize the true reality and what is really
important in this world. We have now seen something very
similar affect humanity—lockdown caused by governmental
controls surrounding the coronavirus—and it lasted longer than
our suggested two week snow storm. Although this outside force
may have frustrated you because you could not go where you
wanted to go or do what you wanted to do, those of you who are
reading this book took the time as an opportunity to be more
quiet, spend time with your families, share the exposing of lies
you have been told, speak up for the truth, and do spiritual work.
It was an opportunity to slow your lives down and experience

_g from a different place, a place of appreciation. This quiet time changed you for the better forever. Because of this change, you are open to a deeper understanding of the concepts we have been sharing with you for many years. Now rather than understanding them at a mental level, you are beginning to live these concepts.

We have based this manual on the principals that are contained in Universal energies, as defined in our earlier book *Pleiadian-Earth Energy Astrology— Charting the Spirals of Consciousness*[1]. We began with the first Universal energy of Initiating and have led you step by step, to the tenth energy of Manifestation because we wish for you to accelerate the manifestation of your own ascension! There are thirteen Universal energies in the Cosmos that build upon each other as they spiral to completion. We have based the steps in this Manual on the first ten of those thirteen energies. You will *fully* experience the 11th (Illuminating), the 12th (Understanding), and the 13th (Completing and Integrating) when you manifest your ascension and become Cosmic citizens, although those energies are very present in the evolutionary and ascension process you are experiencing now. Below, we summarize the steps we have taken you through for your review and integration.

We began with the First Step (Initiation) discussing the importance of Unity Consciousness. We introduced the idea of living your lives through recognizing energy—rather than time— by using flexibility and flow. We set the tone for you to aim for abundance for all and true freedom.

The Second Step (Duality) was presented in a way to help you move beyond your limited perspectives of Duality, which are ruled by separation, fear, and judgment. You came to Earth to experience duality and its opposites in order to learn how to harmonize them. That is the purpose of duality. Humanity has done a terrible job with that, but now that you more fully understand, you can use the dynamic tension of duality to grow and find harmony with one another. We also gave you ways to achieve non-judgment by clearing old traumas and learning to be objective. With this increased understanding, you can finally engage with duality as it has always been designed and intended.

The Third Step (Creativity) took you into a deeper understanding of what you must create to heal, using the power of positive thoughts to raise your vibration and filling your hearts with more joy. We also discussed the ascension process, your liquid crystalline bodies, and the formation of your Rainbow bodies.

In Step Four (Foundation) we told you about the changing structures of your reality and discussed some of the physical changes you are undergoing. We also talked about time, space, and energy as they relate to these changes.

The Fifth Step (Change) offered the chance to discover more about your consciousness and how to make appropriate changes to grow and evolve. We reminded you that consciousness is in *everything* and suggested ways to pay attention to the varying forms of consciousness.

The Sixth Step (Flow) encouraged you to realign with the Divine Feminine within you, talked about androgyny, and gave you suggestions for returning to balance. In a more balanced state, the Divine Masculine can take its place beside the Divine Feminine.

In the Seventh Step (Merging) we prepared you for a different world by explaining the ongoing changes in your third-dimensional reality and offering suggestions about how to prepare yourselves for the world you will be entering. We asked you to step beyond what is familiar to you and understand that *different* does not mean *bad.*

In the Eighth Step (Connecting), we talked about becoming Authentic Humans, as you move into becoming your true selves. We explained that the purpose of your families is to serve as a spiritual training ground. We expanded on the symptoms and process of ascension and talked about your Future Selves. We gave you a definition of what love really is, and we told you how to send light into the dark to lessen its influence.

In the Ninth Step (Harmonizing) we warned you about the extremely negative physical and mental effects of 5G and gave you ways to work with the effects of Cosmic Weather. We explained the effects of light on the evolving mental, physical, emotional, and spiritual aspects of yourselves, and we told you how to work with the light provided by the incoming Cosmic Rays and the energy of the increasing Schumann Resonance to move yourselves to higher vibratory states.

And now in the Tenth Step (Manifestation) we will summarize the most important things you will need to do to actually manifest a higher vibratory version of yourselves!

You have known for a long time that staying in the present with your consciousness is most important and that thinking about, planning for, worrying about, or hoping for the future does not create that future. It just wastes your mental energy thinking about something that may or may not occur. Thinking about, worrying about, or dreaming about the past is equally unhelpful. It keeps you in a mental state in which the future you seek or the past you experienced just does not exist. It's only a mental exercise. In the true reality, there is only the Now moment. The reason this is so important now is because you are moving into an enhanced experience of Liquid Time. You may notice that many of you are feeling really, really heavy, really, really slow, and very, very tired without any energy, as if you are struggling just to be. This has to do with the heightened Schumann Resonance. And as the Schumann Resonance heightens, you are experiencing more of what we call Liquid Time. That is a continual flow of Now moments—one Now moment building upon next Now moment but not planning for a future or looking backwards into the past.

One reason that we created the *Pleiadian-Earth Energy Calendar*[2] was to help you to learn how to let go of linear time and how to experience the Now moment as Liquid Time to accustom you to moving from one energetic moment into the next with flow and grace.

Living in this way creates the future by being present in the Now. You have been taught to live your lives in a fantasy called time, which has caused you to be stuck with an artificial frame of reference, creating the illusion that you can actually plan for a time that does not yet exist—the future. It is really, really important now with the increased Schumann Resonance that you focus your awareness on energy rather than time. Now you may find it a bit ironic that we are telling you to focus on energy when so many of you are reporting that you feel like you have no energy. We want you to understand that the Schumann Resonance amplifies gravity, affecting the density of your bodies, and as the Schumann Resonance increases, you are feeling more of a gravitational pull, which causes you to feel more and more tired. It's the opposite of what you would experience if you were free-floating in space without gravity. There you would feel light and you could float wherever you wanted. Here, on this planet your physical body is experiencing increased density. Simultaneously, the light is pouring in to change you at the cellular level, cell-by-cell, from the dense carbon-based form into the liquid crystalline form of the New Human. We have always told you and we emphasize the importance of understanding that you are waveforms. You are not static particles that stay in one particular shape or formation forever. You change, albeit it has been a very, very slow process in the third-dimensional paradigm. Now you are beginning to expand into multidimensionality, and you are experiencing yourselves changing more and more rapidly. This is why we are emphasizing in this summary the importance of Liquid Time—the Now moment. You must work with the energies that are present in each Now moment in order to manifest all the beautiful and essential experiences we are explaining to you.

You are experiencing more mental, physical, and emotional changes at a faster rate than you ever have before. When the Schumann Resonance goes up over 40, over 60, and into the range of a hundred, you experience such a high vibration that you change at a cellular level in every moment, in each instant. Your energy is changing. The essence of who you are is changing. You are forgetting things because your mind is not working in the frequency to which you are accustomed. Your minds are learning to take orders from your hearts using intuitive, energetic knowing. You cannot fully access your energetic knowing without being fully in the Now moment, without practicing being in Liquid Time and learning to flow from one energetic point to another.

It is more important than ever that you not to feel as though you are not accomplishing anything when you are simply too tired to do anything physical. Remember, remember, remember that your only job at this time is just to be love and send out light, be love and send out light in each Now moment. That's all that's important. Focus your attention on being in the Now moment with trust that if you do everything in a higher vibrational rate in each Now moment, you will be led and guided by the light energies that are here on the planet to show you how to achieve what is necessary for your survival and your evolution. Those energies, light and love, are eternal. They exist forever. They cannot be confined to a past or a future. They cannot be confined to any structure of time. They can only be experienced as abundance and expansion into an ever-growing awareness of more and more light and love. Focusing your energy on this Now moment allows you to move with the flow of abundance towards the freedom that comes from not being confined by the physicality that has been your structured and controlled learning experiences here on this Earth.

You are moving closer and closer toward Rainbow body form. You are moving closer and closer into acknowledging, relating to, and connecting with your light body so that you can meld your light body with your physical form and have a clearer blueprint to create the crystalline form that will support your transformation into Rainbow body. This is a very, very auspicious time, Dear Ones. Liquid Time expresses wave motion. The Now moment means letting go of the past and the future and putting all of your power into being the absolute best you can be; it also means making the absolute highest choices you can make in each Now moment. This means that if you have a bad day, something happens to you that you don't like, you hurt yourself, you don't feel well, or you are experiencing physical or mental discomfort from Cosmic Weather, just acknowledge the experience without going off track by complaining, questioning, or thinking, "This is awful, I don't like it, when is this going to stop, when is it going back to normal?" The answer to those questions, Dear One, is that it is *never* going back to you prior perception of normal; you are moving upward into a new normal. As you start to accommodate and adjust to being in this reality, in multidimensionality, you become more at ease and more comfortable with the idea that you are transitioning into a waveform and leaving the familiar, static, physical body with which you are familiar behind.

Now is your moment. This is the opportunity you have been waiting for to fulfill your mission. Use the light that is radiating your cells as it comes in. Use it to be positive, knowing and trusting that you are going through a positive transformation. You are becoming more crystalline, which means light-bearing. That's what a liquid crystalline body is! It is a light-bearing body. Liquid means honoring the water that you are by becoming so flexible and fluid, mentally and physically, that you are more focused on your increasing waveform state than you are on your old solid physical structure. We have told you that there would come a time when you are able to nurture yourselves on love, light, and water. You will be doing this more and more as the veil of separation closes and falls away through your awakening awareness and the wisdom of your hearts. You will nurture one another with the love you offer unconditionally in unity, in the spirit of *In Lak'ech* (I am another yourself).

Soon you will look at yourself in the mirror and see a change. You will be looking down at your hands and see a change. Your touch will feel a little lighter. Your voice will be a little less vibrant, and yet at times it will carry forth like a crystal bell because you are incorporating the use of tones rather than the sound of words. It is our hope for you that you not be distressed by what you are feeling physically, mentally, or emotionally. Acknowledge the difficulties, acknowledge the challenges, and then congratulate yourselves, because if you are sensitive enough to feel these things, then you are doing something right. It takes slowing down from your habitual fast pace to be able to be in harmonic rhythm with what is occurring on the planet.

The energy that you give to the moment defines who you are, by the ways you focus your thoughts, use your voices, give gratitude, open to your intuition, listen to your hearts, allow all possibilities, and harmonize with one another. This is the

Now moment for which you have been waiting! The increased Schumann Resonance is nothing but good. It is only higher and higher frequencies pouring into you to change you at a cellular level so that your consciousness can expand and you can move into your true waveform. It is a wonderful, wonderful thing, and very soon we'll be congratulating you on having achieved your mission and moving on to the next assignment. Practice slowing down and being in this Now moment. Know that we are with you, as are all other beings of love and light. We are all with you, around you, supporting you and loving you through this transition that humanity has never seen before. You are about to become your Future Selves!

AFTERWORD

A fter reading this book you now have the potential to make a difference in people's lives and change the society in which we live. We have been living in an illusion of pain and suffering, and we have perpetuated that separation and suffering because we have received bad training from all aspects of society: governments, religions, and educational institutions that have promoted the status quo through outdated beliefs and paradigms, rather than supporting a conscious evolution for humanity, based on cooperation and love.

By following the step-by-step guidance within this text, we can move beyond our previous bad training individually, as well as collectively, and make enormous leaps in how we treat each other and our planet. As we begin to see how every thought, every word, and every action affects us all, we can consciously choose to alter the ways in which we think about everything in our lives. We can choose to remain in negative, disempowered, fearful states, contributing even more discord and separation, or we can choose to operate from higher vibrational frequencies to create a more unified and harmonious environment for all. Laarkmaa has shown us how we *can* make a difference in the small ways we choose to think and act, and in even larger ways when we join our positive thoughts, intentions, and actions together. Simple changes in our thought patterns can and do ripple out, positively changing the atmosphere all around us and even reaching further out to affect the entire planet.

This book provides the information that we have been looking for to support our becoming the Authentic Humans we truly are!

I began using the term *my Future Self* as a very young man in search of my highest potential. Now Laarkmaa has lovingly and graciously given humanity the wisdom and guidance to move forward in our ever-spiraling journey to realize the full possibilities that we have to create and embody our Future Selves. All we must do to achieve this advanced state of being is to employ the two simple guidelines of *Ahimsa* and *In Lak'ech*. Then we will truly enter into living our birthright as beings of love and light.

With love and light,
Cullen

APPENDIX A:
THE ASCENSION DIET

We are giving you the Ascension Diet to raise your frequency levels through making higher vibratory choices of how to nourish yourselves. On Earth, there are two ways you can ascend. One is through the traditional method of physical death. The other is through making your physical bodies light enough to match your etheric bodies, so that they may join together to create a Rainbow body. This Rainbow body is less dense and requires a less dense and more conscious way of eating. Eventually, you will be able to nourish yourselves on only the energies of love, light, and water.

We will share the Ascension Diet in steps, so that you may adjust to a new diet. As you move through the steps, improving your diet, you elevate your frequency more and more through your dietary choices, which then is reflected in your other choices. The Ascension Diet is based upon living foods.

STEP ONE is to nourish yourselves through a Plant Based diet. This step moves humanity away from the competitive and aggressive energy that is encouraged by the killing and eating of animals. When you eat an animal that has been killed, you take in the energy of what the animal experiences, as well as the energy of death, which is not in alignment with the energy of ascension into Rainbow body. Evolving beings honor the principals of *Ahimsa*, (Do no harm), for they realize that all life is precious, and killing or taking any life is not a higher vibrational action. Taking this step to change your beliefs and actions about eating animals removes certain levels of separation and fear from your vibration because it eliminates the thought that you are higher or better than any other lifeform. It encourages you to remember that you are aligned with *all* life, as we discussed in our chapter on Unity Consciousness. Begin to see choices to eat or not eat animals through the eyes of *In Lak'ech,* "I am another yourself," and begin to incorporate a diet that is for the highest good of all. Therefore, the first step in The Ascension Diet is to eliminate all meat (including fish and fowl) from your diet. It is also the most important step in the Ascension Diet, because it raises your frequency enough to understand that all life is valuable and should be honored as equal. You will find many sources of protein, such as hemp seeds, legumes, beans, or nuts. Hemp seeds are an excellent choice because they are raw, and they contain all the amino acids you need, easily fulfilling your requirements for protein.

STEP TWO is to eliminate all sugar from your diet. We do not mean honey, maple syrup, fruit, or stevia. We mean cane sugar and high fructose corn syrup. We began telling humanity that sugar is not good for you long before your World Health Organization and National Institutes of Health told you that it is more addictive than cocaine or heroin. We told you more than fifteen years ago to stop eating sugar for several reasons. Sugar tears holes in your light body, and it disconnects you from your ability to listen to your higher self and your intuition. It also is, indeed, extremely addictive, and the addiction to sugar is one of the things that allows you to be controlled. When you stop eating sugar and disengage from the addictive nature of its call, you begin to hear your own intuitive wisdom more often and more clearly, which allows you to more fully awaken to who you really are. Eliminating sugar from your diet encourages you to make higher and better choices in all areas of your life.

STEP THREE is to eliminate alcohol and caffeine from your diet. These substances disconnect you from the natural rhythms of Earth. You are already imbalanced from staying awake past the hours of the setting sun and sleeping past the rising of the sun. You are disconnected from Nature because of your electric lights and your nighttime activities in work or play. Caffeine speeds you up, and alcohol slows you down. You artificially stimulate yourselves with caffeine to help you wake up when you have stayed up too late. And you use alcohol to help you slow down and relax after a stress-filled or exhausting day. We encourage you to eliminate these substances that prevent you from being in harmonic rhythm with your own planet and the entire Universe. It is, of course, your choice.

STEP FOUR is to eliminate all genetically modified material and processed foods from your diet. Choose organic foods that are natural and more full of life energy.

STEP FIVE is to move toward eating more greens and fruit and fewer grains, as you lighten your vibration.

STEP SIX is to incorporate more living, raw foods into your diet. This is something that you should do all along in this Ascension Diet. By Step Six, you should be naturally drawn to more raw foods, juices, and lighter substances.

STEP SEVEN is to drink increasing amounts of clean, pure water. Water is an essential element in your electromagnetic makeup; that's why it is so important to drink ample amounts of water each day. To help your body adjust to some of the higher frequency conditions and ascension symptoms, drinking four ounces of water every hour can be very helpful.

STEP EIGHT is living on love, light, and water. You are primarily made of water (from Earth) and light (from the stars.) You are also beings of love. By the time you reach this step, you will have changed your beliefs about what is required to nourish your bodies. Everything is energy. All matter, including you, is made of energy. Light is the most powerful nutritive energy in the Universe! Like living plants, you will learn to nourish yourselves from the light you receive, the water you drink, and the love you give and receive.

The Ascension Diet supports your moving into Rainbow body. Through higher and more conscious choices, you will eventually sustain yourselves on love, light, and water. The steps that we have provided above for this diet will help you to accelerate your evolutionary journey, feeling lighter and healthier as you evolve!

Pia and Cullen have used the recipes on the following pages on their own path from vegetarianism to veganism towards the goal of living on love, light, and water, as they move towards their Rainbow bodies. These sample recipes offer choices for delightful, healthy foods that promote healing the divisions humans have created between humanity and other kingdoms. When you eat for the highest good for all, not only will you begin to heal yourselves and your planet, you will also accelerate your evolution and your ascension process, which is the purpose of this book.

We love you. Good Always,
Laarkmaa

SAMPLE RECIPES[1]:
VEGETARIAN EATING FOR THE HIGHEST GOOD OF ALL

These are sample recipes to help you transition from a meat-based diet to a delicious and satisfying vegetarian diet, and then to a vegan diet. No animals are killed for these recipes, but the vegetarian recipes do incorporate the animal gifts of natural, organic cheese and eggs (from cage-free, hormone-free chickens). These recipes provide stepping stones from unhealthy diets to a living, plant-based, green diet that Laarkmaa suggests for our evolution. They are sugar-free, gluten-free, alcohol free, caffeine free, and organic. They are intended to introduce you to satisfying foods based on the principles of *Ahimsa* and encourage you to begin your journey to a lighter, greener diet. You will find more recipes on the Blog Page of our website: **laarkmaa.com**

Cullen's Vegetarian Nut Loaf

Cullen shares his recipe for the most protein packed food on Earth!

Three major sources of protein are combined in this delicious recipe suitable for holiday feasts or everyday meals. Be sure to make Cullen's Cashew Gravy (below) to accompany the Nut Loaf. This recipe makes 2 loaves—one for now and one to freeze for later.

3 ½ cups cooked brown rice
2 cup finely chopped walnuts
1 cup finely chopped sunflower seeds

1 ½ large onion, finely chopped
5 cups shredded cheddar cheese
8 eggs, lightly beaten
1 teaspoon sea salt

Preheat oven to 350 (175C). Combine all ingredients and pack into an oiled loaf pan. Be sure to mix with your hands or with a spoon to create an interesting texture. (Do not blend.) Bake for about 50 minutes until firm (sometimes slightly longer) and well browned on top. Let cool in pan for 10 minutes; remove from pan and slice.

Cullen's Cashew Gravy

1 cup finely ground cashews
2 Tbsp. arrowroot flour
¼ cup finely chopped onion
sea salt and pepper to taste
a pinch of thyme
2–3 Tbsp. of sunflower oil
1 ½–2 cups of water

Brown flour and cashews in dry skillet. Remove from skillet and set aside.

Add oil in skillet and heat. Add onion and cook just until golden. Add flour and cashews. Pour in cold water and stir, repeatedly, until the consistency is right. Add sea salt, pepper, and thyme. Cook slowly, patiently, and with love, constantly stirring and adding cold water for about 15-20 minutes. This recipe takes a lot of patience, but the end-product is certainly worth it!

Pia's Green Beans and Pesto

The basil in this recipe has many nutritive benefits. Basil is an excellent source of vitamin K, manganese, iron, vitamin A, and vitamin C. It's also a good source of calcium, magnesium, and omega-3 fatty acids. It is a natural antihistamine, and it benefits digestion, liver function, and even fights depression. Pine nuts are good for the heart.

¼ cup pine nuts
1 pound red potatoes
12 ounces fresh green beans
2 cups basil leaves
1 ounce parmesean cheese
7 tsp. olive oil
2 Tbsp. butter
2 Tbsp. lemon juice

Slice or cube potatoes and steam until done. Steam green beans until tender. Chop basil leaves. Lightly toast pine nuts in a dry skillet. Set aside. Warm olive oil; then add potatoes, green beans, basil, and toasted pine nuts until basil is soft.

Melt butter and combine with lemon juice. Drizzle over the entire dish and serve.

Black Bean & Quinoa Cheese Burgers

Black beans, quinoa, and cheese provide a triple dose of protein in this recipe. Black beans contain fiber, potassium, folate, and vitamin B6.

Be sure to soak the beans overnight to remove lectins before cooking. For those who avoid nightshade vegetables, eliminate the sun dried tomatoes.

1½ cup cooked quinoa
1 ½ cups cooked black beans
1 ½ cups pure water
6 sun dried tomatoes in oil, drained and finely chopped (¼ cup)
1 small onion, finely chopped (1 cup)

sea salt to taste
Sliced cheese of your choice

Preheat oven to 350 (175 C) degrees. Place onion in medium skillet and cook over medium heat for 3–4 minutes until onion has softened. Stir in ¾ cup black beans and 1 ½ cups water. Simmer 9–12 minutes or until most of liquid has evaporated.

Transfer bean-onion mixture to food processor; add ¾ cup cooked quinoa, and process until smooth. Transfer to bowl and stir in remaining ¾ cup quinoa and remaining ¾ cup black beans. Form into patties; Coat baking sheet with oil. Shape bean mixture into 8 patties. Bake for 20 minutes or until patties are crisp on top. Flip with spatula and bake 10 more minutes until both sides are crisp and brown. Place a slice of cheese on each patty and leave in the oven until it melts. Season with sea salt and pepper and cool. Serve with gluten-free buns or with vegetables.

Quinoa Stir Fry

Quinoa is very high in protein, and it contains all the essential amino acids. It also contains quercetin, a natural antihistamine and antioxidant.

The vegetables in this recipe may vary. You may substitute any seasonal vegetable for the carrots and peas; they are all delicious variations!

1 cup quinoa (pre-washed)
2 cups water
1 chopped onion or 2 chopped leeks
1 cup chopped, cooked, carrots
1 cup fresh or frozen green peas
6 ounces Mozzarella cheese
3 Tbsp. olive oil
sea salt and pepper to taste

Rinse 1 cup of quinoa (if not prewashed) and cook it in 2 cups of water. Simultaneously, steam the 2 cups of vegetables until done. Place 3 Tbsp. olive oil in a skillet and warm. Stir in a chopped onion or leeks and cook until golden. Once done, add the steamed vegetables and the cooked quinoa. If using frozen peas, stir them in last. Sea salt and pepper to taste. Finish with 6 ounces of grated cheese on top.

Pumpkin Risotto

Pumpkin is particularly rich in Vitamin A in addition to Lutein, providing protection for your eyesight. Its antioxidant properties promote health.

  1 peeled and seeded pumpkin or butternut squash
  4 potatoes, peeled and cut into large chunks
  2 Tbsp. butter
  Dash of almond or coconut milk
  ¼ cup olive oil
  2 onions, finely chopped
  2 cups Arborio rice
  4 cups boiling vegetable stock[2]
  sea salt to taste

Steam the pumpkin or squash and potatoes in a saucepan until tender. Add sea salt. Drain, reserving liquid. Puree pumpkin and potatoes with half the butter (immersion blender works great). Add enough liquid to make a thick soupy mixture. Keep hot.

Heat oil and the remaining butter in a skillet. Add onions and sauté gently until soft. Add rice and stir-fry for 1–2 minutes until the grains are well covered with oil. Add a quarter of the vegetable stock and simmer gently, stirring until absorbed.

Continue adding vegetable stock until all the stock has been used and risotto is creamy and fluffy (18–20 minutes). Stir the reserved pumpkin puree through the risotto. Top with parmesan cheese.

Warm Lentil Salad[3]

Lentils are high in protein, iron, folate, and fiber. They also contain B Vitamins and zinc. Because they are a low glycemic protein, they help to stabilize blood sugar and guard against heart disease. Pumpkin seeds are loaded with zinc, a mineral particularly important in men's prostate health. Zinc also has beneficial effects on learning and memory and can be used to treat the common cold, to speed wound healing, or for diarrhea,.

¾ cup soaked, rinsed, and cooked lentils
6 handfuls of dandelion, endive, arugula leaves
or greens of choice, torn
2 Tbsp. chopped fresh basil leaves
2 tsp. chopped fresh thyme leaves
½ cup toasted pumpkin seeds

Arrange the greens on an individual plate or large platter. Combine lentils, basil, thyme in a mixing bowl. Wisk together the dressing ingredients in another bowl. Season with sea salt and pepper. Add the dressing to the lentil mixture and toss well. Place the lentil mix on the greens and garnish with ½ cup hulled pumpkin seeds, (previously toasted in a small dry pan).

Dressing[3]

2 Tbsp. organic plain yogurt
2 Tbsp. olive oil
1 Tbsp. lemon juice
1 tsp. honey
sea salt to taste
black pepper to taste

Zucchini with Ricotta Cheese

Zucchini is rich in many nutrients and is high in antioxidants. It contributes to healthy digestion, can reduce blood sugar levels, and can strengthen your vision.

Ricotta cheese is low in sodium, high in phosphorus, vitamin B (which is often missing in Vegetarian diets), Vitamin A, and zinc.

1 ¾ lbs. zucchini (about 4 medium)
11 ounces ricotta cheese
1 large egg
1 Tbsp. chopped parsley
3 Tbsp. unsalted butter
Sea salt to taste

Heat oven to 350 (175 C) degrees. Steam zucchini until tender (3–5 minutes).

Remove ends of zucchini, cut them half lengthwise, and scoop out the pulp.

Drain the ricotta and mix with egg and parsley. Mix with zucchini pulp and fill zucchini halves. Arrange in a baking dish and dot with remaining butter. Bake for 15–20 minutes until golden brown.

ASCENSION DIET VEGAN RECIPES

Vegan Beans & Rice with Vegetables

This meal is a basic on the Ascension Diet and can be varied according to seasonal availability of vegetables and personal taste. Soak your beans overnight to eliminate lectins, rinsing them several times the next day before cooking to eliminate gas or bloating. Mung beans and lentils are easiest to digest. Mung beans are rich in potassium, magnesium, fiber, and antioxidants.

* Beans or lentils of any type, soaked overnight and rinsed

* White or Brown Basmati rice (contains small amounts of protein, unlike other kinds of rice)

* Variety of colored vegetables ––greens, squash, carrots, broccoli, etc.

Cook beans or lentils (beans can take up to 3 hours). Cook the rice. Wash and cut vegetables. Steam them about half an hour before the rice and beans are ready. Add olive oil and sea salt or gomasio (sesame seeds with sea salt) for flavor.

Be sure to eat a balanced amount of vegetables with the rice and beans.

Pia's Veggie Stock

I include Jerusalem artichokes in my stock because they are high in protein, potassium, and iron. Celery is a great source of antioxidants, and it has an alkalizing effect on the body. It helps reduce inflammation and supports digestion. Thyme is a natural antihistamine packed with Vitamin C, Vitamin A, copper, iron, manganese, and fiber. Cilantro is rich in immune-boosting antioxidants, fights infections, and is a unsurpassed as a food that removes heavy metals.

1 cup chopped leeks
5 carrots
3 stalks celery
2 zucchini
10 Jerusalem artichokes
1 yam
1 Tbsp. fresh lemon thyme
2 Tbsp. fresh or dried thyme
4 Tbsp fresh or dried Cilantro
1 ½ tsp. white pepper

Chop all vegetables and place in a pot. Add spices. Cover with boiling water. Simmer for 40 minutes. Drain vegetables and retain liquid. (Freeze leftover vegetables to use in soup later.) The remaining broth is the vegetable stock base. We always make our vegetable stock fresh to obtain the ultimate food value. Laarkmaa tells us that once it has been cooked, all food begins to degrade and does not retain the nutritional value of living food. Freezing stops the decay process, so you may freeze it for later use if you choose. However, we find this stock simply tastes better when made fresh.

Stuffed Avocados—Green & Raw!

Avocados are nutrient rich and healthy for the heart and eyes. Hempseeds are a perfect protein, rich in healthy fats and contain all the essential fatty acids. They also contain high amounts of Vitamin E, phosphorus, potassium, magnesium, calcium, iron, and zinc.

3 small avocados
4 tsp. hempseed
3 small oranges
2 cups radishes, diced
1 ¼ cups finely chopped romaine lettuce
6 green onions, finely chopped
3 Tbs. lime juice
¼ cup chopped cilantro

Halve and pit avocados. Score each avocado half 7 times lengthwise and 7 times crosswise to dice. Scoop out with soup spoon and place diced avocado in large bowl. Reserve shells.

Cut peel and pith from oranges with knife, then cut each orange into 4 slices. Cut each orange slice into 6 small triangular pieces. Add to bowl with diced avocado. Add hempseed, radishes, romaine, green onions, lime juice, and cilantro. Season with sea salt and pepper and gently toss to coat.

Scoop avocado mixture into avocado shells and serve.

Pia's Holiday Chickpea Loaf

Chickpeas are a rich source of vitamins, minerals, and fiber, and they are low in histamines. Chickpea flour is an easy way to receive the benefits of chickpeas.

3 cups finely chopped vegetables
(we like the combination of carrots and broccoli)
1 large leek (or onion) finely chopped
1 cup chickpea flour
2/3 cup water
juice of 1 lemon
sprinkling of oregano, basil, white pepper, sea salt

Preheat oven to 400 (approximately 200 C) degrees. Combine chickpea flour and spices in a bowl.

Add lemon juice and water. Lightly steam the vegetables and leek (be sure all water is drained) and add to the mix.

Pour into a bread pan and cook until a fork comes out clean when you check it (anywhere from 25-60 minutes, depending on altitude).

Feeds 3 people. You can double or triple the recipe to feed more, and it's always a favorite!

Pia's Curried Yams & Cauliflower

Cauliflower is very high in Vitamin C, which fights all kinds of viruses. Rich in phytonutrients that reduce oxidative stress in our cells, it is considered a disease-fighting powerhouse. Yams are an excellent source of potassium, manganese, copper, fiber, and antioxidants. Coconut oil feeds the brain and supports the heart.

3–4 small yams (not sweet potatoes, which
have different properties)
2 ½ cups cauliflower
4 tsp. curry powder
1 ½ Tbsp. coconut oil

Steam yams and cauliflower (separately) until done. Set aside until slightly cool. Chop yams into bit size pieces.

Warm coconut oil in a skillet. Add curry powder to oil. Add yams and cauliflower and stir until well blended. Serves 2–4 people (depending on appetites!)

Goes well with steamed Swiss Chard and lentils or beans.

Pia's Pad Thai

This recipe offers an alternative for people who cannot eat tree nuts because peanuts are a legume. They are an especially good source of healthy fats, protein, and fiber. They also contain plenty of potassium, phosphorous, magnesium, and B vitamins, which are important to Vegetarians and Vegans. The lime in this recipe alkalizes the body and reduces inflammation, as well as supporting the skin, the heart, and digestion.

1 package of brown rice noodles, cooked
½ cup fresh basil
3 Tbsp. olive oil
4 Tbsp. organic peanut butter
1–2 cups assorted steamed vegetables
juice of 1 lime per person

Place olive oil and fresh basil in a skillet and wilt basil. Add peanut butter. Add sea salt to taste. Mix in cooked rice noodles and stir. Serve, pouring juice of 1 lime over each serving.

Spinach and White Beans

Spinach is particularly rich in Vitamin K; it is also an excellent source of Vitamin A, Vitamin C, folate, manganese, magnesium, iron, and vitamin B2. White beans are a nutritional powerhouse, as they're packed with fiber and protein and a good source of numerous micronutrients, including folate, magnesium, and vitamin B6.

Be sure to soak the beans overnight and rinse well the next day to remove lectins.

2–3 cups cooked white beans
3 bunches of fresh spinach, stemmed and cleaned
2 Tbsp. avocado oil
pinch sea salt and pepper

Cook the beans (2–3 hours) and steam the spinach for about 5 minutes. Heat oil in skillet. Briefly stir in cooked spinach and beans and mix together with sea salt and pepper.

Asian Buckwheat Soba Noodles

Buckwheat is a complete protein, high in fiber. Cabbage and broccoli are both great sources of Vitamins C. Broccoli also provides folate, potassium, and fiber.

Be sure that your Soba noodles are pure buckwheat, as many Soba noodles are mixed with wheat.

1 package of pure buckwheat soba noodles
1 stalk of bok choy
2 leeks
1 cup chopped carrots
1 cup chopped cabbage or broccoli (or both)
2 Tbsp. olive oil or avocado oil
sea salt and pepper to taste.

Cover buckwheat noodles in water and bring to a boil. Turn down heat and cook until done (approximately 8-10 minutes, depending on altitude). Drain and set aside.

Combine all other ingredients and sauté in olive or avocado oil until done. Add sea salt and pepper to taste. Add noodles to the mix and enjoy a healthy stirfry. You can also add boiling water and turn this into a delicious soup!

Pia's Blackened Brussels Sprouts

Packed with immunity-boosting vitamin C, Brussels Sprouts are among the most powerful cold-weather superfoods. They are also high in vitamin K and fiber. Ginger is an anti-inflammatory digestive aid. It also relieves pain and supports your heart. I use white pepper over black pepper because it is helps to protect from cardiovascular disease and it prevents the formation of free radicals.

This recipe converts those who have never previously enjoyed Brussels Sprouts!

> 3 cups peeled and washed small Brussels Sprouts
> 3 Tbsp. olive oil
> 1 tsp. ginger powder
> sea salt and white pepper to taste

Steam the Brussels Sprouts. When they are tender, combine warmed olive oil, ginger, and a sprinkle of white pepper in a skillet. Then add the steamed Brussels Sprouts at high heat. Turn them until they are browned on all sides. Delicious!

Roasted Asparagus

Asparagus is a good source of folate and Vitamins A, C, and K. Sesame seeds are an excellent source of calcium and as a seed, provide some protein to this dish. Olive oil is one of the two healtiest oils on Earth (coconut oil is the other.) It contains large amounts of antioxidants, is rich in healthy fats, and is good for your heart.

> 2 bunches of asparagus spears
> 3 Tbsp. olive oil

Trim the ends off of two bunches of washed Asparagus spears. Place on a baking sheet and drizzle with olive oil. Generously sprinkle seseme seeds or gomasio (sea salt and sesame seeds) over the asparagus. Roast in the oven at 415 degrees (215 C) until soft (30-45 minutes, depending on altitude.)

Roasted Leek & Fennel Bisque[4]

Fennel is a magical herb that aids digestion, regulates blood pressure, reduces water retention, improves eyesight, and supports healthy breathing. Leeks contain iron, which supports brain and nerve function and are a good source of vitamins, A, C, and K. Walnuts offer a significantly high concentration of DHA, a type of Omega-3 fatty acid that improves cognitive function.

½ cup coarsely chopped leeks
2 cups sliced fennel bulb
2 cups filtered water
1 cup vegetable stock, made fresh
2 Tbsp. lemon juice or lime juice
1 Tbsp. chopped fresh basil or 1 tsp. dried basil
½ tsp. paprika
5 bay leaves
3 Tbsp. coconut cream
½ cup toasted walnuts for garnish (Omit the walnuts
to reduce inflammation or histamine reaction)

Preheat oven to 400 (approximately 200 C) degrees. Spread the leeks on an oiled baking dish and roast them until soft (about 30 minutes). Put fennel in large saucepan along with water, vegetable stock, lemon juice, basil, paprika, bay leaves, sea salt, and pepper. Bring to a boil over high heat. Reduce heat to a simmer. Stir in roasted leeks and continue simmering for 20 minutes. Add coconut cream, mix, and serve.

Pia's Grapefruit Salad

Grapefruit is high in antioxidants, benefiting your total immune system and improving heart health. Daikon is very high in

Vitamin C, potassium, and phosphorus. It also contains beneficial enzymes that aid digestion.

1 large pink grapefruit
½ cup grated daikon
½ cup grated carrots
¼ cup sautéed scallions
½ cup Brazil nuts, Almonds, or Walnuts
(omit nuts if you have histamine issues)
1/3 cup Lime Juice
Mix and serve

RAW, LIQUID RECIPES

These raw, liquid fruit and vegetable recipes provide a delicious and even lighter diet! Be sure to use only fresh juices, not concentrate or bottled juices, which have lost their healthy enzymes. We often add hemp seed or hemp powder to the vegetable or fruit mix, providing ample protein. Generally the body responds best if you do not mix fruits with vegetables because they do not digest at the same rate. Enjoy them separately!

Vegetable Smoothie

Carrots and Romaine lettuce are both particularly good sources of beta-carotene, which converts into Vitamin A in the body, supporting your vision. Carrots also contain vitamin C, vitamin K, potassium, and antioxidants, promoting eye health. Romaine Lettuce is also high in minerals such as calcium, phosphorous, magesium, and potassium, as well as Vitamin C, Vitamin K, and folate.

2 large handfuls of leaf or romaine lettuce
1 carrot
1 avocado

hemp seed to taste (optional)
Water for liquid

Choose your ingredients and mix with the appropriate amount water.

Fruit Smoothie

Berries are medicine. They are low on the glycemic index and full of vitamins. We recommend wild blueberries and blackberries as our berries of choice; wild blueberries provide support for the brain, digestive system, and vision. Blackberries lower inflammation and support the immune system with their content of vitamins C, K, and manganese. Bananas are rich in potassium and they serve as an effective prebiotic, which helps the body absorb calcium. They increase brain chemicals like serotonin, dopamine, and norepinephrine, which support healthy brain function. Mangos are a natural antihistamine; they promote eye health, aid digestion, and boost immunity. Chia Seeds are filled with protein and healthy fat. They contain plant-based omega 3 fatty acids and are packed with calcium. Adding chia seeds to smoothies thickens them and provides a power-packed breakfast.

1 Ripe banana
1 cup fresh or frozen blueberries or blackberries
1 cup fresh or frozen mangoes
½ cup—1 cup fresh orange juice or an alternative milk (coconut, almond, or hemp)
hemp seed to taste (optional)
1 Tbsp. chia seeds (pre-soaked in equal amount of liquid)

Choose your ingredients and mix with the appropriate amount of liquid, orange juice, alternative milk, or water. (We like coconut milk or almond milk.)

Liquid Gold Shake

We discovered this marvelous shake at a health bar in Whitefish, Montana. The helpful barista wrote down all the ingredients for us, but without the measurements. Play with the measurements, as we did, and find your own delightful combination of this amazing creation! Almond butter is a great source of Vitamin E, magnesium, copper, Vitamin B2, and phosphorous. Maca powder boosts energy. Bee pollen boosts liver health, strengthens the immune system, reduces inflammation, and works as an antioxidant.

raw almond butter
maca powder
banana
golden flax seed
bee pollen
hemp protein
hemp milk
Combine all ingredients in a blender. Blend well. Yum.

APPENDIX B:
OTHER VOICES FROM THE LIGHT

Pia has been a Receiver all of her life. We are including here a few brief messages from other voices from light that come through her, or on occasion, through us together. Their messages match those of Laarkmaa, who at the suggestion of the Pleiadian Elder's Council, invited them to speak on one of our International Live Calls. Below are messages from Mother Mary, Mary Magdalene, Quantamo—the Arcturian Captain of this part of the Universe, a Representative of the Fairy Kingdom, and The Voice. These voices come through Pia's receptive abilities, unlike Laarkmaa, who comes through both Cullen and Pia simultaneously.

Each of the messages from Other Voices From Light included here encourages us to wake up, take back our power and our responsibility, and be grateful for the help we are receiving during this challenging and auspicious time of evolution. As we become our Future Selves, they are all around us, providing encouragement and assistance.

MOTHER MARY

I am Mother Mary, and I come to you with softness, bringing grace and bringing love. I come to you, thanking you for allowing the wisdom of your hearts to rise to the surface. You are called into service to this planet to speak from your hearts, to think from your hearts, to act from your hearts, always with love. I ask you to accept my grace, as I pour the Golden Light of Grace into each and every one of you. You may feel my tears, for I see that you are suffering. I feel your suffering, but I also understand that it is only part of the illusion. I suffered too, until I understood that what I was experiencing was only part of the illusion. So, let your own salt tears wash over you, taking away any pain of what you experience in this Now moment, as you begin to see through the illusion. Trust as my grace pours into you that you will be fulfilled, that you will feel unconditional love because you are deeply loved everywhere in the Universe. You, my friends, who Laarkmaa calls the Light Bearers, are here to do just that—bear the light as you are awakening in increasing amounts. Let your light shine out into the world, and know that I am with you in every moment providing you with grace.

With Love,
I am Mary

MARY MAGDALENE

I am Mary Magdalene. My voice is always present to tell you to fight for the truth and not to be afraid! Always, since I have first spoken to you, I have told you, "Fear not!" There is a great battle waging now against the light and the dark, and you are in position to take up your swords of light and stand up for the truth. Know that fighting with light and with love is the highest calling. It is not a battle of combat against challenging opposites. It is a battle to eliminate fear, to no longer be afraid to speak the truth. It is a battle of standing up and sharing everything that needs to be said. It is a battle of being love in every single moment, recognizing that that is who you are, who you always will be, and you are doing what you have been called to do. You are called to fear not and to spread that message to those who are afraid. The more you can stop the contagion of fear, the more you will be able to move into your position as co-creators for the new world. With this message I tell you again, "Fear not! Fear not! Fear not!"

With Love,
I am Mary Magdalene

A VOICE FROM THE FAIRY KINGDOM

(Bubbling laughter.) I am from the Fairy Kingdom. I come to thank you for what you do for the Earth. I come because I wish no longer to be behind the veil, the veil that prevents life from recognizing life. Fairies have long been hidden from most human eyes because we do not like to be stared at by those who do not understand or accept the energy of light. But we are the energy of light, and our purpose is to bring you joy from that light. Joy, Joy, Joy. (Bubbling laughter.) So, while this is a time that you are experiencing great trouble, I come to thank you, reminding you to laugh often and laugh well. Share the vibration of laughter (Bubbling laughter) with others because when you do this, you help them to raise their vibration also. Know that every time you do this, you are helping to elevate all the vibrations that are necessary for evolution and the ascension of our Beloved Mother Earth. We, the Fairies, are holding our light next to your light, and we are going into this battle together because we are who we are. We are beings of light. (Bubbling laughter.) Laugh, Dear Ones. Cry, if you must, as Mother Mary suggested, but let the tears just be something to cleanse the moment, and then move into holding one another with laughter, with love, and return to the joy that is naturally in your hearts. I am with you, as is all of the Fairy Kingdom.

I love you, (Bubbling laughter.)

QUANTAMO—ARCTURIAN CAPTAIN

Quantamo here, Arcturian Captain of the Earth sector. I am here to give you an overview of your interstellar brothers and sisters positioned around the planet at this time. The Arcturians want you to know that we are doing our part to keep your planet safe as we can from outer influences and protect you from things that do not belong in your atmosphere or magnetosphere. We break up the things into fragments that would fall to your Earth and would be harmful. We deflect things that can cause harm that are set into space, sending them in other directions. We are working as fast as we can to dismantle those things that some humans are inappropriately placing into space. We are working in a task force now to see what can be done—together with your own efforts—to disband the 5G that is so harmful to your planet. However, you are simultaneously receiving impacts of meteors that come very close to your planet. We circle our ships around these potentially dangerous meteors and dismantle them with light beams so that only fragments or pieces fall into your atmosphere, preventing catastrophic situations such as you have experienced a very long time ago on this planet.

The Arcturians wish you to know that now and always we have been on guard against anything in your atmosphere or magnetosphere that can be harmful to your planet. I, Quantamo, and my team do everything that we can to dissimilate everything harmful that is placed in your atmosphere, or things that are about to come into your atmosphere. We do everything we can to dismantle them before they land. We are on your side, ever more present than we ever have been. It is not just the Arcturians here who are speaking of this, but many from across the galaxy. We are all interested and watching, waiting to see how you will step into what is yours to do. I am the Commander of this squadron over Earth. I am Quantamo, but as a commanding officer, I will not give you a command of what to do on your own planet, for you have the power to make those decisions on your own. I will ask you to take back your power. Take charge, take command to do what is necessary in this fight for life, for you are, indeed, necessary in helping to remind the dark that it is part of the light, something that it has completely forgotten. I call you as a brother, calling you to arms, more or less, telling you to take your place; do what you can; stand up for the truth. Be brave. Be courageous and know that everything that you do is in alignment and is in support with the interstellar brotherhood of light.

You are approaching a time of immense change on this planet, of which all of you are aware. Our Pleiadian colleagues, Laarkmaa, are doing a magnificent job of reminding you to remember to be love, to be light, and to be grateful. They also remind you on occasion to do your third-dimensional part.

What I would like to say to you on behalf of all the Arcturians is to, please, take back your power. Do not simply sit by and allow things to happen because you are too lazy to change. If we are going to spend every single moment we can protecting your planet, isn't it about time you spend every single waking moment you have to do the same thing? Sitting around talking about what "they" are going to do next, is *not* going to solve the problem. You need to make major lifestyle changes, and you need to make them *now*, for we cannot protect you from the changes you allow humanity to make. You must do that yourselves. We do everything we can to *stop* the damage of what is being done. But you must implement your own power to stop the damage *before* they implement harmful plans.

So please, from the Arcturian Council, we ask you collectively, "Be active. Be light. Be who you are, and be strong. You are not silly little people sitting on a planet waiting for whatever is going to happen next to you. You are powerful beams of light, and you are our colleagues—our sisters and our brothers. We expect you, as you awaken, to remember this and to act accordingly. We are all here, stationed around your planet to work with you, and you will see us more and more frequently; we promise. Do your part, and know that we are doing our part; we will fight with light until light is all that exists. Do your part, and all will be well. Thank you for allowing me to speak on behalf of the Arcturians.

We send you blessings and love from the Arcturians.

Quantamo

THE VOICE

I am The Voice. I am the V where all wisdom comes together in Unity. I am the V where individuals pour into Unity. I am the V where consciousness awakens. I am here to invite you to be the V yourselves. Be the Voice of Wisdom. Be the place where all opposites come together in Unity. Be that which you are, divine sparks of light. Be the V that is victory for the light, knowing that light is all that is. Be the place where your consciousness suddenly falls into the point of magnification where you are so brilliant that you see the true reality. The truth stands before you now. Do not be dissuaded; do not be blinded; do not be left behind by those lies that are being spread before you. Remember truth is yours just for the asking. Open your hearts, open your minds, and ask all of us who are from love and light to speak, and we will always be available with our energy to shed light on whatever you need in your environment to support you and to help you as you speak your own truth. Remember what Laarkmaa has taught you about In Lak'ech (I am another yourself). And even though I am a Voice from another realm, I am a Voice of wisdom, compassion, love, and higher consciousness. That Voice is you too. You are a Voice from a higher realm. Open your ears and hear yourselves speak the truth. Open your hearts and embrace one another in the spirit of In Lak'ech. Know that we are all one. We are all beings of light, and the light will always be the most powerful and beneficial thing in the Universe. Do not doubt this in times when it seems the illusion of darkness is the greatest. I am The Voice, I am the Wisdom, I am the place where duality merges into unity, and I am your higher consciousness.

With Love and Light,
I am The Voice.

APPENDIX C:
LAARKMAA'S HEART MEDITATION[1]

We would like to invite you to help us, if you choose, to restore the Heart of Humanity through an exercise with color. We would like to remind you as we work with this what the energy vibrations of each color resonate with and how you may utilize that energy. We will lead you through the exercise and ask you to visualize what you can. You are going to begin with recognizing the energy of the heart; the energy of the heart needs to be placed back into humanity. It has been suppressed, ignored for too long. It is time that the power of love, that the energy of the heart come to its rightful place as the leader of humanity. Begin in any way you choose by seeing the pink light of love in a ball of energy in front of you. Feel that ball of pink light in front of you. That is the love from your heart, and that is the love from the Universe, and it is yours. And as you recognize it, and as you feel the energy of that pink light of love, you can begin to feel tingles through your body. You can feel a resonance with love energy. Remember, with love energy, no fear can exist. See the pink light of love emanating all around, as if you hold it in your hands in front of you. See it moving into your heart and back from your heart, and see it moving out across the planet and across the heavens. See it going into the heart of every human being on the planet. Take a moment to breathe in the pink light of love and breathe it out, sending it to the heart of each human on Earth.

Now tone briefly, using the Ahhhhhhhh vibratory sound that opens the heart, while you are holding this ball of pink energetic love light. Use the tones to help carry the love and light you are sending into the heart of every human on Earth. Ahhhhhhhh......

Now feel that energy vibrating through you and know that you are loved and that you ARE love. And as you focus, softly gazing at the pink light, notice that there is a blue light surrounding the pink. It is the energetic vibration of trust, for trust is built upon love. See that soft blue light radiating around the ball of energy you are holding in your hand—pink in the center, blue around it. Feel the energy of trust permeating every cell of your being. You feel calm. You feel peaceful. That is the energy of trust. And as you feel that in yourself, look for us. We always represent ourselves as blue waves so that you can trust that we bring you truth. Our energy carries the energy of trust along with the energy of love. See that blue wavy energy around the pink ball that you hold, and then begin to send those blue waves out across the planet to each human heart that is filled with the pink light of love. Surround that energy now with the blue light of trust so that they may feel what it feels like to be safe, to be calm, to trust. Take a few moments and send that to all of your brothers and sisters across the planet, and send it into your own heart as well, the blue energy of trust.

Now look and you will see the golden light of grace radiating down from the heavens, from the Universe, into the ball that you are holding in front of you—pink love light in the center, trust around it, and golden light of grace beginning to radiate so that you see waves of gold surrounding the blue. This is the energy that releases all karma. This is the energy of grace. This is the energy that both the Christ Consciousness and Mary Magdalene taught, that when you have love and trust, grace can erase everything. Allow the golden light of grace to enter into your own heart. Feel it, knowing that you have the choice to take responsibility with the energy of grace for what comes next. Send the golden light of grace to each human heart across the planet, freeing them from the binding ties of karma, allowing the grace to remove them from pain and suffering so that they may begin to understand how to be different. Send the golden light of grace into each heart. It shimmers and vibrates. It is beautiful. Send it with love and trust—grace for all humanity.

Now see the green healing light. Beautiful, brilliant, emerald green. It is all around the waves of gold, so that you have pink in the center, surrounded by blue, surrounded by gold, and now there is green. Now that you have the energy of love, trust, and grace, you can begin to heal. So, heal yourselves, Dear Ones. Invite in the healing energy to heal every split between you and other, every split between heart and mind, every split between right and wrong, every split between "my way" and "your way." Allow the green energy to radiate healing until there is no more separation. There is only unity. And unity is big enough to hold all aspects so that each human being can follow their path without conflict, using love, trust, and grace. Now send that green healing light from yourself forward into all humans across the planet. Send it with the intention that it heal all splits... all splits of my country, your country. All splits of my oil, your oil, my money, your money. All splits between "I am right" and "you are wrong." All splits between my god and your god. All splits between brain and heart. All splits between you and me. Send that green healing energy out to all humanity. Send your intention on your breath. With love, trust, and grace, may each human being heal.

Now, Dear Ones, notice a brilliant yellow light shining down on you. Notice also the same light, brilliant yellow, is coming out of your own heart, for it is your divine spark, and it is connected with the light of illumination of the Universe. Illumination— this is what the Christ Consciousness was bringing to humanity, the illumination to see the truth. Look at the yellow light. It is brilliant, and it illuminates your way so that you can see how to be fully present in each present moment, listening, looking, and taking responsibility for everything you think, everything you feel, and everything you do so that it resonates in unity for the highest good of all. Feel the golden light of grace reaching out and touching the green light of healing and then touching the yellow light of illumination. They are connected. When you heal because you have accepted grace, you can become illuminated, and when you are illuminated, you can see the truth. Send that beautiful yellow light forward into each human heart, so that each human heart may experience the love, the trust, the grace, the healing, and the illumination that is present. See that light reaching each human heart, from your heart to theirs, and from the Universe into each of you, helping you to awaken to who you are, the new beings, the New Humanity.

Now, Dear Ones, notice the brilliant white Christ light, the light of truth shining into your heart, surrounding, radiating all around this ball of energy you are holding in front of you, the white light of truth that you have reached moving from love to trust to grace to illumination to truth with healing. Notice it is all there, all around you, and send forth into the heart of every human being, the white light of truth, so that they may dispel all of their belief systems and all of their patterns of behavior, moving instead into the foundation that all beings are one, and that you are divine beings of love who have the capacity to trust one another, to be compassionate with one another, to support one another with love. Send forth the white light of truth so that all may awaken, if they choose.

Now, Dear Ones, we approach the final color. It is the violet light of transformation See it radiating around the ball of energy you hold in front of you. It is waving all around. It is the energy of transformation. It is the energy of transmutation. With this energy you can change anything. This is the energy of *change*.

See it all around you. Send forth into each human heart across the planet the ability to change, the ability to transcend their beliefs, the ability to transmute old patterns of behavior and to be different. Send the violet light to each human heart so that they may experience it.

Now notice, if you will, that you have a radiating ball of seven colors in front of you. It is a torus². It is the energy of the human heart. It is time, Dear Light Bearers, that you take this energy and you place it back in its rightful place for the Heart of Humanity. As you send this torus of energy out to each human heart on the planet, you are awakening the heart of all, and you are sending the energy back where it belongs. Send this torus with love and trust—the pink light of love, the blue light of trust, the golden light of grace, the green light of healing, the yellow light of illumination, the white light of truth, the violet light of transformation. Send it forth, and as you send it, you will see sparks of light all across the planet. These are the Light Bearers who are connecting with you through silver threads of connection of light, weaving a web, a net to hold you, as you create the form of a New Humanity.

We love you. Remember this exercise, for it is helping to awaken who you are; use it to bring peace to your world.

We love you. Good Always,
Laarkmaa

END NOTES

PREFACE

1 Laarkmaa defines and explains the Rainbow Body in *Remembering Who We Are—Laarkmaa's Guidance on Healing the Human Condition*, Chapter 8, pages 147 - 153.

2 Laarkmaa explains water communication in *Conversations With LaarkmaaA Pleiadian View of the New Reality*, Chapter 3, pages 17 – 25.

3 First Sense is defined and explained by Laarkmaa in *Conversations With Laarkmaa—A Pleiadian View of the New Reality*, Chapter 2, pages 9 – 15.

4 Laarkmaa offers regular International Live Calls that are announced and can be accessed on www.Laarkmaa.com

CHAPTER ONE

1 Laarkmaa discusses this concept in *Conversations With Laarkmaa—A Pleiadian View of the New Reality*, Chapter 1, page 1.

2 Laarkmaa discusses the "Choice Point" of evolution in many of their Live Calls. Basically, it is the conscious choice to ascend with the planet by choosing higher vibratory living or the choice to follow the wheel of karma through death and rebirth.

3 Laarkmaa first explained Liquid Time in *Remembering Who We Are—Laarkmaa's Guidance on Healing the Human Condition*. Chapter 7, pages 141 – 143.

CHAPTER TWO

1 More information on Laarkmaa's Trauma Clearings is available here: https://www.laarkmaa.com/trauma-clearings

2 Laarkmaa's perspective on judgment can be found in *Conversations With Laarkmaa—A Pleiadian View of the New Reality*, Chapter 15, pages 161 – 163.

3 More detail on Laarkmaa's perspective on "emotions" can be found in *Conversations With Laarkmaa—A Pleiadian View of the New Reality*, Chapter 8, pages 81 - 96 and in *Remembering Who We Are—Laarkmaa's Guidance on Healing the Human Condition*, Chapter 3, pages 60 - 66.

4 Laarkmaa describes the liquid crystalline body in *Remembering Who We Are—Laarkmaa's Guidance on Healing the Human Condition*, Chapter 3, page 79.

5 Laarkmaa explains Shadow Cycles in *Pleiadian-Earth Energy Astrology*, Chapter 11, pages 160 - 178.

CHAPTER THREE

1 A good explanation of the Cosmic Rays and the Kp Index can be found Can be found at Pleiadian Laarkmaa YouTube.

CHAPTER FOUR

1 The Pleiadian-Earth Energy Calendar can be found here: https://www.laarkmaa.com/pleiadian-Earth-energy-calendar

2 Laarkmaa first explained the multidimensional foundation of love, joy, trust, and compassion in *Remembering Who We Are— Laarkmaa's Guidance on Healing the Human Condition*, Chapter 4, pages 83 - 93.

3 A detailed explanation of the Universal and Earth Energies of can be found in *Pleiadian-Earth Energy Astrology—Charting the Spirals of Consciousness*, Chapter 6, pages 60 – 75 and Chapter 7, pages 76 - 92. A good video about the accompanying Pleiadian-Earth Energy Calendar can be found at Pleiadian Laarkmaa YouTube.

CHAPTER FIVE

1 Laarkmaa offers free International Live Calls on a regular basis. You can participate by signing up on our website: **laarkmaa.com**

2 Laarkmaa's suggested supplements to help erase pineal calcification include Vitamin K2–7, Vitamin A, and the herbs Bacopa Monnieri, Suma, and Sea Buckthorn. They also suggest limiting the use of cell phones and other EMFs and completely avoiding exposure to 5G.

3 To explore more wisdom about consciousness, see Pia and Cullen's article *What is Consciousness,* published in Australia's *New Dawn Magazine*: https://www.laarkmaa.com/articles

4 Laarkmaa first defined the Five Pack in *Conversations With Laarkmaa—A Pleiadian View of the New Reality,* Chapter 7, page 56.

CHAPTER SIX

1 Laarkmaa discusses androgyny in *Remembering Who We Are— Laarkmaa's Guidance on Healing the Human Condition,* Chapter 9, pages 170-175.

2 Pia reveals in detail how the patriarchy has caused an imbalance between feminine and masculine energies in her book, *Sacred Retreat—Using Natural Cycles to Recharge Our Lives,* Chapter 3, pp. 41-56.

3 Laarkmaa explains Universal and Earth energies and how to use them in *Pleiadian-Earth Energy Astrology—Charting the Spirals of Consciousness,* Chapter 3, pages 170-175.

CHAPTER SEVEN

1 Information on geochemical engineering can be found here: https://www.geoengineeringwatch.org/

CHAPTER EIGHT

1 Laarkmaa's guidelines to help understand the true nature of reality and to remember who you are can be found in *Remembering Who We Are—Laarkmaa's Guidance on Healing the Human Condition,* Chapter 4, pages. 83-96.

2   More detail on Laarkmaa's perspective on "emotions" can be found in *Conversations With Laarkmaa—A Pleiadian View of the New Reality*, Chapter 8, pp. 81-96 and in *Remembering Who We Are—Laarkmaa's Guidance on Healing the Human Condition*, Chapter 3, pages 60-66.

3   The Energetic Purpose that manifests in one's personality is defined more fully in *Pleiadian-Earth Energy Astrology— Charting the Spirals of Consciousness*, Chapter 14, pages 203-221.

4   Personal Pleiadian-Earth Energy Astrology Charts are available here: https://www.piaorleane.com/pleiadian-energy-charts

5   Laarkmaa defines water communication in *Conversations With Laarkmaa—A Pleiadian View of the New Reality*, Chapter 3, pages 17-25.

6   Laarkmaa frequently addresses what will happen to and on this planet in their Live Calls: https://www.laarkmaa.com/

7   Laarkmaa defines themselves as One of Six and Six of One in *Conversations With Laarkmaa—A Pleiadian View of the New Reality*, Chapter 1, page 1.

8   Laarkmaa has created guidelines for an Ascension Diet, presented in Appendix A.

9   The Pleiadian-Earth Energy Calendar is available here: https://www.laarkmaa.com/pleiadian-Earth-energy-calendar

10   See Appendix A.

11   The Mandela Effect is the experience of a confluence of different perceptions of the same event.

12   More information on Laarkmaa's Trauma Clearings is available here: https://www.laarkmaa.com/trauma-clearings

CHAPTER NINE

1 We have created two Youtube videos on Cosmic Weather; you can find them on Pleiadian Laarkmaa Youtube.

2 Derek Knauss' full article, with referenced links, can be found here: https://prepareforchange.net/2018/12/13/youre-not-dying-its-the-schumann-resonance/

3 Laarkmaa has discussed the twelve strands of DNA in various Live Calls over the last dozen years.
See: https://www.laarkmaa.com/2020-international-live-call

4 The best protection from 5G and EMFs that we have found is Blushield https://www.blushield-us.com/?v=e182ebbc166d Another possible choice for protection is Bioshield, but we have not tested it. https://5gbioshield.com/

5 Water communication is defined by Laarkmaa in *Conversations With Laarkmaa—A Pleiadian View of the New Reality,* Chapter 3, pp. 17-25

6 Information on Continuum Movement can be found here: https://continuummovement.com/

7 See Appendix A.

CHAPTER TEN

1 *Pleiadian-Earth Energy Astrology—Charting the Spirals of Consciousness,* Chapter Three, pp. 22-32.

2 The Pleiadian-Earth Energy Calendar is available here: https://www.laarkmaa.com/pleiadian-Earth-energy-calendar

APPENDIX A

1 Please note the American usage of tsp. for teaspoon and Tbsp. for Tablespoon in the following recipes.

2 The recipe for Pia's Veggie Stock is listed under Vegan recipes.

3 The Warm Lentil Salad and Dressing have been adapted from *Eat, Taste, Heal,* by Thomas Yarema, MD, Daniel Rhoda, DAS, and Chef Johnny Brannigan, page 281.

4   The Roasted Leek & Fennel Bisque original recipe has been adapted from *Eat, Taste, Heal,* by Thomas Yarema, MD, Daniel Rhoda, DAS, and Chef Johnny Brannigan.

APPENDIX C

1   You can listen to Laarkmaa's Heart Meditation here: https://www.youtube.com/watch?v=N6Xc33ZdSdw

2   A torus is a mathematical term for an object of seven colors that exists in dimensionality. More information about a torus can be found here: https://mathworld.wolfram.com/Torus.html

ACKNOWLEDGMENTS

B ecause this text was originally channeled verbally, we owe a tremendous debt of thanks to Vineta Svelch, who helped us to transcribe many of Laarkmaa's original messages from our Live Call recordings. It takes a bit of magic to translate the spoken word into written form. We would like to express our extreme thanks to the invaluable talent and help of the team of editors who helped us to convert Laarkmaa's musical spoken word into a fluid, readable style. Brendan and Sara Bowen, Sharon Swinyard, and Vineta Svelch, each of you did a marvelous job sharing your meticulous expertise and professionalism in grammar, context, and continuity. You have helped us to make Laarkmaa's message more readable, and complete.

Heartfelt gratitude to Rebecca Gretz, our technical wizardess who edits our International Live Calls, maintains our websites, and keeps us sane in the technical world. Rebecca was in Laarkmaa's first Live Gathering audience many, many years ago.

We would like to thank Chris Molé for her beautiful cover design and book layout. Chris, it is such a pleasure working with you! And thanks to Judith Pavlek for providing our Author Photos on the back cover.

Thanks to Derek Knauss for the use of and inclusion of his article in Chapter Nine of this book.

We wish to thank the Host of our International Live Calls, Brian MacIntyre. Your skills and management of these calls are life saving; we couldn't do it without you!

Thank you to all of the Live Call Participants who offered their questions, which we included in this book. Your questions gave Laarkmaa the opportunity to expand more fully and explain more deeply on each topic discussed.

To all our friends and spiritual family, we are grateful for you, and we hold you in our hearts.

With love and light,

Pia and Cullen

ABOUT THE AUTHORS

Pia Orleane, Ph.D. & Cullen Baird Smith are Ambassadors to the **Pleiadian Group Laarkmaa,** a wise and loving group of interstellar beings who share wisdom to support human evolution. They have been working together as a team for almost two decades, although Laarkmaa has worked privately with both of them since childhood in this and other lifetimes.

Co-authors of the Wisdom From the Stars series, which includes the timeless classics *Conversations With Laarkmaa—A Pleiadian View of the New Reality* and *Remembering Who We Are—Laarkmaa's Guidance on Healing the Human Condition,* and the third book in the trilogy, *Pleiadian Manual for Accelerated Evolution & Ascension.* Pia and Cullen, with Laarkmaa's suggestions and direction, designed the revolutionary new Pleiadian-Earth Energy Calendar, a guide for conscious evolution and spiritual advancement using energy rather than time. The accompanying book, *Pleiadian-Earth Energy Astrology—Charting the Spirals of Consciousness,* won the Coalition for Visionary Resources Award for Divination Books.

Awakened since birth, both Pia and Cullen have been communicating with other realms since childhood. Former practicing psychologist, Pia, is a respected intuitive, a Pleiadian-Earth Energy astrologer, and a Receiver of other dimensional wisdom. Trained in Archeology and Anthropology, Cullen is an empathic intuitive and interstellar communicator who has worked with healing energies all of his life. Pia and Cullen have traveled the world, bringing Laarkmaa's wisdom to humanity as keynote speakers. They offer International Live Calls and public gatherings where you may connect directly with Laarkmaa. They also provide private sessions, changing one life at a time.

Lightning Source UK Ltd.
Milton Keynes UK
UKHW020644150921
390618UK00010B/296